Strategic Communication Research Methods

Strategic Communication Research Methods

Marianne Dainton and Pamela J. Lannutti
La Salle University

cognella®

SAN DIEGO

Bassim Hamadeh, CEO and Publisher
Todd R. Armstrong, Publisher
Michelle Piehl, Senior Project Editor
David Rajec, Editorial Assistant
Alia Bales, Production Editor
Jess Estrella, Senior Graphic Designer
Trey Soto, Licensing Coordinator
Natalie Piccotti, Director of Marketing
Kassie Graves, Vice President of Editorial
Jamie Giganti, Director of Academic Publishing

Cover image copyright © 2014 Depositphotos/kristt.

Printed in the United States of America.

cognella® | ACADEMIC PUBLISHING
3970 Sorrento Valley Blvd., Ste. 500, San Diego, CA 92121

Brief Contents

Detailed Contents

CHAPTER 7

Content Analysis and Content Audits   125

CHAPTER 8

Surveys and Communication Audits   145

Part III   Creating a Research Product

Preface

This book is designed to serve as a research methods textbook for upper-level undergraduate and professional master's degree students. It is meant to serve as a practical introduction to the topic for students who are pursuing (or are currently working in) careers in communication-related industries. The primary challenge of instructors teaching research methods to vocationally oriented students is the abstract nature of the topic; many students have difficulty in seeing the relevance of research methods to their professional lives. Accordingly, the goal of this book is to make research methods tangible to students by explaining research methods in a way that makes sense for individuals who are not researchers by trade or training, and by assisting students in seeing how research can be used in careers in public relations, marketing, human resources, corporate communication, social media management, and the like.

There are two different research skills required of professional communicators. First, communication practitioners need to be critical consumers of research. They need to understand the research process, including the unique language of research, and they need to be able to evaluate the quality and ethicality of research. Second, they may be tasked with carrying out research. As such, they need to learn the tools for planning, conducting, and interpreting original research. We believe that this text can assist students with developing both skill sets. To accomplish these goals, there are four unique features to this book.

A Strategic Approach

First, this book contextualizes research as a vital part of any professional strategy. Research is not something other people do; it is a central and necessary part of any position in an organizational setting that requires strategic decision making. As such, we provide an overview of strategy in

Chapter 1 and describe how research is used in every step of the process of developing and assessing strategy. Moreover, examples used throughout the text feature "real-life" professional problems and how research has or could assist in in resolving the problem.

Practical Application

Second, much like any other skill, conducting and interpreting research takes practice. As such, this book provides numerous opportunities for students to practice applying their understanding of research methods. Each chapter concludes with a set of activities asking students to apply what they have learned in the chapter. Some of these activities challenge students to use key concepts to critically evaluate research elements, and some of the activities ask students to produce research elements such as crafting a research question, creating an operational definition, and developing a coding scheme.

A Step-by-Step Process

Third, we have taken a step-by-step approach to methods. We provide the steps involved in conducting research in Chapter 2, and each methods chapter is organized around the discrete steps of how to use that particular method. We believe this step-by-step approach will be of particular value to current students' need for clarity and precision, making the book more accessible and practical than other research methods texts.

Both Academic and Professional Methods

Finally, when describing each research method we have paired a general description of how to do that type of research with a professional application for the research method. For example, we have linked how to conduct observational research with data analytics, we have linked how to conduct a survey with communication audits, and we have linked experimental research methods to A/B studies. In this way, we hope that students understand that both scholarly and applied research use the same methods, better preparing them for success in both their academic and professional careers.

In addition to these features, instructor resources are available that include sample syllabi, PowerPoint slides, and a test bank.

Acknowledgments

There are a number of people we need to thank for assistance in publishing this text. First, we want to thank our colleagues in the Department of Communication at La Salle University for their enthusiastic encouragement. Second, we want to thank Todd Armstrong, our publisher at Cognella, for his continued professional and personal support. Lastly, we wish to thank the reviewers who provided us with important feedback, both critical and congratulatory. The following people have greatly influenced the final product: Sharlee LeBlanc Broussard (Department of Public Relations; Belmont University), Leah E. Bryant (College of Communication; DePaul University), Michelle M. Maresh-Fuehrer (Department of Communication & Media; Texas A&M University–Corpus Christi), Lisa Mikesell (School of Communication and Information; Rutgers University), Margaret C. Stewart (School of Communication and Information; University of North Florida), Katherine S. Thweatt (Department of Communication Studies; State University of New York at Oswego), and Thomas S. Wright (Department of Communication and Social Influence; Temple University).

PART I

Foundations

Introduction to Strategic Research

Completing a marathon is an impressive feat, right? So, in 2017 Adidas decided to capitalize on that by e-mailing all participants of the Boston marathon with promotional offers for Adidas gear. The problem? Their e-mail stated, "Congrats on surviving the Boston Marathon." It appeared that Adidas forgot the horror that struck the Boston Marathon just 4 years earlier, when two bombs went off near the finish line of the race. Three people were killed, and more than 250 people were wounded. The use of the term "surviving" in the e-mail was cringe-worthy at best and likely painful to many who actually did survive the tragedy.

Adidas is not alone in this sort of messaging failure. There are numerous instances of advertisements that have neglected to take into account the social environment. Consider the following tone-deaf examples. In 2018 H&M produced an ad for a hoodie with the phrase "coolest monkey in the jungle" on the chest and used a young Black child as the model. The ad harkened to racial slurs comparing Black people to monkeys. In 2019 Gucci produced a sweater that pulled up over the wearer's face. Its black color and red lips seemed to be an homage to blackface. Lastly, in 2017 Dove aired a soap ad that shows a Black woman taking off her shirt to reveal a White woman (implying that the Black woman was dirty and after using the soap she becomes a "clean" White woman). These incidents point to "brand teams failing to recognize potential racial sensitivities that seem obvious, especially after ads reach wider audiences and are shared on social media" (Schulz, 2018, para. 10).

All of these cases are examples of strategy failures. Whether you work in public relations, marketing communications, social media, or internal communications, at its best professional communication is a strategic function. The main thesis of this book is that research is an important part of developing and assessing communication strategy. For that reason, we believe that professional communicators must develop two skill sets: the ability to be *a critical research consumer* and the ability to be an *effective research producer*. A critical research consumer is able to understand the strengths and weaknesses of the process used to create research and use that understanding to make strategic decisions based on research findings. An effective research producer can engage in the research process to gather and analyze new data in an effort to develop and evaluate communication strategy. Throughout this book, we aim to help you become a better research consumer *and* producer. To get you started, we will describe the nature of strategy, explain some key ideas about the general nature of research, and discuss characteristics of good research.

Communication Strategy

Because professional communication is strategic, we first must address what strategy is and how it is used in various communication professions. Table 1.1 lists four prominent communication functions, the target of their efforts, and what they want as a result of the professional activity. The first major function is **public relations**, which "is a strategic communication process that builds mutually beneficial relationships between organizations and their publics" (Public Relations Society of America, 2019). A *public* is a group of people who share

TABLE 1.1 Communication Functions and Goals

Communication Function	Target Group	Goal
Public relations	Publics	Mutually beneficial relationship
Marketing communications	Customers	Sales
Internal communication	Organizational members	Engagement (productivity)
Media content creation/ distribution	Audience	Reach (sales)

a common interest or problem. Typical publics of concern to public relations practitioners are employees, shareholders, the community, the media, and political groups, among others. At its core, the public relations function creates messages to develop and maintain relationships with these varying groups.

Marketing communications refers to the development of messages to sell a product, service, or idea. For that reason, the target audience is all people likely to purchase the product, use the service, or adopt the idea. In other words, marketing communication seeks to create or maintain customers, and the goal is to enhance sales.

Internal communication includes a number of different professional functions, including human resources, training and development, and change management. Each of these positions focuses on facilitating effective communication among organizational members. The goal of these efforts is to create *employee engagement*, which means that organizational members derive meaning from their work and are committed to the organization and its goals. Although the immediate goal is employee engagement, it would be naïve to imply that organizations strive to create this sort of connection with members simply to benefit employees. Ultimately, the purpose of employee engagement is to enhance the growth and profitability of the organization (Warner, 2018).

Finally, many communication professionals develop or distribute mediated content, including entertainment and news content. Mass media has shifted from broadcasting to *narrowcasting*, which means that the goal is to reach a specific audience. Regardless if you are a scriptwriter, a broadcast news producer, a film editor, or an on-air reporter, your goal is to reach the largest audience within your target audience type. Audiences may be targeted by demographics (age, education, race, income) and psychographics (interests, values, lifestyles). For example, you might be interested in reaching young adults interested in fitness, or the parents of college-aged children, or female science fiction fans. Although these obvious target audiences are helpful, there may be important variations within some of these classifications. For example, Oracle (2015) surveyed over 4,000 Millennials and developed five distinct segments of the generation, suggesting that not all Millennials are alike. Their classification includes the following:

◆ **Up and comers:** Highly educated males who are the life of the party, live in urban areas, and are racially and ethnically diverse

◆ **Mavens:** High-income 30-something moms, live in the suburbs, always on the go

◆ **Eclectics:** Female free spirits, crafty, foodies, dislike the outdoors

◆ **Skeptics:** Often gamers, predominantly male, have a relatively lower income, unlikely to drink alcohol

◆ **Trendsetters:** The youngest Millennials, they are avid social media users, and they are very outgoing

Oracle's (2015) research delineating distinct segments of the Millennial generation may be extremely useful for communication professionals who create and distribute media content when seeking to reach the largest audience within a given target characteristic because the research may help them recognize important variations among and between groups of people.

It should be no surprise that communication strategy varies across these different professional functions. Nevertheless, we will describe a four-step process of communication strategy endorsed by the Public Relations Society of America (PRSA) called the RPIE model, which we believe can be used by all communication functions. The **RPIE model** stands for research, planning, implementation, and evaluation. Table 1.2 highlights the model.

TABLE 1.2   The RPIE Process

Step	What it Entails
Research	Establish the current situation
Planning	Develop goals, objectives, strategies, and tactics
Implementation	Execute the plan
Evaluation	Determine whether the objectives were achieved

First, research means the systematic gathering, analysis, and reporting of information in order to develop or assess communication strategy. Simply put, professional communicators need to gather information to determine the existing situation before they can develop a strategy. In public relations, practitioners often conduct a *situational analysis*, which refers to the identification of economic, political, social, and technological forces that might impact an organization. Internal communication professionals often conduct a *SWOT analysis* in order to assess the effectiveness of internal communications. SWOT stands for an examination of the internal strengths (S) and weaknesses (W) of communication and potential external opportunities (O) and threats (T) that might impact the communication plan. This sort of research is also conducted by media organizations; many newspapers conduct research to determine preferences for distribution (print versus online) and types of content readers wish to see, for example.

The second step is planning, which refers to the development of communication goals, objectives, strategies, and tactics. These activities are listed from the most abstract to the most specific. A goal is a broad statement of organizational intent. Consider the following examples from a public broadcasting station (Maine Public, 2018):

◆ *To be the premier, trusted source of news and educational, cultural, and public affairs programming.*

◆ *To be more relevant to an increasingly diverse audience with an emphasis on future listeners and viewers.*

Although all organizations should have specific goals, we sometimes don't realize that there are goals associated with other types of communications as well. To illustrate, the goal for Ava DuVernay's

2019 Web series *When They See Us* was to shed light on injustices in the criminal justice system (King, 2019).

More specific than goals are **objectives**, which is *what* will be accomplished to achieve the goal. Going back to the public broadcasting strategic plan we described earlier, in order to realize the first goal (to be the premier, trusted source of news and educational, cultural, and public affairs programming) the organization set the following objectives (Maine Public, 2018):

◆ *Continue to build our capacity for reporting and original, local journalism*

◆ *Invest in enterprise reporting that distinguishes us from other news sources*

◆ *Deploy content efficiently and effectively, with fewer barriers, across multiple relevant platforms for maximum impact*

The third element of planning is the creation of strategies. A **strategy** is a coordinated approach to reach an objective. Strategies answer the *how* question. In the case of Maine Public's strategic plan, *how* will they build their capacity for reporting news? Will they hire more reporters? Will they create partnerships with a university to develop journalistic talent? *How* will they deploy content efficiently and effectively? Will they train reporters to create stories that are appropriate for both broadcast and the Web?

Finally, **tactics** refer to the way that you will carry out your strategy. What sorts of information or persuasive appeals will Maine Public use to create a strategic partnership with a university? Will they train reporters to develop stories for multiple platforms in house or will they send the reporters to a training session? It goes without saying that important tactics for communication professionals include creating messages, but crafting a message with a full consideration of the goals and objectives behind the message is what makes communication strategic.

The third part of the RPIE model is **implementation**, which means that the plan needs to be put into action. Messages need to be created, channels selected, and audiences targeted. Often there are unforeseen challenges to implementing a communication strategy, including staffing issues, budgeting problems, or lack of effective leadership.

Nevertheless, if proper research has been used and the strategy is carefully planned, implementation problems can be minimized.

The final component of the model is evaluation. How successful was the strategy? Were the objectives met? How do you know? When developing a communication strategy, an essential part of the strategy itself is determining how you will know if it worked. As Wilson and Ogden (2016) state, the research you conduct here can demonstrate that the activity was warranted because the strategy achieved your objectives.

Types of Research

It should be clear by now that research is an essential part of the strategic process. Recall that we defined research as the systematic gathering, analysis, and reporting of information in order to develop or assess communication strategy. First, note that we are talking about a *systematic* collection of information, which is typically known as formal research. Formal research is meticulously planned and involves the objective collection of data (Stacks, 2002). Contrast this with informal methods of research, which are typically less controlled and more subjective (Stacks, 2002). Examples of informal research include casual conversations with coworkers, randomly scanning newspapers, conducting a Google search, or recollecting personal experiences.

The second aspect of the definition that deserves attention is that the results of the research are *carefully reported* so that consumers of the research are able to understand and potentially even replicate the study. If particular procedures are not disclosed or the nature of the sample is not described, we cannot judge the worth of the study. This highlights yet another distinction between types of research: primary research versus secondary research. Primary research refers to research reported by the person who actually conducted the study. Typically, this form of research is published in peer-reviewed journals, scholarly books, and academic conference papers. Secondary research is a description of a study that was conducted by someone other than the person who conducted the research. In general, most websites, newspapers, popular magazines, and news reports are considered secondary research sources, as are college textbooks.

You may have noticed that we listed only academic sources for primary research. This points to yet another distinction about research types. Academic sources are known as public research, because they are available to anyone who wishes to read about the research results. Research conducted by nonprofit organizations like the Pew Charitable Trusts and a number of government sources might also be considered both primary and public research, such as U.S. Census data. In contrast, proprietary research refers to privately funded research that is not meant for public view. Most research that an organization conducts as part of its strategic planning process can be considered proprietary.

The final aspect of our definition of research is that we are specifically referring to research that is used to develop or assess communication strategy. This focus highlights a final distinction about types of research, which is the difference between basic and applied research. Basic research is conducted by scholars interested in creating or refining a theory. Theory is useful, and we believe it can assist you with decisions in your professional life, but we are not focusing on basic research in this text. Instead, we are focusing on applied research: research that is conducted in order to solve real-world problems. Table 1.3 highlights the different types of research. The types of research we feature in this text appears on the left column of the table.

TABLE 1.3 Different Types of Research

Formal research: Meticulously planned and carefully reported	**Informal research:** Casual, subjective, less planned
Primary research: Research reported by the person who conducted it	**Secondary research:** Research reported by someone other than the person who conducted it
Proprietary research: Research that is privately funded and is not meant for public view	**Public research:** Research that is available for review by the general public
Applied research: Research meant to solve real-world problems	**Basic research:** Research designed to create or test a theory

So, how do these types of research relate to communication strategy? In short, research is necessary to effectively complete the RPIE model. Research is necessary to create a clear analysis of the situation; it is necessary to develop goals and objectives; it drives the crafting of an effective message and the selection of the communication channels; and it is an inherent part of assessing the effects of the strategy. Given the importance of research throughout this process, professional communicators must be adept at conducting and interpreting research. Because being a critical consumer of research is vital to professional success, in the next section we discuss the indicators of quality research.

Evaluating Research

No communication strategy is ever a guaranteed winner, but the likelihood of success increases if appropriate and effective research is undertaken in the process of developing the strategy. However, not all research is good research. In 2017, Pepsi created an ad featuring Kendall Jenner that was widely seen as trivializing the Black Lives Matter protests. Jenner walked among crowds of young people holding placards; eventually she reached a line of police observing the crowds and offered a police officer a can of Pepsi. After the ad was shown, social media exploded with complaints that the ad made light of the Black Lives Matter protests against police brutality and shootings of Black Americans. Although the behind-the-scenes details have not been published, there is evidence to suggest that faulty research might have contributed to the tone-deaf ad. Pinsker's (2017) investigation suggested that Pepsi might have relied on poor marketing research indicating that Millennials were interested in activism (related to the situational analysis) and failed to test market the actual ad with a diverse audience (related to the implementation of the tactic). Estimates are that Pepsi lost about $100 million on producing and promoting the ad (Adams & Telling, 2017). Clearly there can be substantial costs associated with poor-quality research. For that reason, it is important to know indicators of quality research, which are listed in Box 1.1.

BOX 1.1

Indicators of Quality Research

Indicator 1   Establishes a clearly defined purpose

Indicator 2   Provides sufficient background material

Indicator 3   Uses suitable measurement

Indicator 4   Relies on an appropriate sample

Indicator 5   Utilizes the correct method

Indicator 6   Findings are presented accurately and objectively

Indicator 7   Conclusions and recommendations are clearly grounded in the findings

First, good research has a **clearly defined purpose**. Because research takes a lot of time and can use considerable resources, it is important that the goals of the research are explicit and clear before any research is conducted. Moreover, readers of the research should also be able to pinpoint the purpose of the research; for that reason, it is important that the researcher makes identification of the goals of the study as easy as possible. The next chapter describes how to identify research goals.

Second, quality research provides **sufficient background material** to situate the research within already established and ongoing examinations of the topic. It is a rare problem that has not already been researched in some way. Each piece of research can be thought of as part of a larger conversation about the topic at hand. Providing a coherent summary about what is known already about the topic before completing a new piece of research helps to place the new research within that conversation and makes sure the researcher is moving the conversation forward. Offering details about previous research and how your new research is connected to what is already known about the subject in a research report gives a fuller understanding of the topic to decision makers. Chapter 2 describes how to use secondary data, which is part of the process of providing sufficient background material.

Third, quality research uses **suitable measurement**. Effective research involves a clear understanding of key concepts and how they might vary among the people involved in your research. Imagine that a company that runs a social media platform wants to know more about the degree of user engagement with their product. When conducting research on user engagement, it is expected that users will vary, or differ from each other, in their level of engagement. The research will likely also focus on what factors, and variations in those factors, influence user engagement. Researchers also need to decide on the best method for measuring their key concepts. For nearly every concept of interest to those who practice strategic communication, there is more than one way to measure or assess differences in the concept. Think again of user engagement with a social media platform. User engagement could be assessed by interviewing users about their experiences with the platform, by asking users to answer closed-ended survey questions about their use of the platform, by directly observing users on the platform, or by analyzing various metrics generated by the platform. Chapter 3 discusses the process of defining concepts and deciding among types of measurement.

A specific part of research methods that merits its own focus is the use of an **appropriate sample**, which is the fourth indicator of quality research. As we describe in Chapter 4, the term *sample* refers to the people or items that are studied. Typically, a sample is a small group meant to represent the whole, such as studying 200 employees out of a possible of 1,000 employees. To judge the quality of research, consider who has been studied and how closely they represent the group of people who should be studied, as well as how many people have been studied. As we will discuss in the chapter, gathering an appropriate sample for your study has several challenges.

Next, quality research **upholds ethical standards**. Adhering to ethical standards in research is an important part of the researcher's obligation to those who will rely on the research to make strategic decisions. Chapter 5 describes a number of ethical standards relevant to research studies, including fundamental research ethics, ethical guidelines for particular professions, as well as the ethics of proprietary research.

Fourth, the **specific methods** being used should be described in such a manner that others should be able to evaluate what you did in your research and repeat the study if they so desired. Every aspect of the study should be described: what was done, how it was done, when, where, and with whom. You should also fully describe the methods used to interpret the results. Although Chapter 2 provides an overview of typical methods used in communication research, Chapters 6 through 10 provide detailed descriptions about how to use specific research methods such as focus groups, surveys, and several other techniques.

Next, in quality research the **findings are presented accurately and objectively**. This is where knowledge of research methods comes into play. On occasion researchers may be tempted to exaggerate the nature of their findings or present their findings in a manner that supports a particular point of view. Casual readers may not recognize when such distortions take place, but critical readers can see through inflated claims. We discuss the analysis and reporting of results in Chapters 11 and 12.

The sixth indicator of quality research is that **conclusions and recommendations are clearly grounded in the findings** of the study. As we just indicated, researchers can be tempted to overstate their findings, but they can also be tempted to offer conclusions and/or recommendations that do not logically follow from the research findings. Chapter 12 describes how to draw conclusions and make recommendations as part of the research process.

The Barcelona Principles

Many times students believe that what they learn in the university is unrelated to what happens in the "real world." We assure you that research is considered an essential component of strategic communication practice by communication professionals themselves. The Barcelona Principles 2.0 identify the best practices in measurement across a variety of communication professions (Rockland, 2015). These principles, which were approved by organizations such as the Public

Relations Society of America, the Institute for Public Relations, the Global Alliance, and the International Association for the Measurement and Evaluation of Communication, provide a framework for the role of research in effective strategic communications. Each of the principles is described in Box 1.2.

The first principle centers on **establishing measurable goals.** As indicated earlier, an essential part of any strategy is identifying how the strategy will be assessed. One way to do this is through SMART objectives, which is an acronym that stands for **specific** (stated in the simplest and clearest way possible), **measurable** (you establish a way to provide evidence that the goal was achieved), **achievable** (appropriate given the resources involved—not too challenging, but not too easy, either), **results focused** (focused on the outcomes of an activity, not the activity itself), and **time bound** (linked to a specific timeframe). To illustrate, a smart goal for a social media professional would be "Within 2 months our Instagram traffic will add a total of 1,000 unique visitors by increasing our posting frequency from one post per day to two posts per day."

BOX 1.2

The Barcelona Principles 2.0

Principle 1   Goal setting and measurement are fundamental to communication and public relations.

Principle 2   Measuring communication outcomes is recommended versus only measuring outputs.

Principle 3   The effect on organizational performance can and should be measured where possible.

Principle 4   Measurement and evaluation require both qualitative and quantitative methods.

Principle 5   Advertising Value Equivalency (AVE) is not the value of communication.

Principle 6   Social media can and should be measured consistently with other media channels.

Principle 7   Measurement and evaluation should be transparent, consistent, and valid.

Second, the Barcelona Principles 2.0 focuses on **measuring outcomes, not just outputs**. Simply stated, an output is what a communication professional produces: press releases, employee newsletters, a video package, and the like. Historically, people in the communication professions were judged by the quantity and quality of these products. However, just because something has been produced doesn't mean it has been published, or viewed, or understood. Effective communicators instead measure what has happened as a *result* of these efforts, which are the outcomes. Do employees have greater trust in the organizational leadership? Are consumers more aware of your product? Do readers have a better understanding of the issue?

This idea of measuring outcomes is directly related to the third principle, which is that the effect of communication activities should be tied to overall **organizational performance**. One of the *key performance indicators* (KPI) of most organizations is *return on investment* (ROI), which measures net profit associated with the cost of an activity. In marketing communications, it is relatively easy to calculate ROI; to what extent did the cost of a marketing campaign increase sales? In other communication professions, ROI may be more difficult to establish. Possible performance indicators include customer or employee retention, market share, revenue, brand equity, Web traffic, social engagement, and employee satisfaction.

Fourth, according to the Barcelona Principles 2.0, measurement should include both quantitative and qualitative data. The term data simply means information. Quantitative and qualitative data come from differing research methodologies. **Quantitative methodologies** require studying a large sample using precise measurement. The data that are collected by this research typically are analyzed statistically, and results are presented as numerical and statistical comparisons. Quantitative research allows you to draw conclusions and make predictions. **Qualitative methodologies** usually focus on a smaller sample, with a focus on providing an in-depth understanding of an issue. Results are in the form of themes or descriptions. These two methodologies are used for different reasons and provide different types of answers about communication activities. We talk in more depth about these two approaches throughout the book, and especially in Chapter 11.

Next, the Barcelona Principles 2.0 caution professional communicators against relying on **Advertising Value Equivalency (AVE)** as the only indicator of the value of communication. An AVE is a measure that seeks to quantify the benefit to a client from a public relations campaign. For many years, public relations professionals calculated an AVE that implied that public relations coverage was equivalent to purchased ad space. For example, a public relations professional might measure the column inches of a print story and multiply that by the publication's advertising rate to provide an indication of how much the same coverage would have cost if it had been a paid advertisement. Although the intentions were to make public relations comparable to marketing and advertising efforts, the Institute for Public Relations has identified a number of conceptual and logistical problems associated with AVEs (Jeffries-Fox, 2003). Accordingly, best practices suggest utilizing a variety of measurements (often called **metrics**) of your outcomes such as measuring volume of messages, impressions, and reach. These types of measurements will be discussed in Chapter 6 (Observations) and Chapter 7 (Content Analysis).

The sixth principle focuses specifically on **developing goals and measuring outcomes of social media**. In short, social media are just another tool in the professional communicator's tool belt. As such, any decision about how and why to use social media should be tied to a communication strategy, and measurement of social media efforts should go beyond basic calculations of liking or sharing. Both quality and quantity of social media posts are important.

Lastly, the Barcelona Principles 2.0 argue **for transparent, consistent, and valid research**. It is for that reason that this book has been written; all communication professionals should have a baseline understanding of how to conduct ethical and effective research. Indeed, top-level professionals suggest that a solid understanding of the research process is one of the essential skills that all communication strategists should have (Sinickas, 2003). Sinickas (2003) cautions that "as communicators progress up their career paths, they're faced with higher expectations in terms of their understanding of the role of research and measurement in communication campaigns" (p. 1). Clearly, understanding and effectively using the research process is important for your personal career success, as well as the success of the organization for which you work.

Chapter Summary

In this chapter, we talked about the importance of research for developing and assessing communication strategy. Our first major focus was on the nature of strategy. We described the RPIE model of strategy, which includes four steps: research, planning, implementation, and evaluation. We then talked about the nature of research, defining research as the systematic collection of information and careful reporting of results in an effort to develop or assess communication strategy. We highlighted specific features of research, and in doing so differentiated between eight types of research: formal versus informal, primary versus secondary, public versus proprietary, and basic versus applied. Next, we discussed the indicators of quality research: a clearly identified purpose, a sufficient amount of background research, appropriate measurement, upholding ethical standards, clearly described methods, an appropriate sample, objective and accurate findings, and conclusions and recommendations that stem from the findings. Finally, we discussed best practices in strategic communication measurement as indicated in the *Barcelona Principles 2.0* (Rockland, 2015).

PRACTICE ACTIVITIES

1. **Strategy failures:** Search online for the "worst communication failures." There are multiple articles and videos on this topic. For each of the failures, why do you think the strategy failed? What research might the organization have done to prevent or repair the problem?

2. **Creating SMART objectives:** In this chapter, we discussed the SMART objective acronym. Using the SMART objective guidelines, create a communication objective for the organization in which you work or one you have learned more about. In doing so, clearly identify the ways that your objective fits each part of the SMART guidelines.

   Objective:

Specific because:

Measurable because:

Achievable because:

Results-focused because:

Time-bound because:

3. **Differentiating between outputs and outcomes:** We discussed the difference between outputs and outcomes in this chapter. For each of the following outputs, indicate what type of outcome you might expect.

Output	Outcome
a. Brochure	
b. Video news release (VNR)	
c. Organizational chart	
d. Magazine ad	
e. Instagram post	
f. Benefits intranet site	
g. Corporate blog	
h. Direct mail postcard	
i. Product demonstration	
j. Employee handbook	

4. **Quantitative versus qualitative research:** Imagine that you work for a start-up company that is developing an app that will allow you to track the use of a digital photo online. Why might you do qualitative research (studying a small group of people to get an in-depth understanding of the issue) as part of the app development? Why might you do quantitative research (studying a large group of people to draw conclusions or make predictions) as part of the app development?

5. **Evaluating research quality:** Locate a research report from within your company or from a public research source such as the Pew Research Center. After reading the report, evaluate the ways it either

meets or does not meet the standards for quality research discussed in this chapter.

Clearly defined purpose: Is there a clear purpose statement for the research? Do the researchers adhere to that purpose in conducting the research?

Sufficient background material: Ask yourself, Do the researchers adequately discuss what is already known about the topic? Is it clear how this new research study will add to what is already known about the topic?

Appropriate measurement: Do the measures used to assess each concept seem to match the definition of the concept well? Can you think of alternative ways they might have measured the concepts that would have been better?

Upholds ethical standards: Does the way the research was conducted seem to harm anyone?

Uses specific methods: Is the way the research was conducted described clearly and fully enough that someone else could repeat the study? Does the method used to conduct the study seem to make sense given the purpose of the study?

Uses an appropriate sample: Are the people involved in the study the best source from which to gather the data? Does it seem like the amount of people sampled in the study fits the goals of the study?

Findings are presented accurately and objectively: Do you detect bias in the way the data was analyzed or reported?

Conclusions and recommendations are clearly grounded in the findings: Is it clear how the study findings lead to the conclusions and recommendations given in the study?

The Research Process

Few stories demonstrate how rapidly something can shift from a potential public relations nightmare to PR gold than the launch of the Philadelphia Flyers new mascot, Gritty (Madden, 2018). Gritty's introduction caused an explosive reaction not just in Philadelphia, but across the nation. And the reaction was probably not what Flyers senior leadership had expected, at least not at first. For many, Gritty was horrifying. He was described as a "ghastly empty-eyed Muppet" and a "shaggy orange Wookiee-esque grotesquerie" (Yuhas, 2018, p. 14). He became fodder for late-night talk shows and comedians. Yet, less than a month later Philadelphia's City Council approved a resolution declaring that Gritty "honors the spirit and passion" of the City of Philadelphia. *Adweek* deemed Gritty "the internet's most beloved mascot."

If you think this was accidental, think again. The creation of Gritty started with the recognition of a problem. The 2017 NHL all-star game featured a hockey game played by the teams' mascots. The Flyers were only one of three teams not represented because they didn't have

CHAPTER OUTLINE

◆ Step 1: Establishing the Need for Research

◆ Step 2: Determine the Research Objective

◆ Step 3: Formulate Research Questions and/or Hypotheses

◆ Step 4: Select the Method

a mascot, and the son of the Flyers' COO asked his father why not (Fleming, 2018). This question served as the initial impetus for recognizing a lost marketing opportunity. The real scope of the problem became apparent when the Philadelphia Eagles won the 2018 Super Bowl; during all of the publicity events surrounding that win, the mascots of the city's three other major sports franchises were clear and present—the Eagle's own Swoop, of course, but also the baseball team's beloved Phillie Phanatic and the 76ers Franklin. At that point the Flyer's marketing team estimated that a Flyer's mascot could attend between 250 and 300 community events a year, widely increasing brand recognition (Fleming, 2018).

After creating the strategic goal of developing a mascot, the team began crafting the criteria for what an ideal mascot would be (Fleming, 2018). One of their first criteria is that the organization did not want anything that resembled an existing mascot or puppet. Second, they wanted a very big mascot, something larger than life with monster-like features. Third, they wanted it to be as weird as the Phillie Phanatic, a large, green, fuzzy mascot that does not clearly look like any existing creature (Yuhas, 2018). Finally, they wanted it to represent the character of the city of Philadelphia, "a city whose identity is wrapped up in a mix of blue-collar pride, defensiveness and a long history of athletic failure" (Yuhas, 2019, p. 13). In fact, the mascot's name—Gritty—is a frequent descriptor of the city of Philadelphia.

In Chapter 1, we discussed the role of research in communication strategy. As should be evident in the story of Gritty, the beginning of this effort always begins with the development of a strategic goal. Much like there are stages or elements of developing, implementing, and evaluating a strategic plan, there are steps involved when conducting research. Box 2.1 shows the steps that should be taken in the research process.

We provide details about steps 1 through 4 in this chapter: establishing the need for research, determining the research objective, formulating your research questions and/or hypotheses, and selecting your method. The remaining steps in the research process are addressed in detail in other chapters. The fifth step, developing precise measurement, is discussed in Chapter 3. Selecting your sample is

---

BOX 2.1

The Research Process

Step 1   Establish the need

Step 2   Determine the research objective

Step 3   Formulate research questions and/or hypotheses

Step 4   Select the method

Step 5   Develop precise measurement

Step 6   Determine your sample

Step 7   Apply the method

Step 8   Analyze the data

Step 9   Utilize results

---

described in Chapter 4. Each of the specific methods you might apply are discussed in Chapters 6 through 10. Finally, analyzing data and reporting the results are discussed in Chapters 11 and 12, respectively.

Step 1: Establishing the Need for Research

One of the essential roles of a professional communicator is **environmental scanning**, which refers to the process of monitoring, interpreting, and responding to emerging social, political, organizational, and industry trends (Lauzen, 1995). Through environmental scanning, professional communicators can identify and analyze issues in order to make effective decisions. The complexity of the organizational environment determines how formal the environmental scanning process should be. For example, consider a situation faced by Barnes & Noble. The company was facing plummeting stock prices in 2018. However, it was not immediately clear what was causing the falling stock prices because the company faced numerous challenges: the resurgence of independent book stores, falling behind Amazon in e-reader technology, and a sexual harassment scandal involving the company's CEO, among other things (Meyersohn, 2018). The more turbulent the environment, the more formalized the environmental scanning process should be (Lauzen, 1995).

You might recall from Chapter 1 that the first step of the RPIE strategic planning process is research. The need for research is established when professional communicators recognize that they don't have sufficient information to develop a strong strategy. In the case of Barnes & Noble, should they spend money on researching and developing e-reader technology? Or should they develop a public relations campaign to overcome the scandal involving its CEO? Without knowing which issues were most associated with the falling stock prices the company could not develop a rebound strategy.

When insufficient information is available to develop an effective strategy, the professional communicator should consider what type of additional information is needed. Too often, professionals believe that conducting research has to involve collecting new data to address the issue at hand (recall from Chapter 1 that collecting new data is called **primary research**). However, quite frequently the information needed to research the issue is already available. In such cases, it is much more efficient to use existing data than to produce new data to address the issue.

A vast amount of data is available from a number of sources, including government agencies, nongovernment organizations (NGOs), trade associations, commercial information services, and public/ scholarly research. In terms of government agencies, the U.S. Census Bureau publishes a wide variety of data, including demographic and economic data that can assist business launches or complete grant proposals. The Pew Research Center is particularly useful for professional communicators; this nonpartisan think tank conducts research that ranges from social trends to politics, and from science to the media. Similarly, the Gallup organization provides free reports about a wide variety of organizational issues, as well as offering paid consultative services. A large number of trade organizations also provide important data, including the Institute for Public Relations, the American Marketing Association, and the International Association of Business Communicators. There are also commercial services that gather and sell information. You are probably familiar with the Nielson organization, which gathers data about media viewing habits and user attitudes. Similarly, IRI is a company that provides data on consumer purchasing behaviors and attitudes. Finally, although some academic research centers on theory development and testing, there is also a large amount of applied research that might provide data relevant for developing strategy.

If existing data are not available to address the issue, then it will be necessary to design and implement a research project to gather new data. However, it is important to understand at the outset of preparing to conduct primary research that several constraining factors must be considered when designing a new research project. Conducting primary research can be time consuming and expensive. Specifically, it is important to know what resources, both in terms of money and human hours, are available for primary research before designing it. It is also important to consider the time frame in which the data are needed in order to make strategic decisions. Whether a decision needs to be made by the end of the week or sometime in the next 3 months will make a big difference in the way primary research can be conducted.

Another consideration is whether you have the ability to gather the data you need. If your research requires you to collect information from people, do you have the ability to contact those people and are they likely to respond by accepting your request for information? Researchers are often surprised by how difficult it can be to get people to complete surveys and participate in focus groups. Gaining participation from a sufficient amount of people may require incentives that cost money, which should be considered in the overall budget for the research project.

Finally, it is important to consider whether you have the skills within the organization's personnel to adequately analyze the data. While this book will help you gain the skills you need to understand how to develop a research project and to perform some data analyses, oftentimes complex statistical analysis is necessary, which is beyond the scope of this book. If you need complex statistical analysis to address the issue at hand, then it is important to make sure either someone in your organization can perform this type of analysis or you have the budget to hire a consultant to do so. Collecting data that you cannot analyze does not help in the strategic decision-making process.

Despite these potential hurdles to conducting primary research, there are also organizational benefits to doing so. Any data that are collected by an organization will be proprietary, potentially giving your organization an informational edge. Moreover, these data can be used by organizational members to become content experts, providing an additional public relations benefit to the organization. Finally, an organization can sell the results of their research, perhaps resulting in a net profit for the company.

Step 2: Determine the Research Objective

Once a need for research has been established, the next step is to develop a clear understanding of what the researcher hopes to achieve by conducting research, which is called the **research objective**. The research objective is different from a strategic objective. In Chapter 1 we talked about the planning step in the RPIE model, which includes the development of goals, objectives, strategies, and tactics. A strategic objective answers what will be done to achieve the goal. The research objective should include not only the answer to the "what" question (what will be done) but also the answer to the "why" question (why it should be done). One way to accomplish this is to break your statement into two parts:

1. We are interested in studying _____.

2. In order to _____.

To illustrate, check out some sample research objectives in Box 2.2.

Typically there are five overarching goals for research conducted by professional communicators: monitoring the environment, identifying opportunities, diagnosing problems, selecting a course of action, and evaluating the course of action.

BOX 2.2

Sample Research Objectives

To examine current employee attitudes about the organization in order to increase employee engagement.

To measure the sentiment about our organization in social media messages in order to develop a social media strategy.

To gather customer satisfaction data in order to improve our product development.

To ascertain how people have learned about our product in order to determine the effectiveness of our marketing strategy.

Monitoring the Environment

In the first step of the research process we introduced the notion of *environmental scanning*, which involves tracking political, organizational, and industry trends. Because this type of monitoring involves the collection and interpretation of data, it represents a form of research. Monitoring the environment is an essential part of strategic communication. As we address in Chapter 6, more and more customer service issues are arising through social media. Consider the case of Tesco, an international supermarket brand. Like many companies, they had limited employees working on Christmas day 2017. Unfortunately, a large number of rancid turkeys had been sold at the supermarket chain in Great Britain, and customers only realized that the turkey was spoiled when they began to cook them on Christmas day. Because the customer service lines were not being answered, customers took to social media, complaining about the issue, with no company response. Worst yet, Tesco had a scheduled social media post that went out the next day detailing how you might prepare leftover turkey (Rojas, 2017). Needless to say, the customers who had complained to no avail were incensed by the poor management of the issue. Monitoring the environment is an essential part of preventing crises from occurring; it allows proactive rather than reactive responses.

Identifying Opportunities

The story of Gritty at the beginning of this chapter should high-light how research can uncover opportunities to create or enhance relationships. One of the central goals for marketing research, for example, is to identify opportunities. Consider the candy bar Kit Kat, which is sold by the Nestlé Corporation. Although sales of the candy bar are solid around the world, Nestlé was able to greatly expand their market in Japan by recognizing two unique opportunities in that country (Madden, 2010). First, the marketing team at Nestle recognized that the translation of Kit Kat in Japanese is *Kitto Katsu*, which means "surely win" in Japanese. They realized that they could leverage the tradition of sending students good luck wishes for college entry exams by marketing the candy bar as a good luck charm. The second marketing opportunity was identifying different consumer preferences (Madden, 2010). Unlike Americans, Japanese consumers are noted for their interest in exotic tastes and their desire for novelty. Accordingly, there are at least 300 different flavors of Kit Kat bars in Japan, including soy sauce, miso, cucumber, and adzuki bean. Many are manufactured for only a limited period of time, which maximizes demand for the unusual flavors.

Diagnosing Problems

Of course, since the central premise of this book is that research is an essential component of developing a communication strategy, a second major research objective is to investigate organizational challenges and dilemmas. So, do you know what KLM is? If you think it might be a radio station or a brand of milk, you aren't alone (Frederick, 2016). KLM is actually an airline based in the Netherlands that is a part of the Air France group. The airline conducted a brand study before opening additional flight routes in the United States, and what they found was troubling: People had no idea who the company was. The result of this research was a public relations campaign to increase brand awareness by posting a series of humorous videos with the tag line "it's an airline" on social media channels. The campaign resulted in over 120 million views, suggesting that the company's objectives were met (Frederick, 2016).

Selecting a Course of Action

Ultimately, all strategic plans involve actions and activities designed to achieve the objective. Often, this involves choosing the best alternative among several possible courses of action. How do you know which is the best alternative? Research, of course. *Fortune* magazine has listed Wegmans Food Markets as one of the best companies to work for in the country every year since the list was started. Given rising healthcare costs, Wegmans wanted to determine which of the benefits they offered their employees were valued as most important. They conducted a survey of their employees that asked them to rank each of the benefits they offered (Walters, 2011). The company was surprised to learn not only that health care coverage was rated as the deciding factor for employees' decision to stay or leave the company, but that base pay was the least important factor. Learning these preferences allowed Wegmans to make the decision to increase health coverage for employees by holding base pay at a modest rate (Walters, 2011).

Evaluating a Course of Action

The final research goal for professional researchers is to obtain the answer to the question "Did it work?" Indeed, a central element of a public relations or marketing campaign is to ascertain the effectiveness of achieving the campaign's objectives. In fact, given that an organization likely has distinct marketing and public relations goals, it is important to differentiate the results of the two types of campaigns. An example of this sort of nuanced approach to program evaluation was undertaken by London's Victoria and Albert Museum. In 2013 the museum produced a special display of David Bowie memorabilia, with several marketing and public relations objectives, including increasing visitors by 230,000 over a

6-month period, increasing membership, and expanding awareness of the museum (Comcowitch, 2015). By timing different museum activities based on public relations or marketing efforts they were able to isolate the effects of PR versus marketing efforts. Notably, the museum exceeded all of their objectives, but they were also able to establish the ROI (return on investment) of their public relations campaign (Comcowitch, 2015).

Step 3: Formulate Research Questions and/or Hypotheses

Having a clear research objective is an essential part of guiding the rest of the research process. Once the specific goals of the research are understood, the next step is to craft individual research questions (abbreviated as RQ) or hypotheses (abbreviated as H). **Research questions** are much like any other question; they are an open-ended request for specific information. As such, research questions are even more specific than the research objective; although the research objective tells you what you are studying and why, research questions focus your attention on the very specific types of data being sought. To illustrate, consider one of the objectives we presented in Box 2.2: "To examine current employee attitudes about the organization in order to increase employee engagement." The research objective tells us that we are interested in employee attitudes in general. Specific research questions associated with that objective might include the following:

RQ1: How satisfied are employees?

RQ2: How committed to the organization are employees?

RQ3: Does an employee's position influence their organizational satisfaction?

RQ4: Does length of service influence commitment to
the organization?

Each of these research questions addresses a different aspect of the
overall research objective. Moreover, each provides very different sorts
of data, which is important for the researcher to recognize, because
the type of question you ask influences how you will analyze the data
you collect. RQ1 and RQ2 both are seeking to describe a current
state or condition. RQ3 is seeking to compare the satisfaction levels
of people at one level of the organizational hierarchy with those at
other levels of the organizational hierarchy. Finally, RQ4 is looking
to relate two different concepts, which are known as variables. Variables
are concepts that take on more than one value in the research
and will be discussed further in Chapter 3. In RQ4, the research is
seeking to determine if there is a relationship between how long
someone has worked at the organization and how committed they
are to the organization.

Research Questions Versus Hypotheses

Whether the question is seeking to describe, compare, or relate, it is
always phrased in the form of an open-ended question, not a statement.
A hypothesis, on the other hand, makes a testable prediction
about the relationship between two or more variables and is phrased
as a statement of expected results. For example, RQ can be turned
into a prediction:

H1: The longer an employee has worked for the organization, the
more committed they will be to the organization.

In general, there are two types of hypotheses: nondirectional
hypotheses and directional hypotheses. Nondirectional hypotheses
simply predict that two variables will be related to each other in
a predictable fashion:

H2: Employee position influences organizational satisfaction.

In this case, we know that the two variables are related to each
other, but we cannot predict how they are related to each other.
Directional hypotheses specify the exact nature of the relationship.

Compare H1 with H2—you will see that H1 makes a more specific prediction that H2.

When is it appropriate to pose a research question versus a hypothesis? Generally, a research question is posed when you do not have a clear idea of what you expect the relationship between two variables to be. A hypothesis is an educated guess that should be informed by some previous research that suggests how the variables should be related. To illustrate, there is a large volume of published research that has established that the longer an employee's tenure at an organization, the higher the level of the employee's commitment. Knowledge of this body of research would lead someone studying a new organization to propose what we have labeled as H1 rather than a research question. In practice, however, it is common to present research questions rather than hypotheses when conducting strategic communication research. This is because research questions are open to more types of analyses than are hypotheses, which often call for stricter, often statistical, tests of the relationship between variables.

It should also be noted that a single research project may be guided by only one research question or hypothesis, and having both a research question and a hypothesis to guide a project is not necessary. Further, it is also possible that a research project may have multiple research questions, multiple hypotheses, or a combination of research questions and hypotheses. The use of a research question, hypothesis, or multiple research questions and hypotheses in a study should be guided by your objectives for conducting the research and not by any external pressures to have multiple RQs or Hs.

Evaluating RQs/Hs

There are three criteria for developing a useful research question or hypothesis. The first criterion is that the question or hypothesis must be **researchable and answerable**. There are some topics that are neither researchable nor answerable. In some cases, topics are not researchable or answerable because of ethical concerns. It is not ethical, for example, to intentionally expose people to psychologically or physically harmful products or situations. Chapter 5 will provide more information about ethics in the research process. There are other reasons why a topic might not be researchable or answerable, however. If you want to know what your competitor will be doing in 10 years, they (a) are not likely to tell you if they know, but more likely (b) have no idea themselves. We cannot peer into the future, nor can we change the past with "what if" questions. Accordingly, such questions are neither researchable nor answerable. Finally, a research question or hypothesis might not be researchable and answerable because it is not clearly defined. For example, the hypothesis "American organizations will use Twitter more effectively" is not researchable or answerable because the comparison group is not clearly defined (more effectively than whom? What will they do more effectively?). In such cases, making sure the research question or hypothesis is clearly defined may make it usable for research.

The second criterion is that the research question or hypothesis must be **neither too broad nor too narrow**. Quite simply, if a question can be broken down into a series of sub-questions, the research question is too broad. Consider the question "What should we do about fake news?" Certainly, the topic warrants investigation, but given all of the possible things that might be involved in fake news (purposeful disinformation campaigns, distrust of the media, comments from politicians, lack of media literacy, disagreement about the meaning of the term "fake news"), the research question is simply too big to handle with a single research question. Conversely, a research question or hypothesis is too narrow if the information is readily or easily attainable. For example, consider the research question "How many people with graduate degrees work at our organization?" Answering this question requires only a phone call to the human resources department, and therefore it does not warrant further investigation.

The third criterion for good research questions and hypotheses is to be **value neutral**. Simply put, how much faith should you place in research that is funded by an organization that would benefit from the results of the research? Might the researchers have been biased? Most of us who conduct research hope that the results will turn out a particular way. However, it is incumbent on researchers to make sure that their assumptions or biases don't affect the results of the study.

One way this can be addressed is to make sure that the research questions and hypotheses are phrased in a value-neutral way. Consider the following two research questions that might be posed by a researcher working for Instagram:

RQ1: What positive social outcomes are experienced by high-frequency Instagram users as compared to low-frequency Instagram users?

RQ2: How do social outcomes of Instagram use vary for high- and low-frequency users?

In the first research question, the assumption is that Instagram use has positive social outcomes and the research question directs researchers to measure only those positive social outcomes as they compare high- and low-frequency users. Thus, RQ1 is not value neutral. The second research question is value neutral because it allows researchers to assess a wide range of social outcomes, not just positive outcomes, when comparing the effects of Instagram use. Making sure that your research questions and hypotheses are value neutral allows for all possible results to emerge, rather than limiting the results of the study to a preferred result.

Step 4: Select the Method

Once the research questions or hypotheses are developed, the next step in the research process is to select your method. The key thing to remember is that the question you ask (or the hypothesis you pose) determines the method that you use. Table 2.1 provides an overview of each of the methods we will discuss in this book, with the types of information the method can provide.

Too often, people find a method they are comfortable with and then try to conduct all research using that method. However, just because you enjoy conducting surveys does not mean that a survey is really the best way to find the answers to the questions you must address. Instead, a more competent approach is to become familiar with a variety of research methods so that you are comfortable

TABLE 2.1 The Types of Data That Emerge From Various Research Methods

Research Method	Types of Data
Observations	◆ Who, what, when, where, and how people interact within and with an organization ◆ Exposure and engagement with social media and websites
Content analysis	◆ Frequency of messages ◆ Nature of messages ◆ Structure of messages ◆ Impact of messages
Survey research *Questionnaires* *Interviews* *Focus groups*	◆ Attitudes ◆ Beliefs ◆ Experiences
Experiment	◆ Cause and effect

implementing a design that best fits the project goal. Observations, content analysis, surveys, interviews, and experimental methods will be discussed in further detail in upcoming chapters, but a brief overview of each method and the types of research questions and hypotheses best answered by that method follows.

Observations are a means to formally study everyday behavior. These observations allow professional communicators to understand how varying publics interact within your organization and with your organization. Trained researchers might be used to collect observational data, but increasingly organizations are using mechanical means to collect this sort of data. One of the most common types of observations involve social media and Web analytics. Chapter 6 provides an overview of the observational method.

Content analysis is a research method that is focused on the content, nature, or structure of texts. A text is any written or recorded message. Possible texts that professional communicators might study include websites, print advertisements, news broadcasts, and social media posts. Video-recorded conversations also can be considered a text, as might written comments on surveys. Content analysis is best employed to address research questions and hypotheses about the nature of messages. Learning more about existing messages then informs decisions about ongoing and future message strategies. As with digital data analysis, content analysis usually examines public messages that are readily available and rarely involves the direct collection of responses from individuals. Chapter 7 discusses content analysis and the strategic use of content audits, which is an assessment of all of the messages that an organization has distributed.

"Survey" is a broad term that is usually used to describe methods involving asking people a series of questions developed by the researcher. The goal of a survey is usually to address research questions and hypotheses about individuals' attitudes, beliefs, and experiences—not to influence their attitudes and beliefs. There are two general forms of surveys. The first is questionnaire research, in which people respond by writing their answers on paper or online. Questionnaire survey methods are described in Chapter 8, including the specialized use of surveys that are conducted as a part of a professional communication audit.

Like questionnaires, **interview and focus group methods** are also used to assess, but not influence, individuals' attitudes, beliefs, and experiences. Interview methods are the second form of survey research. Interviews are one-on-one conversations between a researcher and a participant in which the participant responds to questions orally. Focus group interviews are group interviews in which multiple participants have a conversation responding to questions developed by the researcher and also to each other. Interview and focus group methods often allow more elaboration and clarification of participants' answers than questionnaire methods, making them especially useful to address research questions and (more rarely) hypotheses requiring rich description of participants' attitudes, beliefs, and experiences. Interviews and focus groups are discussed in Chapter 9. The strategic use of interviews and focus groups is featured.

The final method that we consider are experiments, which are described in Chapter 10. When most people think about experiments they think about Bunsen burners and test tubes. Obviously, that sort of equipment is not a part of professional communication research. What makes something an **experiment** is the rigor involved in the data collection process; when conducting an experiment the researcher carefully controls the situation and tests to see how changes in one variable might influence changes in another variable. For example, you might create two different fundraising request letters and test to see which letter results in a larger number of donations. When researchers use just two variations (such as the different versions of the fundraising letter) it is called **A/B testing**. Although experiments are rarely used in public relations or organizational communication settings, A/B testing is an essential marketing research tool. More importantly, an experiment is the only method that can determine cause and effect, making it an important research method. The experimental method is introduced in Chapter 10.

After we present each of these different research methods in Chapters 6 through 10, we turn our attention to how to analyze the data in Chapter 11. First, we discuss *qualitative* data analysis, which you may recall refers to using words or themes to summarize the results of the research. Then, we provide an overview of basic *quantitative* methods, which are the use of numbers—particularly statistics—as a means for determining the results of the research. In the last chapter (Chapter 12) we describe two different ways of reporting the research: the academic format and the professional format for research reports. We also provide advice for creating infographics, which are visual depictions of research results.

Chapter Summary

This chapter focused on the beginning stages of the research process. The first step is to ascertain the need for conducting research. Typically, the need for research is determined when there is insufficient information in order to develop a strategy. Before conducting primary research, we identified other sources of data that might assist in the decision-making process, including government reports, NGO research, trade group research, commercial data sources, and academic research. If the decision is made to conduct primary research, the second step of the research process is to crystallize your research objective. The research objective should be a statement of not only *what* research will be done, but also *why* the research is being done. Typically, there are five goals for professional research: to monitor the environment, to uncover opportunities, to diagnose problems, to select a course of action, and to diagnose a course of action. The third step is to develop your specific research questions (RQ) and/or hypotheses (H). High-quality RQs and Hs are researchable and answerable, are neither too broad nor too narrow, and are value neutral. Finally, we briefly overviewed various research methods as part of step 4 of the research process, determining your method.

PRACTICE ACTIVITIES

1. **Use secondary research:** Imagine that you are a communication specialist at a new national non-profit focusing on environmental protection. You want to find ways to increase awareness of your organization among key target groups: Millennials, teens, and senior citizens. You are wondering what types of media outlets (social media platforms, television ads, newspaper ads, radio ads, etc.) you should consider for messages about your organization; therefore, you want to know more about how your key target groups engage various types of media. Using publicly available information from the Pew Research Center, what can you learn about how each of your target groups engage with media?

2. **Determine the research goal:** In this chapter we discussed four typical goals for professional researchers: identifying opportunities, diagnosing problems, selecting a course of action, and evaluating the course of action. Which goal do you believe is being achieved in each of the following scenarios and why?

   a. A university's strategic plan calls for infusing service learning throughout the curriculum. However, research indicates that the relationship between the university and its neighbors has not improved.

      Research Goal

b. The director of a nonprofit rape crisis center has left, and the board of trustees is uncertain what the primary skill set of the next director should be, trauma counseling or fundraising.

Research Goal

c. An internet rumor has spread about your product, implying that the use of the product might cause harm or death to pets.

Research Goal

d. Chuckle's ice cream is struggling, facing a double whammy: The economy is down, so fewer people are going out for nonessential items like ice cream, and winter months are typically their lowest sales months. They are desperate to pump up their lagging sales.

Research Goal

3. **Practice writing research objectives:** Using the technique for writing research objectives described in this chapter, use each of the scenarios described in Question 2 to write an appropriate research objective.

a. We are interested in studying:

In order to:

b. We are interested in studying:

In order to:

c. We are interested in studying:

In order to:

d. We are interested in studying:

In order to:

4. **Practice writing research questions:** Now write one open-ended research question and one hypothesis for each of the research objectives you have created:

   RQ1:

   H1:

   RQ2:

   H2:

   RQ3:

   H3:

   RQ4:

   H4:

5. **Evaluating research questions and hypotheses:** We discussed three criteria for evaluating the usefulness of research questions and hypotheses (researchable and answerable, not too broad nor too narrow, identify assumptions and be value neutral). Imagine that you are an internal trainer for a mortgage company, and you are responsible for assessing employee training and development efforts at the company. Consider the following research questions and hypothesis that you may pose. To what degree do they meet the criteria? If the research questions and hypothesis do not meet the criterial well, how would you revise them to better meet the criteria?

   RQ1: How many employees completed federal compliance training modules in 2021?

RQ2: How does our internal training compare to the internal training of all other companies in the United States?

RQ3: How can we eliminate negativity in the organizational climate?

H1: Employees will benefit from internal training, which will lead to greater productivity.

Measurement

One of the most recognized phrases ever to be uttered by a Supreme Court Justice can be attributed to Potter Stewart, who in attempting to define *obscenity* famously declared "I know it when I see it" (Gewirtz, 1996). Many of our personal decisions are based on similar sorts of gut responses: buying a new pair of shoes ("because I know fabulous when I see it") or ordering a bacon double cheeseburger ("because I know yummy when I smell it"). In professional situations, however, when the stakes are higher, we ought to rely on more than just a vague sense that we might know something when we see it. As discussed in Chapter 2, the fifth step in the research process is to develop precise measurement. Measurement provides a mechanism for observing something using a clear standard. Just as we measure the number of teaspoons of sugar in a recipe, or the number of miles between point A and point B, we need to put into concrete terms a way to standardize issues of concern for communication professionals making strategic decisions. For example, what counts as positive press coverage of an event? How do we know whether

CHAPTER OUTLINE

- Conceptual and Operational Definitions

- Variables

- Levels of Measurement

- Reliability and Validity

employees are satisfied? What is satisfactory customer engagement with a brand? In order to start to answer these questions, important aspects of measurement discussed in this chapter must be considered. Specifically, this chapter will discuss conceptual and operational definitions, variables, four different levels of measurement, and two qualities of measurement known as reliability and validity.

Conceptual and Operational Definitions

Like Justice Stewart, communication professionals may also be faced with the sticky task of defining obscenity, or put another way, what violates community standards. In 2018, Facebook provided their first detailed report on the types of content that the company removed from their social media platform because the content was offensive (Facebook, n.d.). Removed content categories were violent content, adult nudity and sexual activity, spam, hate speech and fake accounts (Swant, 2018). But, deciding whether a post falls into one of these categories is not an easy task. For example, is a photo of a mother breastfeeding her child the type of content that should be removed from Facebook? The photo involves adult nudity that some users might find offensive. Yet, other users may think that photos of breastfeeding are natural and would be offended if such photos were removed. So, how does Facebook decide what content "counts" as falling into each category? Or, more broadly, how do any communication professionals decide whether something should be classified in one way or another way? In order to answer this sort of question, a consideration of the terms "concept" and "conceptual definition" is needed.

A **concept** refers to some agreed-on aspect of reality. For example, *time* is a concept, as is *love*, the color *purple*, and what constitutes being *edible*. Notice that all of these terms represent a general idea of something that could be understood differently by groups of people. To illustrate, the date that individuals of the Eastern Orthodox faith celebrate Easter is different than the date that Christians from the West celebrate Easter because of different uses of time; the Eastern

Orthodox faith uses the Julian calendar and Western Christians use the Gregorian calendar. People who have traveled to another country often discover that what is considered edible varies greatly from place to place. For example, many American tourists are shocked to find that a popular drive-through fast food dish in Iceland is svid, a sheep's head cut in half and boiled or cured. Still, despite these variations, we share a common understanding of time and that there are some things humans eat and other things they cannot or should not eat.

Because people may understand a concept differently, concepts used in research should be precisely described so that the measurement developed to assess the concept is focused for both the consumers of the research and the researchers themselves. This definition is known as a conceptual definition. Part of the challenge of defining concepts precisely is that concepts can only be understood by using other concepts. Consider the conceptual definition for time. The Merriam-Webster online dictionary (n.d.a.) defines time as "the measured or measurable period during which an action, process, or condition exists or continues." How many different concepts must you understand in order to understand the meaning of the concept of time? By our count there are eight different concepts in the conceptual definition for time. Of course, time is a very complex concept. What about a simpler concept, such as being edible? The Merriam-Webster online dictionary (n.d.b.) defines edible as "fit to be eaten." In this case, the conceptual definition only requires understanding two additional concepts: what fit means and what eaten means.

But what about providing a conceptual definition of a concept less universal but nonetheless important to a company, such as employee engagement? The dictionary is not an appropriate place to look for a conceptual definition of a concept like employee engagement. Rather, people wanting to measure employee engagement must either rely on a conceptual definition of employee engagement used in previous research or one created by the researchers themselves. For example, Gallup regularly measures employee engagement and defines engaged employees as "those who are involved in, enthusiastic about and committed to their work and workplace" (Gallup, n.d.). The conceptual definition serves as a kind of blueprint for focusing measurement because the conceptual definition tells researchers exactly what the concept they want to measure is. So, if you were creating a research study for Gallup involving the concept of employee engagement, you would need to establish measurement that assesses three concepts: employees' involvement, their enthusiasm, and their commitment. When a concept is complex and involves multiple different aspects (like employee engagement), that concept is considered to be **multidimensional**. Alternatively, when a concept is relatively straightforward, such as your year in college or how old you are, the concept is considered to be **unidimensional**.

Once you have clear conceptual definitions of the concepts you want to study, you have to determine how you are actually going to measure the concept, which is known as the operational definition. The **operational definition** does the job of translating the conceptual definition into a measurement tool you can employ in your research. For any conceptual definition, there are likely a range of possible tools that could be used to measure the concept. For example, if you were trying to measure the degree to which a Facebook user finds some content to be offensive, you could do so in a variety of ways, including asking users to complete survey items about what they consider to offensive, tracking the content of users' comments on content to gauge how often users comment that the content was offensive, or tracking the number of posts a user blocks from their newsfeed. Thus, **operationalization**, or the process of creating an operational definition, is a strategic choice that must be made with three important considerations in mind.

First, an appropriate operational definition will have good conceptual fit. **Conceptual fit** refers to how well the operational definition matches the conceptual definition. Conceptual fit requires two things of an operational definition: (a) that the operational definition encompasses all of the aspects of the conceptual definition, and (b) that the operational definition distinguishes between what is part of the concept from what is not part of the concept. Recall the conceptual definition of employee engagement used by Gallup. To have appropriate conceptual fit, a measure must be able to assess the employee's involvement, enthusiasm, and commitment to encompass all of the aspects of the conceptual definition. However, notice that employee productivity is not mentioned as part of the conceptual definition.

Thus, an appropriate operational definition for employee engagement using the Gallup conceptual definition should not bother with assessing how productive an employee is.

Second, previous usage of a possible operationalization should be considered. Ask, "What possible measurement of this concept has worked well in the past?" If there is a previous measurement that is standard in a field or has been shown to be trustworthy in previous research, then it may be a good idea to use that measurement in your research as well. Later in this chapter, we discuss two qualities of measurement (reliability and validity) that will help you to evaluate whether a measure is trustworthy.

Finally, resources for measurement should be considered when choosing an operational definition. In Chapter 2, we discussed possible constraints that you might face when conducting primary research, including limited time, limited resources, and limited data analytic skills. These limitations should also be kept in mind when deciding which form of measurement you will use to assess a concept in your research. For example, qualitative measurement may not require advanced statistical skills to analyze, but evaluating qualitative responses may take a considerably longer time than it would take to perform some statistical comparisons of data.

You should expect that no measurement will be perfect and that you will have to weigh the pros and cons of measurement options with your specific research goals and resources in mind.

In order to make the best choices about operational definitions, it is important to understand some additional aspects involved in focusing the measurement for research. The remainder of this chapter will discuss these important aspects of measurement.

Variables

One of the central ways that we develop an *operational* definition is by identifying variables. A **variable** is a concept that takes on more than one value within the research project. **Values** are the amount or degrees in which the variable can be represented. Put in other terms, variables always have more than one possible answer and the values are those answers. Think about filling out a questionnaire. You might be asked to indicate your highest level of education. Level of education is a variable; the values for that variable might be elementary school completion, high school completion, college completion, and graduate degree completion. You may be asked to indicate which U.S. state you live in. State residency is a variable and the value of that variable may be any of the 50 states. Other variables might not fall into categories but might instead be measured on scales. For example, self-esteem is a variable; the values of that variable may range anywhere from very low self-esteem to very high self-esteem. Another example is employee engagement, which may range anywhere from low to high. It should be noted that in a research project, all variables are concepts, but not all concepts are variables. Some concepts in a research project do not take on more than one value and are known as **constants**, not variables. For example, if you wanted to research the job satisfaction levels of gig economy workers, then job satisfaction level is a variable (you expect to find different levels of job satisfaction) but being a gig economy worker is a constant (you are only studying this type of worker).

In each research project, you may be assessing one or more variables. In Chapter 2, we discussed research questions and hypotheses and explained how they are used to guide your research because research questions and hypotheses indicate which variables, and which relationships between variables, need to be assessed in the research. Research questions may sometimes involve just one variable. In such cases, the research is usually concerned with simply *describing* an aspect of a situation. For example, a marketing professional might be interested in knowing the degree to which customers perceive the company's products as being safe, or a human resources professional might seek to uncover the reasons why employees use the company intranet site. In each case there is a single variable involved. For the marketing professional, the variable is customer's perceptions of the products' safety, with values of that variable ranging from very safe to very unsafe. For the human resources professional, the variable would be reasons for using the intranet with the values of the variable likely including to find payroll information, to find HR policies, to retrieve documents, and so forth. When there is a single variable, you need to create an operational definition for just that variable.

Other research involves studying how two or more variables might be connected. You may remember from Chapter 2 that some research questions or hypotheses are seeking to *compare* two or more groups and other research questions or hypotheses are seeking to establish the *relationship* between two variables. In these cases, it is often expected that there is a cause-and-effect relationship between two variables. For an example, let's go back to the example of employee engagement. Gallup (2017) argues that the main reason to assess employee engagement is because employee engagement affects business outcomes. Imagine you work for an organization involved in customer service. Within this organization, a person might want to know how the level of employee engagement affects the quality of customer service. In this example, the level of employee engagement is the cause, or input, and the quality of customer service is the effect, or output. In research terms, the "cause" variable is known as the independent variable and the "effect" variable is known as the dependent variable. Thus, in our example, the level of employee engagement is the independent variable and the quality of customer service is the dependent variable.

There are several important things to understand about the relationship between independent and dependent variables. First, the terms identify variables' relationship to each other only in the research question. Thus, a certain variable is not always the cause, or independent variable, of something else. In the previous example, employee engagement was the independent variable because it was expected to affect the quality of customer service. However, in another study, employee engagement might be a dependent variable. For example, the Gallup (2017) State of the American Workplace Study sought to discover which variables (such as benefits, flexibility, and company culture) impacted employee engagement. In this case, employee engagement is a dependent variable, and benefits, flexibility, and company culture are all independent variables. It would be a mistake to assume that a certain variable could only and always be a cause or effect. Second, the identification of independent and dependent variables is critical to data analysis. Data analysis will be discussed further in Chapter 11; however, it is sufficient to say here that knowing which of your variables are expected to be the causes and which are expected to be the effects will guide the choices you make to analyze your data. This is an important part of focusing the measurement in your study.

Levels of Measurement

In addition to understanding your variables, it is important to make strategic decisions about the type of assessment you want for each variable. In general, there are four types of assessment (nominal, ordinal, interval, and ratio) that your measurement can take, known as the levels of measurement. Each level of measurement can provide useful information, but they may not all be appropriate for each variable in your research. The key is to pick the level of measurement for your variables that best fits the goals of your specific research project. Further, it is likely that you will pick differing levels of measurement for different variables in your study. In doing so, more than one level of measurement may be used in any given research project. Table 3.1 provides examples of each of the four types of measurement.

Nominal measurement simply involves placing data into categories. Earlier in this chapter, we had several examples of nominal level measurement. Recall the idea of asking people completing a questionnaire to indicate their highest level of education or in which U.S. state they reside. The result of both of these questions would be categories (either of education level or states) into which people's responses are organized. These are examples of nominal-level data. Nominal-level data is often used to make distinctions between groups of people involved in your research for further comparison. Imagine that you work for an organization that has offices in multiple states and you wish to compare employee engagement at various locations. It will be important for you to use nominal-level data to identify which of the employees who participate in your research come from Pennsylvania and which come from Texas. At the beginning of the chapter we also talked about Facebook and obscenity. In this case, the categories would be "obscene" and "not obscene." As we will discuss

TABLE 3.1 Levels of Measurement

Nominal	During the past 3 months, which of the following types of cuisines have you had? (Check all that apply) ☐ Chinese ☐ French ☐ Indian ☐ Italian ☐ Mexican ☐ Other
Ordinal	Please rank the following types of cuisines from your least favorite to your most favorite. _____ Chinese _____ French _____ Indian _____ Italian _____ Mexican _____ Other

Interval	Please circle the number that matches your opinion best:
	
	I enjoy Chinese food.
	   Strongly disagree 1 2 3 4 5 Strongly agree
	
	I enjoy French food.
	   Strongly disagree 1 2 3 4 5 Strongly agree
	
	I enjoy Indian food.
	   Strongly disagree 1 2 3 4 5 Strongly agree
	
	I enjoy Italian food.
	   Strongly disagree 1 2 3 4 5 Strongly agree
	
	I enjoy Mexican food.
	   Strongly disagree 1 2 3 4 5 Strongly agree

Ratio	In the past month, how many times have you eaten food from the following cuisines? Chinese O 1 2 3 4 5 More than 5 French O 1 2 3 4 5 More than 5 Indian O 1 2 3 4 5 More than 5 Italian O 1 2 3 4 5 More than 5 Mexican O 1 2 3 4 5 More than 5

in Chapters 6 and 7, creating questions to gather nominal-level data and categories to organize nominal-level data can often require careful attention to the ways the categories of data are defined.

Because you want to pick the level of measurement that best fits your research goals, it is important to understand what you can and cannot learn from nominal-level data. Nominal-level data allows you to create categories, but not to understand how those categories rank in comparison to one another. Consider the example in Table 3.1. From this question, we could learn which types of food the people who answered the question had, but not which type of food was the most or least favorite of the people who answered the question. To know about favorite foods, we must turn to the next level of measurement: ordinal-level measurement.

Ordinal measurement incorporates the idea of placing data into categories, as is done in nominal-level measurement, but goes a step further to allow for ranking of the categories. Thus, with ordinal-level measurement, it is possible to understand rankings from most to least, favorite to least favorite, and the like. Refer to Table 3.1 to see how a nominal question can be reformulated to an ordinal-level question. As you can see, ordinal-level measurement allows you to understand the preferences of the people who answer the question in a way you could not with nominal-level measurement. However, it is import-ant to note that you cannot learn from this question *how much more preferred* each type of food is in comparison to each other. This is because ordinal-level measurement does not allow you to assume that the distance between points on the scale (here, the scale from least favorite to most favorite) are equal. It is possible that two people could answer the question the same way (for example, from least favorite to most favorite as Mexican, French, Chinese, Italian, Indian). In this case, you learn that both people indicate that Indian is their favorite cuisine and that Italian is their second favorite cuisine. However, it is possible that person A only slightly prefers Indian food over Italian food, while person B greatly prefers Indian food over Italian food, but you cannot learn this from ordinal-level measurement. To assess rankings in which the distance between points on the scale is considered to be equal, interval-level measurement must be used.

Interval measurement allows for rank ordering with the assumption of equal distance between points on the ranking scale. Thus, interval-level measurement provides more uniform ranking than does ordinal-level measurement. As will be discussed in Chapter 11, this more uniform ranking is especially important for allowing statistical comparisons of the data generated by interval-level measurement. Although it may sound complicated, it's likely that you are already quite familiar with interval-level ranking. Have you been asked to rank your customer service experience at a car repair shop from 1 (unsatisfactory) to 5 (satisfactory)? Have you been asked to read a political statement and indicate how much you agree from 1 (strongly disagree) to 7 (strongly agree)? In each of these cases, you were dealing with interval-level measurement. In each case, you provided a ranking with the understanding that the distance between 1 and 2 on the scale is the same as the distance between 3 and 4 on the scale. This is true of everyone else who answers the question, too. Thus, the rankings provided by interval-level measurement allow us to take abstract concepts, such as satisfaction and agreement, and provide a measure of these concepts in a uniform way. Because of this, interval-level measurement is often appropriate to measure attitudes and opinions. Consider the example in Table 3.1. With interval-level measurement, we can learn of a person's enjoyment level for each type of cuisine and then compare those enjoyment levels across the five cuisines as well.

It should be noted that while interval-level measurement often uses numbers to "stand in" for the points on the ranking scale, these numbers do not have a real mathematical meaning corresponding to them. In other words, a 3 on the scale of 1 (strongly disagree) to 5 (strongly agree) used to answer an interval-level measurement question does not mean anything other than the mid-point of the scale. For measurement in which numbers have real mathematical value, we must turn to ratio-level measurement.

Ratio measurement involves rank ordering with equal distance between points on the scale and real mathematical value assigned to integers. Simply put, ratio measurement is counting. Thus, if we wanted to learn more about people's cuisine experiences using ratio-level measurement, we would phrase the question as we did in Table 3.1. Notice that in ratio-level measurement, the 3 indicates eating the

Chinese food three times in the past month as opposed to 3 indicating the midpoint in opinion about Chinese food as it did for interval-level measurement. While interval-level measurement is appropriate for assessing attitudes and opinions, ratio-level measurement is appropriate for assessing behavior. Ratio-level measurement can give us a uniform ranking of how many times you engaged in a behavior but cannot tell us how much you enjoyed or preferred the behavior. In other words, we can learn that you ate Chinese food three times in the past month, but not if you would have preferred to have eaten more Italian food instead.

Understanding what each level of measurement can and cannot tell you is an important part of focusing the measurement in research. We will now move on to two other important aspects of measurement, reliability and validity, that should be considered when designing your research.

Reliability and Validity

The final two concepts that are important for developing precise measurement are reliability and validity, which are ways of assessing the effectiveness of your measurement. **Reliability** refers to the consistency of measurement. To understand the concept, it may be helpful to think of reliability of measurement in a familiar situation first. Imagine that you are purchasing a bunch of bananas at a grocery store that provides electronic scales for customers to use. You place your banana bunch on the scale, and it reads 1.5 pounds. Now, imagine you lift the bananas up and then place them right back on the scale again, but this time the scale reads 2.4 pounds. Imagine that you place that same bunch of bananas on the scale a third time and it reads 1 pound. Nothing about the bananas has changed, but you have three different weight assessments produced by the scale. Would you be happy with the quality of measurement the scale is giving you? Of course not. Why? Because the scale is not consistent. In other words, it is not *reliable*. If the scale does not give you consistent measurement, the measurement is useless, and you still don't know how much your bananas actually weigh.

Now, let's think about reliability of measurement in a research situation. Consider the measure for employee engagement used by Gallup (2017). Gallup collects data from thousands of people to compile their information about employee engagement. If Gallup is using 12 questionnaire items to measure employee engagement, they want to be sure that those 12 items are consistently measuring employee engagement from person to person (just like a shopper wants to be sure that the produce scale is consistently weighing bunches of bananas). It should be noted that reliability does not mean that the responses to the items measuring employee engagement need to be the same from person to person (just as the weight of different bunches of bananas would not be expected to be the same), just that the measurement itself is consistently understood each time it used.

There are four common ways in which reliability of measurement is assessed: test-retest reliability, split-half reliability, intercoder reliability, and internal reliability. A brief overview of each of these methods is described in Table 3.2.

TABLE 3.2   Ways of Establishing Reliability

Type of Reliability	Description	Example
Test-retest reliability	A reliability assessment in which a variable is measured twice. The two measurements should be equivalent.	Someone who completes a measure of employee engagement should score the same on one day as they do on another day.
Split-half reliability	A reliability assessment in which the researcher randomly divides the items measuring the same concept into two different groups and then compares the correlation between the two groups.	If you ask a group of employees to complete a measure of employee engagement and randomly divide the employees into two groups, the score of one group should be the same as the score of the other group.
Intercoder reliability	A reliability assessment that requires two people to code the same data separately and then compare answers.	If you study the ratings of an organization on Glassdoor.com, two different people will similarly classify the ratings as positive or negative.
Internal reliability	A statistical technique that calculates all possible relationships among the items of a multidimensional scale. The most common of these techniques is called *Cronbach's alpha* (Cronbach, 1951), which provides researchers with a number called a coefficient alpha (α).	Using an established measurement of employee engagement, the researcher uses a statistical package to ascertain whether the measurement achieves an acceptable alpha coefficient.

All four forms of reliability involve calculating a percentage (or a number between 0 and 1.0 that can be translated into a percentage). For example, if the number is .82, this would reflect an 82% consistency. The more agreement, the more consistent the measurement. The general rule of thumb is that a measurement should have a reliability of at least 80% (or .80) to be considered reliable, although on occasion a reliability of 70% (or .70) is acceptable.

The second way that we evaluate the effectiveness of a measurement is through validity. **Validity** refers to the truthfulness or accuracy of the measurement. Essentially, validity refers to how well the measure is actually measuring what it is supposed to be measuring. Think back to the example of measuring the weight of a bunch of bananas using a scale in the produce section. When we discussed reliability, we wanted to know about the stability of the scale. We were asking if the scale will give us a weight measurement that is consistent each time we use the scale to measure that bunch of bananas. When considering validity, our question is different. Now we want to know how we can be sure that the scale is really telling us how much those bananas actually weigh. What if your grocery store is a bit dishonest and they have calibrated the produce scales to add several ounces to each measurement? In such a case, we could put a bunch of bananas on the scale that really weigh 1 pound, but the scale might indicate that the bananas weigh 1.4 pounds. In such a case, the scale would not be valid because it is not giving us an accurate, or truthful, measure of the bananas. Communication professionals rarely measure anything as straightforward as the weight of bananas, but it is still very important that they can be sure that the measurement they are using in research is valid.

There are several ways that validity can be assessed: **face validity, expert jury validity, construct validity,** and **criterion validity.** These forms of validity are defined in Table 3.3.

Before concluding our discussion of reliability and validity it is important to highlight the nature of the relationship between these two forms of assessing a measurement. People often make the mistake of thinking that if a measurement has good reliability, it must also have good validity and vice versa. Instead, the relationship between reliability and validity is as follows: A measure can be reliable without being valid; a measure cannot be valid unless it is reliable.

TABLE 3.3 Ways of Establishing Validity

Type of Validity	Description	Example
Face validity	The researcher assesses the conceptual fit of the measurement. A relatively weak form of validity.	The researcher creates a measure of employee engagement based on their understanding of the concept.
Expert jury validity	A panel of experts reviews the conceptual fit of the measurement.	The researcher creates a measure of employee engagement and asks experts in employee engagement to review the measurement.
Construct validity	Comparing the measurement of a concept to other measurements of that concept that have already been shown to be valid.	The researcher creates a measure of employee engagement and asks people to complete both the new measurement and an existing measurement of employee engagement; the results should be the same.
Criterion validity	Determining how well the scores of a measurement predict the scores on another measurement.	Because employee engagement is predicted to increase work productivity, a measure of employee engagement should predict how productive a person actually is at work.

Let's think about that bunch of bananas and the produce section scale again and start with the idea that measurement can be reliable but not valid. If you put the bananas on the scale three times and it says they weigh 1.4 pounds three times, then we know the scale is reliable. It is giving you a consistent and stable measurement of the weight of the bananas each time you measure. But, we don't know if the measurement is valid because we don't really know if the bananas weigh 1.4 pounds. If the grocer is dishonest and has calibrated the scale to add .4 pounds, then the scale read-out of 1.4 pounds each time we weigh the bananas is consistent (reliable) but not accurate (valid). To see if the scale is valid, we may take a pre-packaged item that is known to weigh 1 pound (say, a package of butter) and put it on the scale. If the scale indicates the pre-packaged 1-pound butter is 1.4 pounds, then we would know it is not valid even though it is giving consistent measurement.

Next, consider the idea that a measure cannot be valid unless it is reliable. Earlier in the chapter we discussed that a produce scale would not be reliable if you placed a bunch of bananas on it three times in a row and it gave you three different weights for that same bunch of bananas even though nothing about those bananas had changed between measurements. If a scale can't give us consistent measurement, then we know it can't give us an accurate or truthful measurement of what we want to know. We cannot trust the scale to give us consistent measurement of the weight of the bananas (it is not reliable), which leaves us having no idea how much those bananas actually weigh (it is not valid).

You can replace the bananas in this analogy with any measurement used in strategic communication research. For example, if you want to conduct a study about leadership effectiveness and communication skills, you will want to identify a good measure of communication competence for people to use to assess their leader. If the items in the measure of communication competence are not understood in the same way from participant to participant, then the measure will not be able to provide consistent measurement of someone's communication competence (it is not reliable). Once you know the items are not reliable, you know that the measure would not be able to provide an accurate measure of someone's communication competence (it is not valid). However, it is possible that the items that are supposed to be measuring communication competence are understood the same way from participant to participant, which would make it a reliable measure. But, it is possible that this reliable measure is really assessing how much people like their leader rather than the leader's communication skills. In such a case, the communication competence measure would be reliable but not valid.

If you are considering using a form of measurement that has been used before, it is important to consider any reliability and validity information available about the measure in deciding whether to use the measurement in your own research. If you are creating your own measurement, you should consider various ways of assessing reliability and validity for the measures you are creating so that you can be sure they are likely to do a good job of measuring the variables you want to study.

Chapter Summary

This chapter discussed key considerations for developing precise measurement in a research project. We first talked about concepts, which are agreed-on aspects of reality. One of the first things researchers need to do when developing a measurement is to provide a conceptual definition so that other researchers know exactly what you mean when you reference the concept. Next, researchers must provide an operational definition, which is how the concept will be measured. The extent to which the conceptual and operational definitions match is known as the conceptual fit. We then turned our attention to variables, which are concepts that have more than one possible value. We explained that when researchers are looking to compare two variables or determine the relationship between two variables, the two variables are labeled independent and dependent variables; independent variables are the presumed cause, and dependent variables are the presumed effect. Our next major focus was on the four levels of measurement. Concepts can be measured using a nominal measurement (which involves placing items into categories), ordinal measurement (which involves both classification and ranking), interval measurement (which involves classification, ranking, and equal distances between the categories), and ratio measurement (which involves classification, ranking, equal distances, and a true zero point). Finally, important ways of assessing the quality of measurement were described, which include reliability, or the consistency of measurement, and validity, or the accuracy of measurement.

PRACTICE ACTIVITIES

1. **Unidimensional and multidimensional concepts:** For each of the following concepts, decide whether the concept is unidimensional or multidimensional and explain why you believe that to be the case. If multidimensional, list the possible dimensions you think might be associated with the concept.

a. School spirit

b. Brand satisfaction

c. Stress level

d. Intelligence

e. Income

f. Religiosity

g. Race

h. Political belief

Identifying independent and dependent variables. For each of the hypotheses or research questions listed, identify the variables and whether that variable is independent or dependent.

H1: Employees who hear a high number of compliments during a performance review meeting will differ in anxiety than will employees who hear a low number of compliments during a performance review meeting.

Independent Variable

Dependent Variable

H2: Mangers who engage in high levels of self-disclosure with employees will be rated as less effective than managers who engage in low levels of self-disclosure with employees.

Independent Variable

Dependent Variable

RQ1: How does corporate charitable giving influence public perception of corporations?

Independent Variable

Dependent Variable

RQ2: How does the social media activity of male and female teenagers differ?

Answers:

Independent Variable

Dependent Variable

2. **Matching conceptual and operational definitions:** Using any of the variables identified in the hypotheses and research questions (except for sex of teenagers; that's too easy!), provide a conceptual definition (you can look this up or create your own) for the variable. Then, identify at least two possible operational definitions for measuring that variable. Make an argument as to which operational definition is the best match for your conceptual definition of the variable.

   Variable:

   Conceptual definition:

   Operational definition #1:

   Operational definition #2:

3. **Level of measurement:** Determine the appropriate level of measurement used for each of the following items, explaining why you believe it is the appropriate level of measurement.

   a. Favorite movies

b. Number of children in a family

c. Job title

d. Frequency of checking Instagram

e. Brand satisfaction

f. Political affiliation

g. Employee engagement

h. Class rank

4. **Reliability and validity:** Do an internet search to investigate the reliability and validity of college entrance exams such as the SAT, the ACT, or the GRE. What forms of reliability and validity have been used to evaluate these tests? How reliable and valid are they?

Sampling

4

A re there differences in the coverage of climate change based on the political slant of the news source? What about differences in opinion about climate change based on the political affiliation of the person? Although we might assume that we know the answers to these questions, these are actually **empirical** questions: Rather than assuming we know the answer, we can determine the answer by conducting primary research. Certainly there are measurement decisions that would have to be made to conduct this study. What do we mean by *differences in coverage*? Do we mean frequency, or do we mean tone? What do we mean by *opinions about climate change*? Do we mean whether someone thinks that it is a major or minor problem, or do we mean whether someone believes that it is occurring or not? In addition to making conceptual and operational decisions such as the ones we described in Chapter 3, there are additional decisions that would have to be made before conducting these studies. In Chapter 2 we introduced the steps that need to be taken to undertake a research project. We discussed the fifth step in

CHAPTER OUTLINE

◆ Key Concepts About Sampling

◆ Probability Sampling Techniques

◆ Nonprobability Sampling Techniques

◆ Sample Size

the process in Chapter 3: develop precise measurement. This chapter focuses on the next step in the process, which is to determine your sample.

In an ideal world we would be able to study every message that focuses on climate change, or every person who holds an opinion about climate change. Perhaps with enough time and money this could be possible, but as you might imagine, it would be a difficult endeavor. Google the phrase "climate change" and see just how many hits you get. Then conduct a Web search for "climate change opinions" and check out how many studies have been conducted on this topic, as well as how many people were included in each study. Because it is not always possible or practical to study every single instance associated with a particular message or attitude, researchers rely on a **sample**, which is a small group that is meant to represent the whole. How you go about selecting your sample has important ramifications for the validity (or accuracy) of your study. In this chapter we describe the key concepts associated with selecting a sample, as well as the different types of sampling procedures. We then talk about how many objects (messages or people) in your sample you need to feel confident about the results of your study.

Key Concepts About Sampling

One of the most important considerations when conducting research is exactly who or what you will study. In the case of the communication professionals, the most likely answer to this question is that you will study the content, nature, or structure of messages (through data analytics or content analysis) or that you will study people (through observation, a survey technique, or an experiment). If your research interest is in messages, the first thing you need to determine is the **universe** of messages, which means all messages that meet the desired criteria. So, in the study about coverage of climate change we just talked about, the universe of messages might be all news articles about climate change (eliminating blogs, social media posts, and other sorts of messages that are not news articles). If you are a public relations professional tracking social media mentions of your organization, the universe might be all social media posts with #your organizationname. If you are a human resource professional you might be interested in studying employee engagement with the company intranet site; in this case the universe is all content on the company intranet.

If instead of messages you are interested in the thoughts, feelings, attitudes, or behaviors of people, you need to identify your population, which is all people who possess a desired characteristic. A population is in essence the same thing as a universe; the terms are just different when your focus is on people rather than messages. In the case of our climate change study, our population would be all people who have an opinion about climate change. That is a huge population! Not all populations are as large. You might be interested in all people who work for your organization; depending on the size of your population, the number of employees in your population might be more manageable. Your population might be even smaller—all students in your strategic communication research class this semester. In short, the population consists of all people who share an important characteristic.

As we indicated earlier, in the ideal world you would study everything in your universe or everyone in your population. Research that does so is called a census. Most of us are familiar with the United States Census, which is a decennial (it occurs every 10 years) count of the population in the United States. The goal is to collect information of every household in the country so that the government can make decisions about resource allocation and adjust the number of state representatives to the House of Representatives. It is a massive endeavor that accumulates huge amounts of data.

In professional communication research, conducting a census is rare because it is unlikely that the entire population or universe is available and accessible to the person conducting the research. When a census study is not possible, a sample from the population or universe must be selected. With sampling, the goal is to have a high-quality, representative sample so that you can generalize what you learn to the larger population or universe. A representative sample is when the small group that you study matches the characteristics of the larger group. To illustrate, Shen, Jiang, Jin and Sha (2015) wanted to learn about work-life balance among public relations professionals, so they devised a survey about work-life conflict experiences and coping strategies for PR practitioners. However, the population of PR professionals is very large—it's estimated that there were 259,600 PR jobs in 2016 in the United States alone (United States Department of Labor, n.d.). Accordingly, Shen and colleagues (2015) used the survey responses from a sample of 565 PR practitioners to represent the experiences of the entire population of PR practitioners.

Although conducting a census can drain resources, the process of sampling might also be resource intensive, especially when studying people. Depending on the objective of your study, selecting a representative sample can also take a large amount of time and money. Thus, creating a sample for a study is a strategic decision that greatly impacts the effectiveness of your overall research. For that reason, in the next section we will discuss different types of sampling techniques and their advantages and disadvantages. For ease of understanding, we will focus specifically on sampling people rather than sampling messages. The techniques are roughly the same for both.

Probability Sampling Techniques

Probability sampling techniques are those that use random selection of individuals from the population to form the sample. Random selection means that every individual in the population has an equal chance of being chosen for the sample. If there were 1,000 people in the population and you used random selection, then each person in the population would have a 1 in 1,000 chance of being chosen for the sample. There are three instances of random selection that you likely already know about. First, random selection is the process used by most lotteries. Every single person who purchases a lottery ticket has the exact same chance of winning as every other person who purchases a lottery ticket. In the case of major lotteries in the United States such as the Powerball or Mega Millions, you have about a 1 in 300 million chance of winning the jackpot for every ticket you purchase. Second, the American jury system is based on the premise of random selection.

Each American citizen presumably has an equal chance of being selected for jury duty. Note that this does not mean that every citizen has an equal chance of actually being *selected* as a juror; it just means that the system of generating a jury duty summons is conducted randomly. Finally, if you have ever put people's name in a hat and picked names from the hat, you have actually created a random sample.

There are online tools to help with the process of random selection, such as www.random.org. Random selection is meant to ensure that bias does not enter the process of sampling, which helps make sure the sample is representative of the population. Because of this, probability sampling methods are most desirable and should be used whenever possible. There are many types of probability sampling methods, but we will discuss some of the most common for strategic communication applications (see Table 4.1 for overview).

Simple random sampling is the process of randomly selecting individuals for the sample from a sampling frame, a master list that identifies all members of the population. As the name would suggest, this sampling method is straightforward. If there are 1,000 people in your population and you want a sample of 100 people, you would assign a number to each person in your population, use a random number generator such as the one at www.random.org to select 100

TABLE 4.1   Probability Sampling Techniques

Simple random sampling	Starting with a master list of everyone in the population, numbers are assigned to each person and a random number generator is used to select the sample.
Systematic random sampling	Starting with a master list of everyone in the population, numbers are assigned to each person and every nth person on the list is selected.
Stratified random sampling	Also known as proportional random sampling, a simple or systematic sample is conducted that allows for control over how subgroups of the population are represented within the sample.
Cluster random sampling	Involves multiple levels of random selection, starting with large areas of the population and moving to smaller areas of the population to create a sample.
Stratified cluster sampling	Similar to random cluster sampling but adds a stratification process that divides the population into subgroups.

numbers, and then choose the people who have been assigned to those numbers to get your sample. A **systematic random sample** is similar to a simple random sample, but instead of using a random number generator, the researcher uses every nth person (for example, every fifth person for a small population, or every 115th person or 2,200th person for a larger population).

Although these two types of sampling are simple, what is often less straightforward is creating the sampling frame itself. Do you really have the ability to identify every member of the population for your study? You might if the population is employees at your organization or your organization's clients. You won't if your population is all Twitter users or all potential customers for your product. Without a sampling frame, neither simple random sampling nor systematic random sampling are possible and a nonprobability sampling technique (discussed later in the chapter) may have to be used instead.

Another useful probability sampling method is **stratified random sampling**, also known as proportional random sampling. Stratified random sampling is useful when you want control over how subgroups of the population are represented within the sample because you want to examine differences in your results based on subgroup classification. For example, if you were interested in studying employee engagement you might want to make sure that your sample included both frontline workers and managers. To do this you would first determine how many frontline workers the company employs and how many managers the company employs. Imagine an organization that has 1,000 frontline workers and 100 managers. Your sample should include 10 times the number of frontline workers than managers. In stratified random sampling, the sampling frame is first divided into subgroups based on your target characteristic. In our example, you would divide the individuals in the sampling frame list by job type (frontline worker or manager). After the sampling frame is divided by subgroup, the next step is to randomly select from each subgroup, consistent with your target subgroup proportions for the sample. In our example, we desire a sample of 100 frontline employees and 10 managers. Therefore, we would use either simple random sampling or systematic random sampling to randomly select the correct proportion of participants based on job title. In stratified random sampling, every individual has an equal chance of being selected for the sample as every other individual *within the subgroup.* As with simple random sampling, stratified random sampling cannot be used without a sampling frame.

A type of probability sampling that does not require you to first identify every individual in the population (sampling frame) is **cluster random sampling**. Cluster random sampling involves placing members of the population into different groups, called clusters. For example, consider a bank that has 1,200 branches. If the bank wanted to survey employees, rather than starting with a list of all bank employees they might start with a list of all branches, and then randomly select a sample of branch offices for their study. As you can see, cluster sampling does not require a sampling frame that would list all employees that work at the organization, but it does require information to inform the sampling such as a list of locations and information about who works in those specific locations.

Finally, **stratified cluster sampling** is similar to random cluster sampling but adds a stratification process that divides the population into subgroups and uses layers of random selection within the subgroups. Imagine a multinational company located in North America, Asia, and Europe that wants to survey its employees about the effectiveness of their onboarding process for training new employees. The company employs approximately 60,000 people in North America (100 offices), Asia (50 offices), and Europe (50 offices). Ultimately, a sample of 1,000 employees is desired for the survey. The company wants to ensure that the sample proportion is similar to the proportion of offices in each region. To create the sample, the company may create a list of all office locations and organize them by region. The first sampling step may involve stratified cluster sampling in which offices from each region subgroup are randomly selected to create a list of 50 North American offices, 25 Asian offices, and 25 European offices. Next, a list of employees at each of these 100 offices may be used to perform random cluster sampling by randomly selecting 100 employees from each office to participate in the survey. In this way, a sample of 1,000 employees (50% from North America, 25% from Asia, 25% from Europe) is randomly selected using a combination of stratified and cluster sampling.

Nonprobability Sampling Techniques

Nonprobability sampling techniques are those used to draw a sample from a population without employing random selection. Lack of random selection means important differences between probability and nonprobability sampling arise. With nonprobability sampling techniques, some individuals from the population have a greater chance of being included in the sample than others. The chance that a specific individual has of being included in the sample cannot be accurately calculated when using nonprobability sampling techniques. Because some individuals have a better chance than others of being included in the sample, nonprobability samples are vulnerable to bias derived from the specific sampling technique used. In other words, the way a researcher chooses a nonprobability sample may make certain individuals over-represented in the sample such that the study results may be less representative of the entire population than if a probability sample method had been used. However, nonprobability sampling techniques are used much more frequently in professional communication research than are probability samples. Why? Because in many professional communication cases, the researchers do not have the resources needed to perform probability sampling, including access to a master list of all individuals in the population (sampling frame), or the time and money that is sometimes needed to perform probability sampling. If probability sampling is not possible, there is still a great deal to learn from a well-performed nonprobability sample. As with probability sampling, there are many types of nonprobability sampling methods. We will discuss some of the most common nonprobability sampling techniques for strategic communication applications (see Table 4.2 for overview).

Convenience sampling is a technique of creating a sample from the most readily available members of the population. There are many specific ways you can create a convenience sample, such as asking clients who visit your office to complete a survey, asking people who visit your website to take part in a study, or asking the coworkers you interact with on a daily basis to participate in the study. In short, a convenience sample means that you use people who are in close personal (or virtual) proximity to participate in the sample. Volunteer sampling involves

TABLE 4.2 Nonprobability Sampling Techniques

Convenience sampling	Creates a sample from the most readily available members of the population.
Volunteer sampling	Involves distributing information about your study and asking people who qualify to participate.
Judgmental sampling	Chooses a specific group of people for your sample because of some information you know about them. Also known as purposive sampling.
Network sampling	Relies on members of the researchers' own networks to take part in the study.
Snowball sampling	Relies on participants in the study to identify additional participants in the study.
Quota sampling	Involves using other nonprobability sampling techniques to create a sample in which subgroups of the population are represented in the sample along desired proportions.

distributing information about your study and asking people who qualify as part of the population to participate. Volunteer sampling commonly involves posting calls for participants on websites, posting flyers asking for people to participate, or taking out advertisements asking for people to participate. Both convenience and volunteer sampling have the advantages of being easy to accomplish and requiring few resources, and because of this, these sampling methods are commonly used in academic as well as applied communication situations. However, Baxter and Babbie (2004) warn that these sampling methods are "risky" because they are very vulnerable to bias. For example, the people you work with may be of a similar educational level and socioeconomic background to you, and these factors may differ from the average educational level and socioeconomic background of the entire population for your study. Further, people who volunteer for a study are likely those who have stronger opinions on the topic than those who do not volunteer. Therefore, caution should be used when generalizing from these types of samples to the entire population.

Another type of nonprobability sampling method is **judgmental sampling**, also known as purposive sampling. In judgmental sampling, a specific group of people is chosen for your sample because of some information you know about them. For example, Turnbull and Wheeler (2016) wanted to learn more about how organizations choose an advertising agency. They decided to interview senior marketing managers at multinational organizations because these individuals were most likely to have expertise in this topic. While judgmental sampling is especially useful in ensuring that the members of the sample meet the study population criteria, Baxter and Babbie (2004) point out that the sample may represent a subgroup of the population better than the population as a whole. For example, in Turnbull and Wheeler's (2016) study, marketing managers in multinational organizations might use a different decision-making process than marketing managers at smaller organizations or those that operate in only a single national market.

The third form of nonprobability sampling, **network sampling**, means exactly what you might assume. Network sampling involves asking members of the researchers' own personal and professional networks to take part in the study. One of the most common ways that this is achieved by researchers who are university professors is asking students to be research participants. However, the advent of social media has made this type of sampling common for all researchers; one common way of network sampling is for researchers to post a link to a survey on their social media accounts. Participants are therefore drawn from the researcher's own social media network.

Snowball sampling is a nonprobability sampling method in which each person who completes your survey does "double duty" not only as a participant in your study but also as a recruiter for more people to participate. In snowball sampling, the researcher identifies an initial group of participants from the population using any of the sampling methods we've already discussed. This initial group of participants is not only asked to participate in the study, but also asked to identify and/or invite other members of the population who can participate as well. Because all participants are asked to recruit additional participants, the sample grows larger and larger as it expands out from the original group of participants, just like how a snowball rolling downhill picks up more snow and grows bigger as it falls. Snowball sampling is most effective and most commonly used when members of the target population are difficult to find using convenience or volunteer sampling (Heckathorn & Cameron, 2017). For example, it is estimated that 4.3% of American adults identify as lesbian, gay, bisexual, transgender, and queer (LGBTQ) (Jones, 2017). One of your authors used snowball sampling to recruit a LGBTQ sample for surveys about same-sex marriage by asking LGBTQ people originally identified through judgmental sampling if they would ask other LGBTQ people they knew to also complete a survey (Lannutti, 2014).

Although snowball sampling is often effective, precautions must be taken to make sure that those recruited via this sampling method truly fit the population criteria through screener questions because the researcher becomes more and more distanced from the point of recruitment for the sample as the sample grows. To illustrate, in Lannutti's (2014) studies with LGBTQ participants it was important to make sure that all people recruited by other participants really identified as LGBTQ. Additionally, bias may be introduced into the sample as individuals are more likely to recruit those like them in ways beyond the population criteria. For example, while participants in Lannutti's (2014) same-sex marriage studies may have been recruited because they identified as LGBTQ, it is likely that whichever participant recruited them was similar to them in terms of socioeconomic background, region, education, and other demographic factors. Thus, when using a snowball sample, a researcher must be sure to record demographic factors and use caution when generalizing to the overall target population.

Finally, **quota sampling** is the nonprobability equivalent of stratified random sampling. In quota sampling, the researcher wants subgroups of the population to be included in the sample in certain proportions and then uses any of the other nonprobability sampling methods to gather participants until those proportions are filled. For example, Schumann, Bowman, and Schultheiss (2016) wanted people who play video games to complete a survey about game quality, but they wanted the sex and ages of the people who completed the survey to fulfill certain pre-set quotas based on marketing information about who purchases and plays video games. That is, they wanted their sample to closely relate to the marketing research about sex and age of video game players. After establishing how many people per age group and sex group they wanted for their survey, Schumann and colleagues (2016) distributed an announcement about their study on gaming websites and recruited via this volunteer sampling method until their age and sex quotas for the sample were full. Quota sampling has many of the advantages of stratified random sampling in that both methods give a researcher more control over the proportions of subgroups in their sample, but because quota sampling does not use random selection it is vulnerable to the bias that may affect all nonprobability sampling methods.

Sample Size

No matter which sampling technique you choose, you must address the question of how many people you need to include in your sample for research to be successful. Including too few people in your sample may mean that you do not have the ability to make the comparisons you wish to make or that you might miss vital information in your data because not enough of the population's opinions, beliefs, experiences, and behaviors were examined. Having too many people in your sample may result in a waste of resources, an unnecessary extension of the time it takes to complete your study, and an overestimation of the significance of relationships among the variables you are assessing. The answer to how many individuals is appropriate for your sample depends on factors unique to your specific research project and often requires weighing the ideal sampling conditions against the limitations you are faced with when completing your research. Still, there are some general guidelines to consider when assessing the necessary sample size, and these guidelines differ depending on whether you are collecting qualitative or quantitative data.

Sample Size for Qualitative Data

When you are collecting qualitative data using methods such as interviews or focus groups, your goal is rich description of the data you are collecting rather than the ability to make claims about patterns or compare trends as you would when collecting quantitative data. Therefore, you will need a sample size that allows you to fully explore the topic at hand, provide detailed and nuanced descriptions of what you learned about the topic, and make connections among the things you learned from the data. As we will discuss further in Chapter 11, analysis of qualitative data involves a process of identifying themes within the data and meaningful connections among those themes. In qualitative research, the analysis of themes in the data usually begins before all of the data are collected so that the researcher may know when they have reached a sample size that is sufficient for the study. The point where enough data has been collected is known as saturation. Saturation occurs "when no new categories or relevant themes are emerging" from the data (Corbin & Strauss, 2008, p. 148). As Corbin and Strauss (2008) explain, saturation means that any new data you collect seems to confirm the themes and relationships among themes that you have already collected instead of indicating a new theme or relationship among themes. In other words, saturation is a judgement call that you must make based on what you are learning in your study as you go. Saunders and colleagues (2018) point out that while saturation is considered the standard for determining sample size in qualitative research, researchers vary widely in the exact processes they use to determine whether they have reached saturation. We believe that for professional communication situations, the bottom line regarding saturation is whether you can adequately address the question "How do you know that you have collected enough data to answer your research questions?" with the answer "Because I am getting the same answers to my questions when I conduct a new interview, focus group, and so on as I got from the previous data I collected."

Sample Size for Quantitative Data

Unlike qualitative data, your goal in collecting and analyzing quantitative data is the ability to show and compare trends in your data through statistical reasoning. The sample for quantitative data needs to be appropriately sized for the measures and analyses you are using in your study and is therefore determined by those factors. To illustrate, have you ever seen a political poll released during an election season? Typically the poll will indicate the number of people supporting Candidate A and the number of people supporting Candidate B. However, these polls don't survey all voters; they rely on a sample of voters. For this reason, the poll usually provides something called a **confidence interval** and the **margin of error**, which are indications of how precise the poll is likely to be. A confidence interval is usually expressed in a percentage, and it is an indicator of how likely the results from your sample would match the results if you studied the entire population. Ideally, a confidence interval of 95% is achieved. The margin of error is how much the specific result is likely to vary from the actual result. So, if 45% of voters in your poll prefer Candidate A and the margin of error is +/- 3%, the actual support of the candidate is likely to fall somewhere in between 42% and 48%.

The strongest way to determine the needed sample size for a quantitative study is to conduct a **power analysis**. A power analysis considers key factors about the research, such as desired effect size, level of measurement, and type of statistical test to be performed, to calculate how large a sample is needed to maximize success of the desired comparisons (Wiedmaier, 2017). There are many statistical packages available to help researchers conduct a power analysis, including free online resources such as G*POWER. While conducting a power analysis is the most recommended way to determine an appropriate sample size for a quantitative study, it may not always be possible to do so if the researcher does not know key information about the measures or expected effect sizes. In such cases, there are a few generalizations to keep in mind when determining sample size. First, examine what researchers working on a similar topic have done in the past. Knowing about previous successful sample sizes for studies similar to yours can be used to estimate a similar sample size for your study. Second, understand that as the number of variables you have in your study and the number of comparisons of the relationships among those variables you want to analyze increases, needed sample size also increases.

Finally, when researchers use probability sampling, the actual number of people who need to participate in a study might be smaller

TABLE 4.3   Sample Size for 95% Confidence Interval Using a Probability Sample

Population Size	Needed Sample Size
1,000	278
2,000	322
3,000	341
5,000	357
10,000	370
50,000	381
100,000	383
500,000	384
Infinity	384

than your think. Consider the guidelines presented in Table 4.3. The representativeness that is achieved through the use of a random sample means that even relatively small samples might accurately reflect a population with a 95% confidence interval (Stacks, 2016). If you want an even higher confidence interval (say 99%), you still don't need any more than a sample of 500 people for a very large population. Of course, this is dependent on the use of a probability sample. These numbers are not accurate for nonprobability samples because they are less likely to closely represent the population as a whole.

Chapter Summary

This chapter discussed the process of sampling, selecting messages from a universe or individuals from a population to include in your research study. Key concepts central to the sampling process were explained, including a sample frame and a census. Various probability sampling techniques (those that include random selection) and nonprobability sampling techniques (those that do not include random selection) and their advantages and disadvantages were explained. The specific probability techniques we discussed included simple random samples, systematic random samples, stratified random samples, cluster random samples, and stratified cluster samples. The nonprobability techniques we described were convenience samples, volunteer samples, judgmental (purposive) samples, network samples, snowball samples, and quota samples. The chapter concluded with a discussion of the appropriate sample size for qualitative and quantitative research.

PRACTICE ACTIVITIES

1. **Create a simple random sample:** Identify a population with at least 100 people for which you have access to a sampling frame. Perhaps it is people who work in your office or fellow students in your program. Using random selection (remember, there are online tools such as www.random.org), create a sample of 25 individuals. Do you see any potential bias in your sample? Why or why not?

2. **Compare convenience sampling to simple random sampling:** Using the same population you used for practice activity 1, create a convenience sample of at least 25 people by asking the people most easily available to you if they would agree to take part in a study if you were conducting one. Keep track of who agrees until you reach 25 people. How do the characteristics of this convenience sample compare to those of your simple random sample created for practice activity 1? Which sample is likely to be more representative of the population and why?

3. **Identify the sampling technique:** Identify which type of sampling is being used *and* why you believe this to be the case. Remember, there are two overall types of sampling (probability and nonprobability) and then subtypes under each.

   a. The governor of Pennsylvania is interested in surveying all Democrats in the state to determine if there is a difference between wealthy and non-wealthy individuals' support for him. He gets a list of all Democrats, and then divides that list into wealthy and non-wealthy groups. Everyone on the list has an equal chance of being surveyed. A sample is drawn, representing the correct proportion of wealthy and non-wealthy individuals in Pennsylvania.

b. A student is interested in finding out how students at their university feel about the alcohol policy on campus. They go to three dorms and survey students who answer their doors.

c. A researcher wants to study married persons' use of supportive communication. They ask students to convince a married person they know to fill out the questionnaire.

d. A researcher is interested in finding out whether verbal abuse accompanies physical abuse in dysfunctional relationships. He goes to a shelter for battered women and surveys a sample of women who are living there.

e. A market researcher is interested in whether newspaper subscribers want "Cathy" or "Sally Forth" to appear in the cartoon section on Sundays. She obtains a list of all *Inquirer* subscribers and calls every fourth person on the list.

4. **Develop a sampling strategy:** Identify the members of your population and a realistic sampling technique for each of the following situations:

a. A manufacturer of a new cereal wants to find out cereal preferences in Chicago.

b. ABC wants to determine households' viewing habits and programming preferences.

c. The Palomar Company wants to know how often its employees eat in the company cafeteria versus going out for lunch.

d. A manufacturer would like to survey users to determine demand potential for a new power drill. The drill can be used by automobile, construction, and major appliance manufacturers.

e. The Dainler Group wants to determine the effectiveness of their recent campaign to increase brand awareness.

5. **Critique a sampling method:** Find a communication research article. Answer the following questions about the sampling techniques used in the study:

   a. What is the population from which the sample was drawn?

   b. What sampling technique was used?

   c. How was an appropriate sample size determined?

   d. What are the strengths of the sampling decisions that were made?

   e. What are the weaknesses of the sampling decisions that were made?

5

Ethics and Strategic Research

In early 2018 news broke that Cambridge Analytica, a political consulting firm, had accessed 87 million people's Facebook pages without their consent. It did so by posting an app on the social media platform that appeared to be a personality test; when users completed the personality test the consulting company gained access to everything posted on the user's Facebook page, as well as everything posted on their friends' pages. The consulting company then used data mining techniques to create psychographic profiles, which, combined with the location data available from the social media platform, allowed the company to create targeted political ads to influence political opinion. In summarizing this scandal, *PR Daily* asserted that "news about Cambridge Analytica's 'problematic' (some might prefer the term 'morally bankrupt') approach to data analysis has left consumers on Facebook feeling suspicious and defenseless." For this reason, "It's more important than ever to talk about ethics in research" (Young & Musyi, 2018, pp. 2–3).

When considering the ethics of conducting research, it is typical for textbooks to focus on

CHAPTER OUTLINE

◆ Basic Research Misconduct

◆ Ethical Research Codes of Conduct

◆ Ethical Guidelines for Research That Involves Human Participants

◆ Ethical Guidelines for the Use of Digital Data

◆ Unique Ethical Concerns of the Professional Communication Researcher egregious examples of unethical research, what some scholars call "ethical horror stories" (Dixon & Quirke, 2018, p. 12). You have likely already learned about the Tuskegee syphilis studies, Milgram's obedience studies, and Zimbardo's Stanford prison experiment. These shocking examples make it relatively simple to identify the ethical principles that have been violated. However, often ethical issues that arise when conducting research are far less dramatic. Dealing with ethical issues in research requires the ability to understand and apply ethical guidelines. This chapter will introduce you to a wide variety of ethical principles developed from government requirements, academic societies, and professional organizations. We will start by describing the three basic forms of research misconduct. Then, we identify some ethical statements and codes of conduct that inform the professional research process. Next, we will highlight ethical guidelines for research that involve human participants and ethical guidelines for the use of digital data. Finally, we conclude with unique ethical dilemmas that occur when conducting proprietary research.

Basic Research Misconduct

Before discussing the unique ethical concerns for conducting professional communication research, there are several universal ethical guidelines that require explicit mention. Plagiarism is an ethical violation. Plagiarism involves using another person's words, in whole or in part, without citing the source of the work or using quotation marks; paraphrasing someone else's work without citing the true author; imitating a source's syntax or phrasing; or not including the names of authors who contributed to the document, or, conversely, including the names of people who did not contribute. Not only is plagiarism a violation of most professional communication codes of conducts, it is fundamentally deceptive and can be considered a form of intellectual theft.

Two other forms of deception are data fabrication and data falsification. Data fabrication is when a researcher makes up some or all data reported in a research study. Data falsification is changing or omitting data in order to achieve desired results. These forms of research misconduct can have profound implications. Consider Andrew Wakefield's research that purported to show a link between the measles-mumps-rubella vaccine (MMR) and autism. Although originally published in a well-respected medical journal, we have subsequently learned not only that Wakefield's methods were unethical, he also fabricated data and engaged in biased and misleading interpretations. Moreover, he failed to disclose that he was provided a financial incentive by attorneys who were seeking to file lawsuits against vaccine manufacturers (College of Physicians of Philadelphia, 2018). The result of his unethical conduct (and widespread media coverage of the study) was a drastic reduction in the number of children receiving the vaccine. In the United Kingdom, there were over 12,000 cases of the measles. The United States declared that measles had been entirely eradicated by the year 2000, but subsequent to the Wakefield study more parents refused to vaccinate their children, leading to large-scale measles outbreaks in recent years (Quick & Larson, 2018). Clearly, these forms of research misconduct can have significant implications.

Ethical Research Codes of Conduct

Virtually every professional society in the communication industry has its own code of ethics. For example, the International Association of Business Communicators (IABC) identifies 11 ethical behaviors for professional communicators, which include statements such as "I communicate accurate information and promptly correct any errors," "I protect confidential information while acting within the law," and "I do not guarantee results that are beyond my power to deliver" (International Association of Business Communicators, 2018). IABC members are asked to sign a statement indicating that they will abide by these 11 ethical standards. Although most organizations have a general code of ethics, despite the increasing importance of making data-based decisions, relatively few professional organizations have a specific code of ethics for conducting research (Bowen & Stacks, 2013).

A **code of conduct** refers to guidelines for action that provide a way to handle the typical dilemmas faced in a profession (Bowen & Stacks, 2013). They are differentiated from legal requirements; the law references what is permissible, whereas ethical codes provide a way of viewing what is right or wrong. Professional associations affiliated with the communication industry that do have a research ethics code of conduct include the American Association for Public Opinion Research (AAPOR), the American Marketing Association (AMA), and the Insights Association (which represents corporate marketing research and data analytics professionals). Table 5.1 highlights elements of the research code of conduct for the AAPOR (American Association for Public Opinion Research, 2015). The large number of possible stakeholders they reference in their code makes it particularly noteworthy.

The Institute for Public Relations (IPR) has embraced an alternative approach to acknowledging the ethical dimension of conducting professional research. IPR developed a research ethics statement that identifies core principles, which include "intellectual honesty, fairness, dignity, disclosure, and respect for all stakeholders involved, namely clients (both internal and external), colleagues, research participants, the public relations profession, and the researchers themselves" (Bowen et al., 2012, p. 2). Bowen and Stacks (2013) argue that an ethical statement such as that developed by the IPR is preferable to a formal code of conduct because ethical statements allow for values-based decision making rather than a prefabricated canon.

In addition to the ethical standards created by professional organizations, globally there are over 1,000 different laws, regulations, and guidelines associated with conducting research (Department of Health and Human Services, 2018). The majority of these are **regulations** (which are rules developed by a government agency) and **guidelines** (which have no force of law). Regardless of whether a researcher is a member of a professional organization that has distinct ethical guidelines, there are clear standards that influence research decisions throughout each stage of the research process: planning the research, conducting the research, and reporting the research. We turn next to ethical guidelines for research involving human participants.

TABLE 5.1 Highlights of the AAPOR Research Code of Conduct

I. Principles of responsibility in dealing with people	◆ We will avoid harming, endangering, misleading, or humiliating participants ◆ We will not conduct other activities (such as sales, fundraising, or political campaigning) under the guise of conducting research ◆ We will make no false misleading claims about a study's purpose or sponsorship ◆ We will keep information conducted for a client confidential except where explicitly authorized by the client ◆ We will correct factual misrepresentations or distortions of the data or analysis, including those made by our research partners, co-investigators, sponsors, or clients ◆ We will recognize that differences of opinion in the interpretation of analyses are not necessarily factual misrepresentations or distortions and will use professional judgement in handling disclosure of differences of opinion
II. Principles of professional practice	◆ We will be careful in our research design, samples, and instruments, as well as in collecting, processing, and analyzing data to ensure reliability and validity of the results ◆ We will not knowingly draw conclusions that are inconsistent with the data available, nor will we tacitly permit such interpretations ◆ We will not engage in data fabrication or falsification
III. Standards for disclosure	◆ We will disclose sufficient information about how the research was conducted to allow for independent review and verification

Ethical Guidelines for Research That Involves Human Participants

At least in part because of the unethical horror stories alluded to earlier (e.g., Milgram's obedience study and Zimbardo's Stanford prison study), the U.S. government passed the 1974 **National Research Act**, which identified ethical principles to be followed when conducting research involving human beings (Horner & Minifie, 2011). When the law was passed the National Commission for the Protection of Human Subjects of Biomedical and Behavioral Research was created, and they were given the charge of creating a set of ethical guidelines for research that involved people. The result of this effort was the **Belmont Report**, which identifies three overarching ethical guidelines: respect, beneficence, and justice. In 1981 the Belmont Report was used to develop the **Common Rule**, a set of specific rules and procedures for conducting research with human participants, which governs research at all U.S. federal agencies and American universities (Department of Health and Human Services, 2018).

Respect for Persons

The first element of the Belmont Report specifically says that because human beings are autonomous, they have the right to decide whether they wish to participate in research (Department of Health and Human Services, 2018). However, it also recognizes that some people are members of **vulnerable populations**, which are groups of people who may not have the ability to make the decision to take part in research. There are two reasons why people might be a member of a vulnerable population. First, they might have **decisional impairment**, which means that they do not have the mental capacity to make the decision to take part in research. Examples are children and people with cognitive impairments. Second, there might be **situational or positional vulnerability**, which means that the individual might be susceptible to coercion to take part in the study. Prisoners, for example, might be rewarded or punished for their participation in research. More subtle coercion can occur as well; employees might feel pressured to take part in a study because they wish to safeguard their job. Researchers must take steps to protect members of vulnerable populations from undue coercion.

The implication of this ethical guideline is that all participants must give **informed consent** to take part in research. Informed consent means that the research participant has been presented with sufficient information about the research and that they voluntarily agree to take part in the study. The information must be presented in a way that participants can understand, so technical jargon should be avoided, and levels of language comprehension should be considered. Typically, the informed consent process involves the completion of an informed consent document, which both the participant and the researcher sign. Box 5.1 includes an overview of the elements of an informed consent document.

Earlier we indicated that children are considered to be part of a vulnerable population. For this reason, researchers must have signed parental or guardian consent for anyone under the age of 18 to be a part of the research process. In addition, researchers should take the time to explain the research in a way that children can understand and receive the child's assent, which is a verbal agreement to take part in the study.

One common exception to the required use of signed consent forms is the use of anonymous surveys. If the population of interest are adults who are not a member of a vulnerable population, if the study itself is unlikely to cause any emotional or social harm, and if no information that could identify individuals who participate in the study is collected, then the research may be considered exempt. In exempt survey research, researchers may be given permission

---

BOX 5.1

Elements of an Informed Consent Document

Name and Contact Information of the Researcher(s)

Purpose and Background of the Study

Procedures of the Study, Including Duration

Possible Risks or Discomforts That May Occur as a Result of the Study

Expected Benefits of the Study

Alternatives to Taking Part in the Study

Statement That Participation Is Voluntary

Statement of Right of Privacy

Statement of Right to Withdraw from the Study

Information About Data Storage and Disposal

Signatures of the Researcher and Participant

to include all elements of the informed consent information at the beginning of the survey but not be required to have the participant sign a consent form.

Finally, we should note that on occasion providing true details about the nature of the study might influence the results of the study. For example, imagine you were testing messages from a new marketing campaign that uses humor and you want to see which of the possible messages you are considering make people laugh. If you tell people you are examining whether they think something is funny, they might intentionally or unintentionally monitor their reactions, making it impossible for you to really evaluate message humor. In this case, researchers are permitted to be deceptive in the informed consent process by not fully informing the participants about the purpose of the research (but they still need to complete the other elements of the informed consent process). We should note that deception is not typical in professional research; it is generally a very rare practice, and it is usually associated with experiments. When deception occurs, researchers are ethically bound to engage in **debriefing**, which is explaining the true nature of the study to the participants immediately after the study has taken place. During debriefing, the participant might choose whether they want any data associated with them to be included in the study.

Beneficence

The second guideline set forward by the Belmont Report is **beneficence**, which means having the interests of the research participants in mind. In practical terms it means that the researchers must maximize the benefits and minimize risks to participants. In general, there are rarely direct benefits to participants in communication research studies. This is especially true because any payment a person might receive for being in the study is not considered a benefit of the research, but rather an incentive for participation. Communication studies are not usually like medical studies where a participant's health might improve as a result of the treatment being tested in the research. At best, we might be able to say that the knowledge gained by the research might benefit "people like you." This form of indirect benefit is perfectly acceptable. The bigger concern is minimizing risk.

All research involves some level of risk. Unlike medical research, rarely is there the possibility of causing physical harm in communication research. Nevertheless, we do sometimes study sensitive issues that might cause emotional or social harm. For example, human resources professionals might study employees' attitudes about their manager, or experiences with discriminatory or harassing behavior. In those cases, participants might be justifiably concerned about their privacy. For this reason, researchers are ethically obligated to either assure their participants of anonymity or confidentiality. **Anonymity** means that there is no way to connect the data to an individual participant. In anonymous research, even the researcher cannot link a specific participant to the data they provided in the study. **Confidentiality** means that the researcher does have the ability to link identifying information to specific participants, but the researcher promises not to make links between specific participants and their data known. For example, interviews are often video recorded. These data can clearly connect a participant with what they said to the researcher. In these cases, researchers seek to protect participants by giving them pseudonyms in the research report and otherwise shielding identifying details.

A final consideration associated with beneficence is **data protection**. Given that there are no legal protections for research participants, researchers are ethically obliged to treat data with the utmost care. Data must be stored in a secure location so that confidentiality can be ensured, and data should be deleted or destroyed at an appropriate time after the study has been completed (organizations and publishers may have guidelines about the specific amount of time appropriate for data destruction).

In order to make sure that beneficence is achieved, the Common Rule sets the requirement that all organizations that benefit from federal funds (directly or indirectly), including universities, research institutions, and health care facilities, must have an ethics board called an **Institutional Review Board** (IRB). The IRB is responsible for approving and monitoring all research that is conducted at that institution, making certain that the guidelines set forth in the Belmont

Report are followed. IRBs are particularly focused on the extent to which a research study might put participants at risk. Moreover, the Common Rule has set forth very specific guidelines about the composition of the board, as well as the review process.

Justice

The final ethical principle set forth by the Belmont Report is **justice**, which focuses on the balance of benefit and harm across groups of people. In general, the guideline suggests that there should be fairness of distribution. Individuals from particular social groups should not be excluded—or disproportionately used—as research samples as a function of their place in society. Researchers must demonstrate that the recruitment of participants is fair and impartial. Note, however, that this refers to general principles. It is perfectly appropriate to use only a certain social group in the study if that is in fact the purpose of the study. If the goal of the research is to ascertain lesbian, gay, bisexual, transgender and queer (LGBTQ) individuals' perceptions of a new product or service geared to their needs, then the sample should focus exclusively on individuals who are LGBTQ.

Ethical Guidelines for the Use of Digital Data

In contrast to the very specific guidelines associated with the use of human participants in research, there is no agreement about the ethical rules for using digital data, making the combination of widespread use of digital data coupled with the lack of clear standards for the use of these data a "perfect storm of ethical risks" (Vallor & Rewak, 2018, p. 8). The use of digital data for research purposes challenges ethical conduct throughout the research process, from the decision about how and where to gather these data, to the security of these data, to providing access or selling these data to third-party organizations. Although there are no agreed-on ethical standards, we believe that researchers should be aware of and make explicit research decisions based on a number of ethical concerns associated with using this type of data. In this section we discuss the ethical use of social media data, as well as the use of HTTP cookies to gather information.

Using Digital Data

At the beginning of this chapter we talked about Cambridge Analytica's use of Facebook data. However, Facebook itself has used its users' data without consent, as have other platforms. In 2012 Facebook conducted an experiment to determine if the valence of posts (positive or negative) a user saw influenced the user's emotions (Dewey, 2014). For 1 week, roughly 700,000 users saw proportionately more positive posts or proportionately more negative posts than average. Facebook then analyzed the words used by the users in their own posts. The results showed that, as predicted, people who saw more negative posts also used more negative words in their own posts, and vice versa (Dewey, 2014). All of this was done without the user's consent. Moreover, one of the key elements of research ethics involves minimizing potential harm to participants; Facebook did not take into consideration that some of the people who had been exposed to negative posts might suffer from clinical depression. Viewing a disproportionate number of negative posts might have affected their mental health (Vallor & Rewak, 2018).

There are two ethical questions that arise when using digital data such as social media posts. First, are those data public or private? Traditionally, observation of behavior in public settings has not required informed consent because it is assumed that people in public know that they can be observed. However, the issue of internet data is not quite as clear cut. On the one hand, because information on the internet is public, some people argue that informed consent is not needed. As Bortree (2003) suggests, "Lurking in chat rooms and reading discussion boards is like 'hanging out on the street corner'" to observe public behavior (p. 7). Others, however, argue that any communication intended to be private should be considered private, even if it has been conducted on a public platform. For example, Facebook's study of emotional contagion was conducted without any consideration of the privacy settings of its users. (Facebook later added language about conducting research to its data use policy.) A best practice for this quandary is to make certain that users of digital platforms must opt in to have their data used for research purposes rather than opt out (Vallor & Rewak, 2018).

A second question related to the use of social media data is "To what extent do these data include **personally identifiable information** (PII)?" Recall that whenever using human participants the goal is to protect the participants' privacy. What is considered PII varies by U.S. state and across different countries. In most of the United States PII includes a person's name, address, phone number, Social Security number, and credit card number, among other things. However, the EU takes a much broader view of PII; they include physical, mental, economic, and social elements of an identity. Regardless of how restrictive a definition of PII might be, there are ethical responsibilities associated with protecting any PII data. Indeed, even when researchers claim that all identifying information has been deleted, there may be characteristics of individual responses that prevent anonymity from being achieved (Zimmer, 2010). To illustrate, in 2016 researchers used OKCupid's site to analyze the profiles of 68,000 users. When the researchers published the study, they included their entire data set; even though the actual photos and names of the users were not published, the data set included usernames, biographical information, age, sex, sexual orientation, religion, personality traits, interests, and answers to the dating site's survey questions (Vallor & Rewak, 2018). Many people consider this to be an ethical breach, since identifying the participants from these data would be relatively easy to do. Interestingly, and related to the question of whether digital data are public or private, the study's lead author claimed that the study was ethical because members of the dating site have the expectation that other members of the dating site will view their profile, making the data public.

Using HTTP Cookies

A second ethical concern regarding digital data involves the use of **HTTP cookies** to track Web users' browsing history. An HTTP cookie (also called a Web cookie, a browser cookie, or an internet cookie) is a small piece of data that is placed on a user's computer by the browser that they are using. Their intended use is to record important pieces of information such as the pages the user has visited in the past, whether the user is logged in, and information that the user has previously entered into fields such as their name, address, and so forth. However, an ethical issue surrounds the use of **third-party cookies**, which is information placed on the computer from a domain other than the one shown on the address bar. Third-party cookies are often embedded by advertisers, who are collecting data about individual users' browsing histories. Advertisers then use this information to target ads based on consumer behavior. How many times have you searched for information on a product only to find ads for that product or similar products splashed across websites you access for the rest of the day? As John, Kim, and Barasz (2018) conclude in their study of public perceptions of this activity, "When it comes to ad personalization, there's a fine line between creepy and delightful" (p. 68). John and colleagues' (2018) study of public perceptions of targeted ads concluded that there are five best practices for the ethical use of these data: don't target sensitive information such as health conditions or sexual orientation; be transparent about data use practices; use data sharing only when it benefits the user; justify your data collection to users; and try traditional data collection first.

Unique Ethical Concerns of the Professional Communication Researcher

You may recall from Chapter 1 that we differentiated between *public research* (which is research conducted by academics, the government, or think tanks and is publicly available) and *proprietary research* (which is research conducted by an organization that is not meant for public view). Because of the nature of proprietary research there are four potential ethical tensions for researchers engaged in proprietary research, each of which centers on best practices for research versus organizational or client interests. The first tension focuses on the motivation for conducting the research, the second tension involves the interpretation of the research findings, the third tension involves obligations to the organization/client versus obligations to the public or other important stakeholders, and the final tension centers on data security.

Motivations for the Research

One of the essential values identified by the Institute for Public Relations' statement of ethical research is that the researchers must have *good intentions*. Certainly, all individuals who engage in research should make certain that their motivations for conducting research are authentic and unbiased. However, meeting the goal of good intentions might be particularly challenging for professional communicators, who must balance ethical standards with organizational goals. Stewart (2014) created an ethics checklist for marketing research that focuses on determining if there are good intentions for doing the research. We have modified the checklist to include other forms of professional research in Table 5.2.

Two specific ways that professional communicators might have to grapple with good intentions is *conducting unnecessary research* or *performing the wrong research* (Stewart, 2014). In the case of unnecessary research, remember that research should assist organizations

TABLE 5.2   Checklist for Avoiding Unethical Research Decisions

Answering "yes" to any of the following questions suggests that the research decisions may be unethical.
1.   Does the decision to engage in this research practice treat the organization as an "exception to the rule"?
2.   Would the decision to conduct this research lose profits if customers were aware of what we had done?
3.   Would qualified job applicants be unwilling to work for the organization if they knew about the research practice?
4.   Does the decision to engage in this research practice benefit some parts of the organization without benefiting others?
5.   Would I prefer avoiding the consequences of the decision to engage in this research practice?
6.   Did I avoid fully answering any of these questions?

with identifying and solving problems. Research that does not accomplish these goals is likely to be unnecessary. To illustrate, Malhotra and Peterson (2006) described a situation in which a pie manufacturer wanted to conduct market research to understand the purchase of pies in convenience stores. Before collecting any new data, the researchers looked at the company's sales numbers. They determined that less than 1% of all sales were made at convenience stores, making market research—which is often time consuming and costly—unnecessary.

Unnecessary research often takes the form of collecting digital data. Vallor and Rewak (2018) caution that the practice of collecting data and storing it just in case the data might be useful at a later time is also unethical. Data should only be collected when needed, stored as long as it is needed, and deleted when it is no longer needed.

As for performing the wrong research, the issue is making certain that the actual research conducted is aligned with the goal that is driving the research. Numerous organizations and industries have demonstrated questionable intentions for engaging in research. One example is research conducted by Johnson & Johnson; during lawsuits associated with the company's hip replacement devices, internal documents demonstrated that clinical trials were not really centered on the safety of the product but were actually efforts to gather marketing information (Steffen et al., 2017). Steffen and colleagues conclude that if marketing objectives influence the conception or design of a study that is not intended to be a marketing study, the ethicality of the research is questionable. Indeed, this issue violates one of the central elements of the American Association for Public Opinion Research's ethical code of conduct (refer to Table 4.1 for an overview of their code).

Interpretation of the Findings

A second distinct tension for professionals engaged in proprietary research involves the objective interpretation of the data. Recall from the AAPOR's ethical code of conduct that interpretations of research should be consistent with the data. Remember from earlier in the chapter that one of the basic forms of research misconduct is data falsification. The ethical challenge is that when an organization has spent a large amount of time or money to conduct the research, it should come as no surprise that they want the results to support whatever initiative they are investigating. Consider the impact of eating oats on cholesterol. Many of us have seen Quaker Oats advertisements that claim that eating oats can lower cholesterol. These ads are the results of research funded by the Quaker company. According to Pratt (1988), the original study involved just over 200 people who ate a low-fat diet for 6 weeks. After that period of time, one-third of the participants were instructed to continue eating the low-fat diet for another 6 weeks; one-third of the participants ate a low-fat diet supplemented with 2 ounces of oatmeal every day for an additional 6 weeks; and the final group ate a low-fat diet supplemented with 2 ounces of oat bran every day to complete the 12-week study. All three groups lowered their cholesterol, with those who ate the oatmeal lowering their cholesterol about 9.3%.

Quaker Oats pounced on these results, launching an advertising campaign that stated "In recent clinical studies, where Quaker Oats were a daily part of a low-fat, low-cholesterol diet, total serum cholesterol levels dropped on average almost 10 percent" (Pratt, 1988, para. 5). Unfortunately, this isn't exactly what the research found. Although the group that ate the oatmeal did reduce their cholesterol by 9.3% (which might be rounded up to 10%), only 3.2% of the decrease came after oatmeal was introduced into the participants' diets—most of the decrease came from the first 6 weeks of eating the low-fat diet. Moreover, all three groups reduced their cholesterol levels, providing further evidence that the diet played a more significant role than the oatmeal (Pratt, 1988).

Obligations to the Public and Other Stakeholders

The Quaker Oats example highlights not only the tension associated with data interpretation when conducting proprietary research, but also ethical obligations to the public. In response to the Quaker company's advertising, the Center for Science in the Public Interest filed a petition with the Federal Trade Commission, accusing Quaker of misleading the public. In 2007 the company agreed to tone down their claims (Center for Science in the Public Interest, 2007). Current claims on boxes of Quaker Oats state, "As part of a heart healthy diet, the soluble fiber in Oatmeal can help reduce cholesterol." Of course, the typeface for the first 12 words is significantly smaller than the typeface for the final five words, and the capitalization of Oatmeal certainly suggests that readers are meant to start reading at that point.

Returning to the research ethics statement published by the IPR, researchers should demonstrate respect for all stakeholders. Similarly, the AAPOR code details responsibilities to the public and the profession. Unfortunately, there are multiple examples of failures to comply with this ethical guideline. Readers need to look no further than the tobacco industry. Despite public claims to the contrary, tobacco companies not only had been researching the addictiveness of cigarettes, they had actually researched how to make cigarettes even more addictive by increasing the speed with which nicotine enters the bloodstream (Henningfield et al., 2006). Unfortunately, the fact that proprietary research is not publicly available makes this form of unethical research behavior challenging to uncover.

One last way that communication professionals might fail in their obligation to their stakeholders is through the use of unsupervised machine learning. Organizations sometimes use computer algorithms to make predictions. If algorithms are completed only by unsupervised data mining, organizational members might be making decisions without understanding why they are making the decision. Vallor and Rewak (2018) describe a case in which a bank could use unsupervised machine learning to predict who to accept for home loan applications. In doing so, if a customer is denied a loan, they have no idea why they have been denied the loan—and neither do the loan officers of the bank. These sorts of situations represent a failure of organizational members to understand the needs of their clients.

Data Security

The final ethical tension for professional communicators is data security. Vallor and Rewak (2018) point out that the problem of too many people having access to data is a challenge to responsible professional research. Much like crime scene analysts document every person who has access to evidence, so too must professional researchers be careful with the chain of responsibility for data. Moreover, even if ethical guidelines have been followed in the initial collection of data, when digital data are involved researchers need to be concerned about the reuse of the data later. This is especially the case if there is any risk of emotional or social harm from the data. Vallor and Rewark (2018) encourage us to think, "I should be asking myself where that data might be five or ten years from now, in whose hands, for what purposes, and with what safeguards. I should also consider how long that data will remain accurate and relevant, or how its sensitivity and vulnerability to abuse might increase over time" (p. 49).

Chapter Summary

Chapter 5 focused on the importance of ethics throughout the research process. Three forms of basic research misconduct were identified: plagiarism, data fabrication, and data falsification. Ethical codes of conduct were described, with a specific focus on two professional organizations' approaches to providing ethical guidelines for doing research. We then focused on ethical standards for using human participants in research, highlighting the Belmont Report's principles of respect, beneficence, and justice. Given the increase in the use of digital data, we then turned our attention to highlighting ethical concerns with the use of digital data. The question as to whether digital data were public or private, as well as the question of how to handle personally identifiable information, were addressed. We also talked about the use of HTTP cookies and the challenge of how to ethically engage in targeted advertising. We concluded with the unique ethical tensions associated with conducting proprietary research. These include the motivations for conducting the research, the interpretation of the findings, and the obligations to the public and other stakeholders.

PRACTICE ACTIVITIES

1. **Creating a strategic plan:** Go back to the model of strategic planning in Chapter 1. For each step in the RPIE model, identify what specific ethical threats might be present using the concepts described in this chapter.

2. **Examples of unethical professional research:** Conduct additional research about each of the examples provided in this chapter. Then, articulate what ethical principles have been violated and which have not, including why you believe the research to be ethical or unethical:

   ◆ Cambridge Analytica's use of Facebook data

   ◆ Wakefield's study linking the MMR vaccine to autism

   ◆ Facebook's emotional contagion study

   ◆ The OKCupid study

   ◆ Quaker Oats cholesterol claims

3. **Complete an IRB application:** Find your university's IRB information. Try to complete the application form for a study that you might conduct about a topic of interest to you. What elements where difficult to complete?

4. **Professional ethical codes:** Find the ethical code of conduct for a professional association associated with your (desired) employment industry (e.g., Public Relations Society of America, American Federation of Television and Radio Artists, Social Media Association, etc.). Do they have any specific ethical guidelines for research? If not, how might the elements of their code of conduct translate to the research setting?

5. **Research with human participants training:** Check to see if your university IRB offers any kind of training or certification to conduct research with human participants. Complete the training. Keep track of which parts of the training seemed particularly important for communication research.

PART II

Applying Research Methods

Observation and Data Analytics

6

Have you ever run into a supermarket to pick up just a couple of things, and by the time you get to the register you have a cart full of items? You should know that this is not a personality flaw, but the result of careful research into consumer behavior. Major retailers have conducted extensive research into the design aesthetics that will influence customers to spend more money. For example, it is no mistake that after entering a store you are forced to walk through much of the establishment before you get to the registers and the exit (Rupp, 2015). Retailers are counting on you making an impulse purchase because you encounter so many items on your journey. Nor is it just dumb chance that you walk through the bakery, produce, and floral departments of a supermarket first, as each of these departments present a sensory experience that is designed to foster positive emotions—and therefore stimulate the desire to make a purchase. Nor is it accidental that the dairy section is placed as far away from the entrance as possible, since most people have at least one dairy item on their shopping list (Rupp, 2015). In fact, one

CHAPTER OUTLINE

◆ Step 1: Develop Your Research Question

◆ Step 2: Determine the Nature of Your Observation

◆ Step 3: Decide on the Role of the Observer

◆ Step 4: Decide on Your Method of Observation

◆ Step 5: Record the Data

◆ Step 6: Conduct a Test Run

◆ Step 7: Make the Observations

◆ Step 8: Analyze the Data

◆ The Strategic Use of Observations: Digital Data Analytics

◆ Advantages and Disadvantages of Observation

study found that people spend significantly more time (and more money) in supermarkets that play music, but the tempo of the music is important—nothing too fast, or customers will literally boogie right down the aisle and out the door (Milliman, 1982). In short, the reason why virtually every supermarket (or every big box store) looks and sounds the same is not because of a lack of imagination, but because of careful research.

Observation is a research technique that involves surveillance of naturally occurring behavior. The focus on behavior is what makes the method unique; the observation method is not distorted by what people *say* they would do, or what they *think* should be done. It focuses on what people actually do. To make this distinction clear, how often do you *intend* to work out or *say* you are going to wake up early to finish some work, and then somehow don't go to the gym or get out of bed? Observations are the only method to determine what people have actually done.

Data collected through observations can be either *quantitative* (using precise measurement and numbers) or *qualitative* (in-depth understanding and themes) in nature. There are eight steps for conducting observational research (Franz, 2012), which are highlighted in Box 6.1. We will walk you through these steps one at a time.

BOX 6.1

Steps in Conducting Formal Observations

Step 1   Develop your research question

Step 2   Determine the focus of the observation

Step 3   Choose the appropriate role for the observers

Step 4   Decide on your method of observation

Step 5   Determine the method for recording data

Step 6   Test run the observation

Step 7   Observe

Step 8   Analyze the data

Step 1: Develop Your Research Question

Observation is a formal research technique. As such, it requires systematic planning and careful measurement. We are not talking about insights based on professional experience or casual conversations. As with all research studies, observation starts with the creation of a research objective and a research question. You might recall from Chapter 2 that there are five typical professional communication research objectives: monitoring the environment, evaluating opportunities, diagnosing problems, selecting a course of action, and evaluating the course of action. In Chapter 2, we also talked about three different goals for conducting research: to describe communication, to compare differences between groups, and to relate communication to some other variable. The goal of observational research is almost always to *describe* the nature of interaction, with a specific focus on *monitoring the environment* or *diagnosing problems*.

Step 2: Determine the Nature of Your Observation

After developing the research question, the researcher needs to determine the focus of the observation and how it might be best achieved. There are a series of decisions that need to be made in this step. The first decision is whether the people who will be observed are aware that they are being observed. Recall from the ethics chapter that ideally people provide informed consent for participating in research. In non-disguised observations the people being studied are indeed aware that they are being observed and why they are being observed. For example, Moon (2018) studied how members of an NGO (non-government organization) conducted media relations. The members of the organization were aware that she was conducting research on the topic and that they were being observed. However, one of the challenges of non-disguised observations is the possibility of the Hawthorne effect taking place. The Hawthorne effect is named after research that was conducted in the 1930s at a Western

Electric factory in Hawthorne, Illinois. Researchers were investigating whether employee productivity would change based on manipulating things like the lighting in the plant, the timing of breaks, and the cleanliness of workstations. They found that productivity increased when any change was made, at least temporarily. These changes were interpreted as evidence that people often change their behavior when they know they are being observed.

If the researchers believe that any shifts in natural behavior might unduly influence the results of the study, they might choose to use **disguised observations** instead, which is when the people being observed are not aware that they are being observed. This might include the use of surreptitious cameras or two-way mirrors. Disguised observations might also take place in public places. Droms (2013), for example, observed 300 product returns at retail establishments in order to develop a model for the prototypical patterns of interactions during returns and exchanges. In describing her method she asserted, "The researchers were careful to blend into the store so that consumers were not aware of our observation and, as a result, change their behavior. This involved standing in the return line and waiting among consumers, observing from an enclosed area behind the return and exchange counter, and pretending to apply for a job in the retailer's kiosk" (Droms, 2013, p. 83). Although using disguised observations helps to overcome the Hawthorne effect, there are ethical challenges associated with these sorts of interactions. You might recall from the chapter on ethics that all participants must give informed consent to be a part of the study. One exception is when observations take place in a public place, because people expect to be observed while in public. Nevertheless, researchers must use caution when disguising their observations.

After determining whether observations will be disguised or non-disguised, the researchers must decide between using direct versus indirect observations. **Direct observations** focus on observing the actual behavior. This behavior might occur online, or it might occur face to face. For example, the researcher might sit in on a department meeting and track each participants' type of comment (e.g., question, statement of fact, statement of opinion, and so forth). In Moon's (2018) study of media relations activities of an NGO, she directly observed workplace interaction and had access to Web conferences.

Direct observations are preferred, but not always possible. Consider highly personal behaviors (e.g., things that occur in the bedroom or the bathroom); observing such interactions might be considered intrusive or an invasion of privacy. Other reasons for not being able to engage in a direct observation is if the interaction or the interactional partners are hostile or dangerous, or if the costs of directly observing the interaction is prohibitive. In such cases you may need to conduct an indirect observation. In indirect observations the research centers on the symptoms or effects of the behavior. For example, the condition of a book is an indicator of how frequently it has been used, or the number of service calls made is an indicator of the quality of an appliance. To illustrate the use of indirect observation, Vraga, Bode, and Troller-Renfree (2016) examined people's eye movements while viewing social media content. Although they had direct evidence of *where* their participants' eyes went while viewing the social media content, they had no idea *why* their eyes tracked in that way. As such, eye tracking is only an indirect measure of interest; people might have looked at specific content not because they were interested in it, but because they had difficulty seeing the information, difficulty interpreting the information, or because they were surprised by the information.

Once these elements have been decided, there are a number of question about exactly *how* you will conduct the observation research. These decisions center on the role of the researcher, the type of observation that will take place, and the method of recording your observations.

Step 3: Decide on the Role of the Observer

Once the nature of the observation has been determined, the researcher then needs to decide what role he or she will play in the research process. If the decision is made to conduct a disguised observation, typically the researcher takes a complete participant role; the people being observed believe that the researcher is simply another person taking part in the activities being observed. For example, "secret shoppers" are people who investigate the shopping experience by pretending to be just another shopper. Similarly, in Droms's (2013) study of product returns the research assistants who collected data pretended to be other customers.

If the decision is made to conduct non-disguised observation, the people being observed are aware that they are being observed. There are two types of non-disguised observations. The researcher can be a **complete observer**, which is when it is clear that the researcher is not participating in the activities under investigation. In the eye tracking study we discussed earlier, Vraga and colleagues (2016) played the role of researchers; there was no pretense that they were also participating in the activity. Alternatively, the researcher can play the role of a **participant observer**, which is when the researcher is simultaneously taking part in the activities being observed and also playing a researcher role. In Moon's (2018) study of NGO media relations, she both volunteered at the organization and conducted her research at the same time. Participant observation is particularly challenging, since the observation itself can influence full participation and vice versa. For this reason, participant observation tends not to be used very frequently for professional research (Cooper & Schindler, 2008).

Step 4: Decide on Your Method of Observation

The next step in conducting an observational study is to determine the procedures being used to collect the data. As with many types of research, observation can be either qualitative or quantitative in nature. If qualitative, the researcher records observations and then determines themes that will help to make sense of the experience (Chapter 11 describes how to analyze qualitative data). Such research efforts are typically called **unstructured observation**, because there are no predetermined types of behaviors that the researcher is looking for. To illustrate, Smith (2014) conducted an ethnography of decision-making processes during crises at a mental health facility. **Ethnography** is the term for a type of observation that involves an in-depth analysis of the communication practices of particular communities or contexts. Because of this specific focus, all ethnographies involve observation, but not all observations are considered ethnographies. In this case, Smith (2014) observed over 1,500 hours of interaction over 13 months at a children's treatment center. Rather than seeking to identify a fixed set of decision-making strategies, Smith instead watched what happened in times of crisis and developed a model of decision-making that emerged from her observations.

Conversely, researchers can choose to conduct a **structured observation**, which involves creating an observation checklist similar to the coding scheme of a content analysis. These checklists might come from previous research or theory that has identified the important variables to be measured. When data are gathered using this type of checklist, the researcher typically does a quantitative analysis of who, what, when, where, and how the behaviors in question were observed. For example, in Droms's (2013) study of product returns the checklist included the sex of the customer, his or her approximate age, the type of interaction (sale, exchange, return), and whether a receipt was present. These items came from previous research that identified the routine patterns of exchanges and returns. Table 6.1 provides an example of what Droms's (2013) checklist might have looked like.

Step 5: Record the Data

There are two main ways of collecting observational data: mechanical data collection and human data collection. **Mechanical data collection** simply means that machines are used to record the behavior. This might entail the use of audio or video recording, or computer tracking of behaviors. For example, returning to our example of grocery store design, researchers have used radio frequency identification technology (RFID) to track the movement of grocery store shopping carts. This allows researchers to track customers' movements so that a retailer can maximize store design and product location (infsoft, 2017). As we will discuss shortly, social media and Web analytics use digital data as a form of mechanical observation.

Human data collection relies on trained researchers to observe interaction. The researchers can use an observation log if the study

TABLE 6.1 Observation Checklist Sample

Adult sex	Male	☐
	Female	☐
Age range	Under 18	☐
	18–25	☐
	26–40	☐
	41–50	☐
	51–60	☐
	61 or older	☐
Group size	Single adult	☐
	Combination of adults	☐
	Adult with one child	☐
	Adult with multiple children	☐
	Family (2 adults with 1+ children)	☐
Interaction type	Return	☐
	Exchange	☐
	Other	☐
Presence of a receipt	Yes	☐
	No	☐
	Unknown	☐
Notes		

is structured, or field notes if the study is unstructured. **Field notes** are detailed notes that a researcher writes either during or immediately after the observation. These notes often involve both *descriptive information* about what was observed, but also *reflective information*, which involves the researcher's interpretations about what he or she has observed. Field notes might also include sketches or diagrams.

Ideally, field notes include the following information:

◆ A description of the people who were observed, including, at minimum, basic demographics, but if possible, people's formal and informal roles in the interaction

◆ The setting of the observation, including the physical setting as well as times and dates

◆ The purpose of the interaction, especially if the interaction was a planned event (e.g., an organizational meeting)

◆ A description of the communication or interaction that occurred. What are people doing? How exactly are they doing it?

◆ Thoughts or feelings that occur to the researcher as she or he is doing the observation

Step 6: Conduct a Test Run

Because naturally occurring interactions can't be repeated, researchers must make sure that their observation system "works" in the real world. For that reason, researchers should test their observation scheme before collecting data. If conducting unstructured observation, how well can the researcher capture the information? Is she or he able to capture everything that might be useful? Are additional camera angles necessary, or additional voice recorders? Does she or he need to work on developing detailed field notes? If using structured observation, does the observation sheet work? Are there extraneous elements or elements that are missing? In addition to making sure that the data that are collected will be useful to answer the research question, conducting a test run also allows the researcher to practice making observations, potentially making the researchers more skilled and efficient at collecting the data. As such, test runs allow the researcher to make adjustments so that actual observations are high quality.

Step 7: Make the Observations

Once you have conducted a test run you are ready to start making your observations. The number of observations that you need to make varies depending on whether you are conducting a qualitative or a quantitative observation. If conducting a qualitative observation, much like with interviews and focus groups, you need to continue making observations until you have achieved saturation, which is the point at which you are no longer observing anything new. If conducting a quantitative observation, you need to collect sufficient data to allow for the appropriate statistical tests that you will conduct. For those interested in the way to determine this statistically, you might review Wilhite (2017), who provides a technical description of determining the number of observations required for a probability sample.

Step 8: Analyze the Data

As with all research methods, the collection of data is not enough; the researchers also have to make sense of the data, especially in terms of how the data answer the research questions. Unstructured observations tend to be qualitative in nature, and so qualitative techniques such as thematic analysis will likely be used. Structured observations tend to be quantitative in nature, allowing for the use of statistics to draw conclusions with the data. Both techniques for data analysis—qualitative and quantitative—are outlined in Chapter 11.

The Strategic Use of Observations: Digital Data Analytics

Two important ways that organizations use the observation method are through social media analytics and website analytics. **Social media analytics** refers "to all activities related to gathering relevant social media data, analyzing the gathered data, and disseminating findings as appropriate to support business activities such as intelligence gathering, insight generation, sense making, problem recognition/opportunity detection, problem solution/opportunity exploitation, and/or decision making" (Holsapple et al., 2014, p. 4). In short, social media analytics refers to an organization's ongoing efforts to monitor and measure social media traffic that is related to the organization and its practices. **Website analytics** is very similar to social media analytics, but the focus is specifically on collecting and analyzing the use of websites.

When analyzing social media activity, communication professionals must differentiate between **monitoring social media** (which means engaging in surveillance of the social media environment, and attending particularly to mentions of an organization, its product or services, and its stakeholders), and **measuring social media** (which means determining how well an organization's social media activities are achieving organizational goals (Blanchard, 2011). Both activities involve the systematic collection of data, which means that both are formal research processes. However, the type of data collected, and how those data are used, varies considerably. Accordingly, professionals must have an awareness of organizational goals in order to best undertake social media analytics.

Monitoring Social Media

Monitoring social media involves tracking mentions of your organization or brand, comments about products or services, references to stakeholders, and, perhaps most importantly, customer complaints. A survey of 1,000 consumers conducted by the software company Sprout Social found that almost half of their respondents have complained about a company on social media (Hutchinson, 2017). Research also indicates that 84% of consumers expect companies to respond to a social media complaint within 24 hours. The expectation rises for complaints posted on Twitter; 72% of consumers expect their Twitter complaint to be acknowledged within an hour (Hutchinson, 2017). The importance of social media monitoring—and effective social media responses—cannot be overstated. To illustrate, you may recall seeing social media posts about a United Airline's passenger being forcibly removed from a plane in 2017. Videos of the encounter spread quickly, but United Airline's social media responses only exacerbated the public relations crisis by failing to address the concerns that were posted on Twitter and a variety of other social media platforms (Ohlheiser, 2017).

When monitoring social media, professional communicators should also pay attention to *who* is posting about the organization. If the person posting about the organization is a **social media influencer**, the impact of a social media post is likely to have much more of an impact than a post by the average user. Consider the example of Heather Armstrong, a professional blogger with over 1.5 million Twitter followers who was unhappy with the customer service she received after purchasing a Maytag washing machine. Her negative tweets about the company resulted in 2,500 comments within a few hours. Clearly, negative social media posts by any customer can be damaging to a company, but Armstrong's role as a social media reporter made the post especially detrimental for Maytag (Olson, 2009).

Measuring Social Media

In contrast to monitoring social media, measuring social media involves assessing such important considerations as stakeholder engagement, attitudes about the organization, the impact of events and sponsorships, and of course, linking the use of social media to sales. Using a strategic approach to measuring social media requires using an organization's goals or objectives to identify the most important data to collect (Driver, 2018). In gathering these data, professional communicators use **metrics**, which are numeric values assigned to the output or outcomes of social media efforts (Michaelson & Stacks, 2017).

The International Association for the Measurement and Evaluation of Communications (AMEC) has generated a set of standards for social media measurement in the communication industry that has been endorsed by a large number of professional organizations, including the Public Relations Society of America, the Institute for Public Relations, the Global Alliance for Public Relations and Communications Management, the International Association of Business Communicators, as well as major multinational organizations and major communications agencies. These standards focus on five overarching communication goals: exposure, engagement, preference, impact, and advocacy (AMEC, 2019). Key measurements of each goal are listed in Table 6.2.

TABLE 6.2 Key Social Media Metrics

Goal	Metric
Exposure	Audience growth rate
	Impressions
	Post reach
	Social share of voice
Engagement	@mentions
	Amplification rate
	Applause rate
	Average engagement rate
	Conversation rate
	Likes
	Shares
	Virality rate
Preference	Bounce rate
	Click-through rate
	Cost per click
Impact	Attendance
	Downloads
	Positive evaluations
	Sales
	Subscribers
	Votes
Advocacy	Customer satisfaction score
	Net promoter score
	Testimonials

Exposure

Exposure is the most fundamental element of assessing social media activity; it refers to the extent to which an audience has encountered social media content. Simple metrics for exposure include impressions, which are the number of people who saw the post; post reach, which is the number of people who have had a social media post on their screens; and audience growth rate, which is the change in the number of followers over time. A more advanced metric of exposure is social share of voice, which is all social media activity referencing an organization, brand, product, or service as compared to social media activity of competitors.

Engagement

Most communication professionals are more interested in engagement than simple exposure. **Engagement** refers to interaction that occurs in response to social media content (AMEC, 2019). It can reference the number of times followers talk *with* organizational members, or it can simply refer to the number of times people talk *about* the organization or its brand (Luttrell, 2016). There are a large number of metrics associated with engagement. Simple metrics include **@mentions**, which is the number of times an organization, brand, product, or service is mentioned on social media using the @ symbol, and **likes**, which are the number of times a post has been liked or favorited. Although these measures provide some insights, most professionals agree that such indicators are "vanity metrics," which means everyone reports how many they have, but ultimately they mean very little in terms of engagement). Better indicators of engagement include the **applause rate**, which is the number of approvals (e.g., likes, favorites) a post receives in proportion to the total number of followers; the **average engagement rate**, which is the number of engagement actions (e.g., likes, favorites, shares, comments) a post receives in proportion to the total number of followers; and the **conversation rate,** which is the number of visitors who click on a link on a post and then take action on the page as compared to the page's total number of visitors. The strongest levels of engagement can be measured by the **amplification rate**, which is the ratio of **shares** per post as compared to the overall number of viewers, and the **virality rate**, which is the number of people who share a post relative to the number of unique views of that post.

Preference

The third type of social media goal centers on actions that take place as a result of social media content. The AMEC (2019) calls this goal **preference**, although others have called it *influence* (Luttrell, 2016) or **conversions** (Driver, 2018). Preference metrics typically center on responses to calls to action, which are links on a post that bring the audience to additional content. Sample calls to action are links that ask people to fill out a contact form, sign up for a newsletter, become a member of an organization, or browse a catalog of products or services, for example. The key indicator of this goal is the click-through rate, which is how often people complete the call to action. A second major metric is the bounce rate. A bounce is when a visitor views a single page of a website before leaving. To illustrate, if a large number of followers click on your call to action, see the landing page, and immediately leave, you have a high bounce rate. Finally, in the case of paid calls to action (i.e., sponsored ads on social media sites), the cost per click is the amount paid per individual click on the call to action.

Impact

Impact is one of the strongest social media analytics. It refers to measurements of the direct effect of a social media message, campaign, or program (AMEC, 2019). Most of these items are readily understood metrics: for marketing efforts, the number of downloads, subscribers, or sales; for events, the number of people who attended the event; for campaigns, the number of votes received; and for public relations efforts, an indication of positive evaluations of the organization. Note that most of these metrics are not derived from the social media platform itself but are additional measurements that need to be linked to social media posts. For example, there are two major ways that positive evaluations of an organization can be measured. First, a content analysis of social media posts can be undertaken in order to determine sentiments about the organization. The method for conducting a content analysis will be described in Chapter 7. Second, public relations professionals can conduct a survey of stakeholder attitudes about the organization. Survey techniques are described in Chapter 8.

Advocacy

Although impacts can rarely be measured directly though social media platforms, the final goal can be. Advocacy occurs when followers provide recommendations or positive reviews of an organization, its brand, or its products and services (AMEC, 2019). One major metric of advocacy are testimonials, which are reviews or endorsements of an organization, brand, product, or service posted on social media. Consider the websites Yelp, TripAdvisor, Glass Door, and Rotten

Tomatoes. Each of these websites is designed with the sole intention of providing a place for people to review businesses, workplaces, and films. Other websites, like Amazon and other retailers, encourage customers to provide reviews of items and services. Finally, beyond websites that are dedicated to reviews or channels that allow testimonials, reviews often happen organically. Positive reviews should be tracked and reported. Conversely, wise social media managers do reactionary monitoring using keywords such as the company name and "sucks," "fail," "WTF," and "hate" so that negative reviews can be addressed immediately with the person who posted it.

More formal measures of advocacy include a **customer satisfaction score (CSat)**. Typically, CSats are acquired through a pop-up window after a user has visited a site asking them to evaluate their satisfaction with the visit. These data are relatively easy to collect and interpret. Slightly more complicated are **net promoter scores (NPS)**, which are measures of customer loyalty. Again, users are typically asked a single question about how likely they would recommend the company/product/service to a friend with a range from 0 (not at all likely) to 10 (extremely likely). In reviewing these data, communication professionals would be striving for average scores of 9 or 10.

The metrics described in this chapter are just a few of the possible ways that social media can be measured. Because there are so many different metrics that need to be monitored, professional communicators tend to use what is known as a **dashboard**, which is a digital interface that displays a variety of distinct social media metrics simultaneously in order to provide a centralized report of social media activity (Luttrell, 2016). Much like the dashboard of a car, which includes a speedometer, a tachometer, fuel gauge, odometer, and even oil level and tire pressure indicators, a social media dashboard allows you to see a number of different measurements simultaneously.

Tools for Collecting Social Media Data

Collecting social media data can be as simple as using the built-in platforms associated with a social media platform. YouTube, for example, has an analytics tool that provides 15 different pieces of information, including the number of views of a video, the demographics of those who have viewed it, playback locations (for example, whether the video was viewed on the YouTube Watch Page, a You Tube channel, or on another website), traffic sources (that is, other sites that viewers have used to find your video), audience retention, subscribers, favorites, likes and dislikes, comments, sharing, estimated earnings, ad performance, watch time, call to action (i.e., whether people have clicked on any links you have embedded), and live events (which includes things like the number of people viewing a video at a particular time, how many times a video was played back, and whether there were any playback issues or failures to launch). All of this information is uploaded daily. Although the type of information available varies, every social media platform provides some form of application programming interface (API) that provides analytics for free to the users of that platform.

There are also a variety of social media monitoring software packages that can be used. The benefit of these software packages is that they allow for greater customization and integration of data. Examples of paid platforms include Hootsuite, Sprout Social, Buffer, Social Bakers, and Simply Measured. Free analytics tools include Google Analytics, Cyfe, Klout, and Peakfeed. Finally, professional communicators can collect data from a social media firehose, which is open access and provides all of the data that comes from a social media platform. Major social media firehoses include GNIP and Datasift.

Web Analytics

Web analytics is quite similar to social media analytics, but the focus is on how individuals use a website. Web analytics seeks to explain not only how many people have frequented a website, but *why* they have gone to the website, *how* they found the website, *what* they do when they get to the website, and whether they *return* to the website. There are typically five goals associated with engaging in Web analytics: keyword insight, which is an analysis of the search terms that drive people to a website; audience insight, which provides information about who the audience is and how they behave; channel insight, which allows you to identify which social media channels drive visitors to the site; page quality, which is an indication of how well a site is meeting viewers' needs; and **trends**, which is the ability to track these data over time.

Many of the same metrics identified in the social media analytics section are used for website analytics, such as click-through rate and bounce rate. However, there are also some metrics that are unique to Web analytics. These metrics are listed in Table 6.3.

One of the major challenges of Web analytics is determining actual Web visits by a person versus Web visits initiated technologically by robots or **website crawlers** (which are also called spiders, spiderbots, bots, ants, and automatic indexers). Crawlers are programs that are used to "scrape" data from a website. In fact, many of you have probably had the experience of having to type in a code to prove to the website that you are not a robot. Web crawlers are used most often to index internet content, and they are both beneficial and problematic for professional communicators. On the one hand, you want the content of your website to be easily retrieved by stakeholders doing an internet search. On the other hand, you also want real data about the use of your website that has not been inflated or distorted by visits from Web crawlers.

TABLE 6.3 Common Web Analytic Metrics

Metric	Data
Unique visitors	Page views
	Visits (number of page views per session)
	Unique visitors
Visit characterizations	Entry page (first page visited)
	Exit page
	Visit duration
	Click-through/Click-through rate
Visitor characterizations	Location
	New visitors
	Visits per visitor
	Recency
	Frequency
Engagement	Page exit ratio
	Bounces/Bounce rate
	Page views per visit

Tools for Web Analytics

The granddaddy of all Web analytics tools is Google Analytics, which is a free tool that provides reams of information; in fact, one of the biggest criticisms of Google Analytics is that it is overly complicated for anyone other than a Web analyst (Bigby, 2018). Other Web analytics tools include Adobe Analytics, Clicky, eTracker, Hubspot, and KISSmetrics.

Advantages and Disadvantages of Observation

The main advantage of observation as a research method is that it provides insight into the way that people actually interact without the biases (intentional or unintentional) that occur when people report on their own behavior via a survey. You might recall from Chapter 1 that conducting a survey is the only method we can use to determine what people think or feel. However, many researchers also use surveys to determine how people behave. Unfortunately, how people say they behave and how they behave can be quite different from each other.

The major disadvantage is that when human observers are used, the observers own biases and interpretations can affect the results. In addition, although observations allow researchers to determine *what* people do, they do not provide an understanding of *why* they do it. Ultimately, understanding why is what allows for more effective strategic decisions.

Chapter Summary

This chapter introduced the observation method of research, which is a technique for surveilling naturally occurring behavior. We talked about the various types of observations (non-disguised versus disguised, direct versus indirect, structured versus unstructured), the various roles of the researcher (complete participant, complete observer, or participant observer), and ways of recording the data (mechanical versus human). We then focused on digital data analytics as a strategic form of observation research used in professional settings. We specifically described the role of social media analytics for monitoring social media posts about an organization, as well as for measuring the extent to which social media activities are achieving organizational goals. We discussed specific metrics that can be used to measure exposure, engagement, preference, impact, and advocacy. In addition, we identified both public and proprietary means to collect this data. Next, we focused on website analytics, which provides professional communicators with data not only about how frequently a website is used, but also how it is used, why it is used, and how users found the website. We also identified public and proprietary tools for Web analytics.

PRACTICE ACTIVITIES

1. **Conduct an unstructured observation:** Try to be a participant observer in another class or at your workplace. Try to simultaneously be a participant in your class/workplace *and* take field notes about patterns of interaction. How good were your field notes? How well did you perform as a participant? Submit your field notes and a reflection of your challenges to the professor.

2. **Develop an observation checklist:** Create a RQ focusing on monitoring behavior in a particular location. Then develop a checklist that would assist you in your observation.

3. **#hashtags:** Trace the hashtags of an organization (e.g., search for #americanairlines). Are the comments primarily positive or negative? How responsive is the organization to this feedback?

4. **Measuring a social media campaign:** A recent survey indicates that large numbers of college students experience food insecurity, which is a lack of consistent access to nutritious food. Knowing that large amounts of food are wasted at your university, you and a group of your

friends have created an app that can connect hungry students with high-quality food leftover from campus events. Of course, you have to communicate that the app is available and how it works, so you create a social media campaign.

a. How might you measure awareness of the app?

b. How might you measure how engaged people are with the app?

c. How might you measure how often people saw your social media post and then downloaded your app?

d. How might you measure how effective your app was in assisting students with food insecurity?

5. **Google Analytics:** Create a Google Analytics demo account (https://support.google.com/analytics/answer/6367342?hl=en). Create your own custom dashboard. Create the name of your dashboard, add or remove widgets, and rearrange them on the page. Submit this to your instructor.

Content Analysis and Content Audits

Perhaps no other trend has influenced professional communicators more in recent years than public perceptions of "fake news." Traditionally, fake news was defined as "news articles that are intentionally and verifiably false, and could mislead readers" (Allcott & Gentzkow, 2017, p. 213). We all likely can agree that tabloid stories centering on UFO abductions and manufactured celebrity scandals constitute fake news. Recently, fake news has taken on the meaning of false information about political figures on social media. This form of fake news is highly problematic because the majority of Americans now get their news from social media sources (Allcott & Gentzkow, 2017). Moreover, since the 2016 presidential election, the meaning of fake news has shifted, with many Americans believing that politically slanted or biased information is also fake news (Finneman & Thomas, 2018). According to the Pew Research Center, 87% of Republicans and 53% of Democrats believe that news organizations demonstrate political bias in their coverage (Barthel & Mitchell, 2017). This lack of trust in the objectivity of the news media has

125

profound implications for professional communicators. But is it true? Are mainstream media sources biased?

The method to determine whether any media outlet is biased is to conduct a content analysis. **Content analysis** is an objective research method that is focused on the content, nature, or structure of messages. So, in order to determine if media coverage is biased, you would need to classify media content into categories of favorable, neutral, or unfavorable toward a political candidate or platform. Of interest, formal content analyses have found very little evidence of media bias (e.g., Budak et al., 2016), but a content analysis of trust in the media finds that the most common reason for mistrust is perceived bias (Newman & Fletcher, 2017). This gap points to the differences between the results of objective research and subjective perceptions.

In the communication professions, content analysis is an important research tool. Content analysis helps communication professionals better understand existing messages, which then informs their decisions about ongoing and future message strategies. For example, public relations professionals use content analysis to assess sentiments about an organization, as well as the prominence and quality of coverage (Michaelson & Stacks, 2017). Marketing professionals use content analysis to determine public perceptions of brands (Liu et al., 2017). Having a way to measure the communication about an organization or brand that already exists helps point the way forward to future messaging.

Fundamentally, content analysis involves the development of categories into which messages can be placed and counting the number of times each category occurs in a selected group of texts. Recall from Chapter 2 that a **text** refers to any written or recorded message. Accordingly, in order to better understand messages professional communicators might analyze newspaper stories or television newscasts; organizational media such as websites, newsletters, or annual reports; social media posts; or print, broadcast, or digital advertisements, among other things. In this chapter we discuss the process of conducting a content analysis. We specifically feature the differences between human coding and computer-assisted coding in the process. We will also discuss the role of content analysis in communication strategy. Finally, we highlight the advantages and limitations of this method. Box 7.1 includes a summary of each of the steps involved in conducting a content analysis.

BOX 7.1

The Steps for Conducting a Content Analysis

Step 1   Develop your research question

Step 2   Select the appropriate texts to analyze

Step 3   Select whether you are interested in manifest or latent content

Step 4   Determine your units of analysis

Step 5   Develop your categories

Step 6   Create your coding procedures and decision rules

Step 7   Establish intercoder reliability

Step 8   Code the messages

Step 1: Develop Your Research Question

Because content analysis focuses on the nature and structure of messages, most content analyses start with a research question that seeks to *describe* the nature of messages. Sample research questions associated with content analysis are the following:

RQ1: What is the sentiment of tweets about Organization X?

RQ2: What types of stories are covered on network news?

Note that both research questions are simply asking about the kinds of message content that exist. However, as a technique, content analysis can also make *comparisons*. To illustrate, consider the following research questions:

RQ3: Are there differences in the sentiment of social media posts about Organization X on different social media platforms?

RQ4: How does story coverage vary across television networks?

These research questions seek to compare content based on the source of the messages (Facebook versus Twitter versus Instagram, or CNN versus Fox News). You can also compare content based on different groups of people (messages about men versus women, or different racial or ethnic groups), or over time (coverage in 1990s, 2000s, 2010s, and 2020s).

Step 2: Determine Your Texts

Because content analysis focuses on existing messages, once you have developed your RQ the next step is to identify which specific messages you will need for your analysis. For example, the Pew Research Center, a nonpartisan think tank, conducts numerous content analyses to provide information about contemporary issues and attitudes. In their overview of methods, they state that "choosing a sample involves both a focus on thoroughness, representativeness and the purely practical question of availability. Depending on the scope and goals of a project, we might code every story in a given news outlet, or we might use various search techniques to find specific articles relevant to our analysis" (Pew Research Center, 2018, para. 4). In general, there are three considerations in selecting the text for a content analysis. First, the researcher needs to select *forms* (e.g., magazine articles, social media posts, television broadcasts) and *genres* (e.g., political news, online reviews, reality shows) of a text. Second, the researcher needs to identify *target issues or dates* (e.g., articles published in volume 191 of *Time* magazine, reviews posted in the month of January, reality shows broadcast on the four major broadcast networks over a 2-year period). Finally, the researcher should determine whether she or he will analyze all messages that fit the criteria (which is called the universe) or some sample of messages that fit these criteria. Recall that sampling techniques are described in more detail in Chapter 4.

Consider the example of a study of media bias in political news stories conducted by Budak and colleagues (2016). They started by identifying the top 13 U.S. news outlets and two highly rated political blogs. From this list, they compiled over 800,000 news articles published in these outlets over the course of a year, which they then reduced by classifying the articles as to whether they were news articles about U.S. politics or not. From their original list they identified approximately 115,000 political stories. Finally, to reduce the sample even further, the authors randomly selected two political stories from each news outlet for every day of the year, resulting in a final sample of just over 10,500 stories. These stories were then coded as to whether they were positive, negative, or neutral toward members of the two major political parties.

Before moving to the next step in conducting a content analysis, several cautions related to technological advancements are worth acknowledging. First, Lacy, Watson, Riffe, and Lovejoy (2015) suggest that content analyses of internet material can be challenging not only because of the sheer amount of content on the Web, but also its ephemeral nature. All of us have likely had the experience of clicking on a URL only to find that the content is no longer available. Second, Lacy and colleagues (2015) caution about using key word searches in order to develop the universe of content. The choice of which key words are selected can influence which results are (and are not) identified. Researchers should identify which key words they used to gather the sample of messages in the report of their research.

Step 3: Identify the Type of Content

The second step in conducting a content analysis is to determine the characteristics of the content that are of interest. The content of messages can either be manifest or latent (Keyton, 2015). **Manifest content** is the observable words, phrases, or images that appear in the text. An example is a list of trending hashtags on social media sites; these compilations search for specific hashtag phrases and identify the number of times that hashtag has been used over a specific period of time. In essence, these lists are an informal version of a manifest content analysis. Relatedly, in Chapter 6 we introduced you to the notion of social media monitoring. This type of scanning of social media for mentions of an organization, product, or brand can serve as the foundation for a manifest content analysis as well. Note that even images can serve as data for a manifest content analysis. Hu,

Manikonda, and Kambhampati (2014) classified a random sample of users' Instagram images into one of eight categories: friends, food, gadgets, captioned photos, pets, activities, selfies, and fashion. The most frequent post type (not surprisingly) was a selfie, and the least frequent type was a picture of a pet.

Latent content, on the other hand, requires interpretation on the part of the researcher. Rather than a focus on an observable, physical entity such as a word or a photograph, latent content analysis focuses on the implicit meanings of message content. For example, Cho, Furey, and Mohr (2017) studied the organizational Facebook pages of *Fortune* magazine's "world's most admired companies" to understand their corporate social responsibility (CSR) messages. Their categories included environmental stewardship, philanthropic contributions, educational commitments, community/employee involvement, public health commitments, and sponsorship of cultural/sports activities. The researchers weren't looking at the posts for the number of times these specific words were used, but, rather, any post that suggested one of these categories. For example, a post suggesting that the organization had donated $1 million to a local nonprofit would be counted as a philanthropic contribution, whereas a post indicating that the organization had donated money to the local food bank in order to combat food insecurity would be counted as a public health commitment. Cho and colleagues (2017) found that the most admired organizations tended to post CSR content about community/employee involvement and philanthropic contributions most often, although CSR messages were not posted as frequently as other types of information.

One type of latent content of concern to professional communicators is called **sentiment analysis** (also called tonality analysis), which focuses on the valence (positive, negative, or neutral) of a message author's views on the topic of interest. In the example of biased news coverage, Budak and colleagues (2016) used sentiment analysis to classify the valence of political stories about Republican and Democratic politicians. In the marketing arena, Liu and colleagues (2017) focused on social media posts about several different brands and found that the posts about New Balance shoes were more positive than posts about Adidas, for example, and that posts about Burger King were more negative than posts about Wendy's. Notably, social media posts tended to be more negative than positive for all 16 brands Liu and colleagues (2017) studied.

In addition to sentiment analysis, there are a host of other types of latent content that might be of importance to professional communicators. Michaelson and Stacks (2017) suggest that public relations practitioners might also conduct prominence analysis, quality of coverage, and competitive analysis. Prominence analysis focuses on the nature of an article, including the reputation of the publication (e.g., the *New York Times* has a better reputation than the *Daily Mail*) as well as factors associated with the article such as the length of the article and where in the publication the article appears. Quality of coverage involves measures of sentiment, prominence, as well as the overall volume of articles generated. Competitive analysis refers to conducting a content analysis both for one's own organization as well as for a competitor. In this way, professional communicators can benchmark how well they are doing relative to competitors.

Step 4: Unitize

Fourth, the researchers need to determine which units of the message they will consider, which is called unitizing. Units are those elements within a message that are actually counted. There are four types of manifest units (Stacks, 2002). Among the types of manifest units are *symbols* or *words* (e.g., your organization's name or corporate logo); *individuals* or *roles* (e.g., a particular person's name, an occupation, or even a demographic category); *time/space* (e.g., length of story, amount of airtime, or size of photo); and *physical units*, which refer to the entirety of a text (e.g., an advertisement, a website, a news story, a social media post).

Latent content, on the other hand, always involves the creation of a theme as the unit. So, Cho and colleagues' (2017) study focused on the themes of philanthropic contributions, employee or community involvement, and so on. Sentiment analysis focuses on the themes of positive, negative, and neutral coverage. Given the fact that interpretations vary between individuals, when using a latent unit of analysis the researchers need to carefully identify the characteristics that would determine what "counts" as that theme. We will turn to this important issue when we discuss the fifth step. When unitizing latent content, the researchers must establish whether they will use a physical unit (i.e., each article or post or website will be placed into only one theme) or a thematic unit (i.e., there might be multiple themes or multiple incidences of a single theme in one physical unit).

Step 5: Develop the Coding Scheme

The fifth step in conducting a content analysis is to develop the **coding scheme**, which is the categories that will be used to classify the messages. In the case of manifest content, the unit is the same as the category. That is, if the unit is a word, the category is the word itself. Imagine a researcher is interested in determining the relative frequency with which universities in Philadelphia are covered in the *Philadelphia Inquirer*. In this case, the categories would be the names of all universities in the city (La Salle University, Temple University, University of Pennsylvania, etc.) and the researcher would literally comb through the newspaper, counting every time that a university was mentioned. Other manifest categories work in a similar fashion; instead of counting the number of times La Salle University is mentioned, you could count the number of articles that mention La Salle University. Since it is likely that the university would be mentioned more than one time in an article, this would give you two different counts. Which manifest category scheme to use should be determined by the specific goals of the study.

An interest in latent content makes the development of a category scheme more complex. The best practice would be to start by looking to see if any previous research has already developed categories that might be used in your research; there is no need to reinvent the wheel. Using an existing category scheme is a **deductive method**. For example, the content analysis conducted by Cho and colleagues

(2017) used an existing classification of types of CSR for their categories, and content analyses using sentiment analysis use the existing themes of positive, negative, and neutral coverage.

Sometimes, however, previous research will not provide you with the exact categories that you need to answer your research question. In this case, the researcher reviews the data and identifies themes that emerge while reviewing the data. Note that the researcher does not actually count the frequencies with which these themes emerge at this time; rather, he or she is simply carefully reviewing the data for all possible themes, which is called an **inductive method**. To illustrate, Clark, Michel, Early, and Baltes (2014) interviewed 50 working adults about their coping strategies for work and family stressors. First, the researchers individually reviewed the data, looking to uncover "strategy dimensions." After the individual efforts, the researchers met as a group to discuss the strategy dimensions each had derived, and then collaborated to finalize the 11 coping strategies they used as their final coding scheme.

Regardless of whether the category scheme is inductively or deductively derived, there are three rules for content analysis categories. First, the categories must be **equivalent**. For example, one category can't be the genre of a movie (e.g., romantic comedy) and another category be an evaluation of a movie (e.g., blockbuster). The categories must exist at the same level of abstraction. Second, the categories must be **mutually exclusive**. Each unit must be placed into one and only one category. If your categories are equivalent, there is less of a temptation to code things into more than one category, but the decision about which category to place each unit in can be challenging. We will describe a way to overcome this problem when describing the next step of content analysis. The final requirement in developing content categories is that the categories should be **exhaustive**. Categories must cover every possible occurrence of a relevant theme. One way to overcome this problem is to create a category called "other," into which unusual or outlying content can be placed. A general rule of thumb is that if more than 5% of the data are coded as "other," the category scheme needs to be revised or the coding process reexamined (Keyton, 2015).

Step 6: Create Coding Procedures and Decision Rules

As we explained in the development of categories, the sixth step in content analysis provides a mechanism for making sure that categorizing data is mutually exclusive. This step is the development of coding procedures, including decision rules. **Coding procedures** are an explicit set of policies about which types of content should be placed into which categories. This is accomplished by providing very clear descriptions for each theme, including definitions and examples. For example, if you are interested in conducting a sentiment analysis, you might use the following definitions from the Institute for Public Relations:

Positive: An item leaves the reader more likely to support, recommend, and/or work or do business with the brand.

Neutral: An item contains no tonality at all, just reports the facts. If the news is negative, an article can be neutral if it just reports the facts, without any editorial commentary. In an unfavorable environment, neutral may be the best that can be achieved. Coding should be based on whether the clip makes people more or less likely to do business with an organization.

Negative: An item leaves the reader less likely to support, and/or work or do business with the brand.

Balanced: An item with both negative and positive information in roughly equal proportion can present a balanced profile, which would be considered neutral overall. (Eisenmann, O'Neil, & Geddes, 2015, p. 11)

Decision rules refer to a set of rules for what should be done in the case of uncertainty. Consider again the themes in Cho and colleagues' (2017) categories of corporate social responsibility. Philanthropic contributions can refer to donations of money, products, or services to a wide range of possible recipients, including public health organizations, environmental organizations, educational organizations, and cultural or athletic organizations. However, because these specific organizational types have their own categories, the researchers likely created a decision rule that only contributions that did not specify one of these types of organizations should be placed into the philanthropic contribution category. Decision rules provide an objective measure of content that others could duplicate simply by following the rules.

When conducting a content analysis, researchers create a code book, which is a document that details the coding scheme (the list of categories), the coding procedures (definitions and examples of the categories), and a list of decision rules.

Step 7: Establish Intercoder Reliability

The creation of a code book is one way to ensure that the research can be replicated. However, quality content analysis research requires additional evidence for the reliability of the research. Recall from Chapter 3 that reliability refers to the consistency of the measurement. In the case of content analysis, researchers are expected to provide evidence of intercoder reliability, which is a measure of the consistency with which two different coders place content into the same categories. Not surprisingly, coding manifest content usually results in very little error in placing content into categories, but errors are still possible. To illustrate, count the number of times the words "code" or "coding" occurs in the key terms section of this chapter. Did you get 15? If not, you made a mistake. Coding latent content can be much more challenging, and so a measure of reliability is very important.

To develop a measure of intercoder reliability, two different people must code the same texts using the same coding procedures. Typically, one of the individuals is the researcher who has developed the code book. Ideally the second individual has not been involved with the creation of the code book; in this way you can determine how effective the code book is. That is, if the second coder can follow the code book and use the coding scheme in a way that is consistent with the primary researcher, then the code book is of sufficient quality to allow for replicability. The amount of texts to be coded to establish intercoder reliability depends in part on the size of the data set. A good rule of thumb is that at least 50 units should be coded, or 10% of the entire sample (Lombard et al., 2002).

The most basic indicator of intercoder reliability is simple agreement. The calculation for simple agreement for two coders is as follows:

$$\frac{2 \times A}{N_1 + N_2}$$

"A" refers to the number of agreements, so the numerator is two times the number of times the two coders agreed on the placement of content. "N" refers to the number of units coded; N_1 references the number of units coded by the first coder, and N_2 references the number of units coded by the second coder. The number of units coded by the two individual coders might not be the same; if the unit is a theme, one coder might see five instances of a theme on a website, and the other coder might see fewer themes on the website. However, if you are coding physical units it is likely that both coders will code the same number of units.

To demonstrate the calculation of reliability, imagine you are using Cho and colleagues' (2017) CSR categories to code 100 social media posts. You agree on 82 of the 100 posts. Your reliability would be

$$\frac{2 \times 82}{100 + 100} = .82$$

Remember from Chapter 3 that measures of reliability typically range from 0 (meaning the measurement is completely unreliable) to 1.0 (meaning the measurement is perfectly reliable). Acceptable reliability is usually between .80 and 1.0 (Lombard et al., 2002). Your reliability of .82 indicates a solid measure of consistency in your coding. If you do not establish an acceptable level of reliability, you may need to refine your coding procedures and/or create additional decision rules in order to increase the likelihood of achieving adequate intercoder reliability. After making these adjustments, you go through the process again to see if your intercoder reliability has improved.

Although simple agreement provides a good indicator of consistency, most published research uses more complicated statistics to indicate intercoder reliability. Scott's *pi* and Cohen's *kappa* are statistics that take into consideration the possibility that agreement might occur because of chance and not because the two coders have successfully agreed on the placement of the message. More information about how to calculate these statistics can be found in Stacks (2002). Most statistical software packages will allow you to calculate these types of reliability.

Step 8: Code the Data

The final step is straightforward; once an acceptable level of reliability is achieved you place each unit into one of your categories, keeping a count of how frequently each category occurs. Ideally, one or more people code all of the data. However, in large data sets the task might be divided and individual coders given a distinct part of the data to code once intercoder reliability has been achieved.

Although we will talk more about data analysis in Chapter 11, it is important to highlight an essential feature of virtually all content analyses. For ease of understanding, the appropriate way to summarize the results of a content analysis is through a frequency table, which is a chart that identifies each category and the frequency with which content was assigned to that category. In its ideal form, the content categories are listed in order of descending value, although that is not strictly necessary, especially if the categories themselves have a logical order. Table 7.1 depicts an example of a frequency table.

TABLE 7.1   Example of a Frequency Table for Sentiment Analysis

Category	Frequency (Percentage)
Positive tone	66 (35.3%)
Neutral tone	21 (11.2%)
Negative tone	84 (44.9%)
Balanced tone	16 (8.6%)
Total	187 (100%)

Human Versus Computer-Assisted Coding

Thus far we have discussed the process of conducting a content analysis as if all the work is being done by people. However, many organizations rely on computer coding of data. There are three advantages of using computer-assisted coding rather than human coders (Lacy et al., 2015; Pew Research Center, 2018). First, computer-assisted coding can handle much larger data sets than human coders. Second, computer-assisted coding reduces the time and cost of conducing a content analysis. Finally, computer-assisted coding is very reliable; as long as the software itself has no glitches, the coding will be 100% reliable. Nevertheless, there are major disadvantages as well. First, the content must be digital. If it is not digital content, then the researchers need to digitize it. Second, the content must already be available before the content analysis begins. The messages to be content analyzed might have already been gathered through another research process, such as when focus group participants are asked to comment on a product and those comments are then to be content analyzed. Alternatively, the content to be analyzed may be publicly available. That means that copyrighted material like some television and radio broadcasts can be difficult to acquire. Finally, computers can only do what they have been programmed to do and programing a rich understanding of language is incredibly difficult. For this reason, computer coding is best suited for coding manifest content.

Despite this limitation, an increasing number of software packages have been developed for analyzing **unstructured content** (i.e., the content available on social media, websites, or organizational reports, for example, as compared to content in a structured database). These software packages vary from software based on manual coding of dictionaries (e.g., creating a list of words and synonyms to "count") on the one hand to data-driven open-vocabulary methods of analysis that involve machine learning on the other hand (Schwartz & Ungar, 2015).

At its most basic, **text mining** is a rule-based software system that uses a dictionary of terms or topics created by the researcher. In its classic form, if the researcher is interested in positive emotions he or she would generate a list of all possible emotions (e.g., happy, joyful, cheerful, pleased, and so on; Schwartz & Ungar, 2015) and the software program would scan the texts for evidence of these terms. More recent software packages require the researcher to feed the computer pre-coded data, and the computer creates an algorithm based on those data. Uncoded data can then be scanned, and the software classifies that data based on the algorithms it derived from the already-coded examples. These examples are considered supervised learning, since the researcher is ultimately the person who has generated the content categories, either directly or indirectly.

On the other end of the spectrum of computer-assisted coding is machine learning (Scharkow, 2011). In this scenario, the computer software analyzes groupings of words in order to uncover meaning. Specifically, advanced software packages can sift large quantities of text-based data and classify content based on categories developed by the software itself. This is called unsupervised learning. There are challenges to these types of programs, however. For example, imagine that someone has posted about a Happy Meal at McDonalds. The software program cannot differentiate between the emotion of happiness and the proper name for a child's meal at the chain restaurant.

There are a wide variety of open source and proprietary software systems that can engage in computer-assisted coding of data. Proprietary software includes Nvivo, Microsoft Text Analytics, and DiscoverText. Open source programs include KNIME, RapidMiner, and Open Calais.

The Strategic Use of Content Analysis: Content Audits

A content audit is a method for professional communicators to identify and evaluate the nature of an organization's owned media, which means content produced and controlled by an organization. Although it is most often associated with Web content, a content audit can also include blog posts, social media content, white papers, brochures, or any other documents produced by the organization. There are typically two steps for conducting a content audit: creating a content inventory and conducting a content assessment. A content inventory involves creating a complete and thorough description of all content being reviewed. This typically means creating a spreadsheet that lists each unique piece of content. For websites, it might mean focusing on each page or URL as a separate piece of content (Lieb, 2015). For each piece of content, you should create a thorough description of the content, including the following:

◆ Title of the content

◆ Type of content (text, image, video, press release, etc.)

◆ Authors (in house employee, agency, etc.)

◆ Original publishing date and any update dates

◆ Intended audience

◆ Metrics (such as page views, shares, conversions; see Chapter 6)

TABLE 7.2 Common Evaluations Made During Content Assessment

Usefulness and relevance	Does the content meet organizational needs?
	Does it meet stakeholder needs?
	Is the information still relevant?
Clarity and accuracy	Is the content correct?
	Is the content organized logically and coherently?
	Do images/video meet technical standards?
Influence and engagement	Do the metrics support the usefulness of the content?
	Are the persuasive techniques appropriate?
	Are the persuasive techniques effective?
Completeness	Does the content include all information stakeholders might need?
	Does the content provide too much or too little information?
Voice and style	Does the content use a consistent voice?
	Is the tone of the content appropriate for the context?
	Does the content look, read, and sound professional?
Usability and findability	Is the content easy to find?
	Is the content easy to read/view?
	Is the content in a usable format?

Adapted from Jones (2009b).

Once you have completed your inventory, you then conduct a content assessment, which is an evaluation of the content. Is it accurate and up to date? Does it support strategic objectives? Table 7.2 provides an overview of some of the most common evaluations made during a content assessment. Jones (2009a) suggests that not only should you evaluate existing content, you should also identify any gaps or opportunities that the existing content does not address. These evaluations might be done qualitatively, by making expert judgments, or quantitatively, by assigning numeric evaluations to each category that is being evaluated (such as 1 = very weak and 5 = outstanding).

Advantages and Limitations of Content Analysis

There are a number of benefits of content analysis. The primary benefits are that it is unobtrusive, which means that it does not involve direct contact with people, and that it is nonreactive, which means that responses (in this case texts) don't change because they are the focus of a research study. In Chapter 6 we talked about the Hawthorne effect, which is when people alter their behavior because they are aware that they are being observed. Content analysis is free from this threat to validity.

Content analysis is also a very transparent research method. Recall from Chapter 1 that the Barcelona Principles 2.0 (Rockland, 2015) call for transparent, consistent, and valid research. Because of the precision necessary in developing a coding book, content analysis allows those who are reading the research to fully understand exactly what was done and allows for replicability.

Third, content analysis allows for an investigation of messages over time, which is termed longitudinal research. By definition, a text is a written or recorded message. As such, researchers can retrieve older messages to compare the nature of the content over time. For example, remember Hu and colleagues' (2014) study of the most common Instagram posts? In 2014 they found that 24.2% of all Instagram photos were selfies. Those interested in shifts in the way the social media platform is used can easily replicate their study later to see if selfie posts have increased over time.

However, there are also some significant limitations of content analysis. Michaelson and Stacks (2017) argue that there are two general problems with communication professionals' use of content analysis, both of which are associated with strategy. The first problem is that in focusing on objective classification of messages, the accuracy of the message is not considered. Specifically, the extent to which basic facts, misstatements, and omissions occur in messages are typically not considered when conducting a content analysis. However, a thorough understanding of these issues may be important information in order to ascertain the nature or scope of a problem and might impact any strategies that are developed to resolve the problem.

Second, communication professionals often fail to connect the messages that are being analyzed to communication goals (Michaelson & Stacks, 2017). Yes, it is important to know the sentiments in social media posts or the prominence of news coverage. However, these data should be used to ascertain the extent to which specific goals are being achieved. Remember that in the creation of SMART goals, one of the essential elements is *measurable*. The results of content analyses can provide these measurements.

The results of a content analysis can only be as good as the code book with which a researcher works. If the coding scheme is incomplete or flawed, or if there are insufficient or unclear coding rules, the content analysis will fail the criterion of replicability. Similarly, if the sample of texts being analyzed is too small or is skewed in some way, the results will not be valid.

Third, if the content analysis is of latent content, natural variations in interpretation might affect the reliability and/or the validity of the study. Although the use of computer-assisted coding can increase the reliability, it does not necessarily increase the likelihood of validity. Computer-assisted coding can be no more accurate than the program that is being used, and programming for an understanding of natural language use and emotion is very challenging.

Finally, content analysis can only answer the *what* question: what is being said, what texts are saying it, and what the frequency with which it is being said is. The strength of being unobtrusive and nonreactive means that we cannot ascertain *why* the messages are being crafted in a particular way and *how* people are responding to them. To answer the why question, researchers would have to use survey methods (questionnaires, interviews, or focus groups).

Chapter Summary

This chapter introduced the method of content analysis, which is a technique for uncovering the content, nature, or structure of messages. Eight steps for conducting a content analysis were described. They include developing your research question, selecting the appropriate texts; determining whether the interest is in manifest or latent content; identifying the unit of analysis; developing categories, coding procedures, and decision rules in the creation of a code book; establishing acceptable intercoder reliability and then coding the data into the categories. We also talked about the rising use of computer-assisted coding and compared it to human coding. Next, we discussed the use of content audits, which is a strategic use of content analysis that professional communicators use to classify and evaluate owned media. A content audit includes two parts: a content inventory and a content assessment. Finally, we talked about the advantages and limitations of content analysis as a research method.

PRACTICE ACTIVITIES

1. **Media bias:** As indicated at the beginning of the chapter, despite evidence that mainstream media sources evidence very little bias, many members of the public perceive political bias. Go to the original article published by Budak and colleagues (2016) and critically evaluate the methods and results that they used.

2. **Inductive coding scheme:** Create an inductive coding scheme for latent content. Go to an online review site (e.g., Yelp, Open Table, Angie's

List, Amazon, Trip Advisor, etc.). Select a product or organization, and review the evaluations. Based on those reviews, attempt to create an equivalent, mutually exclusive, and exhaustive coding scheme that is not based on manifest content. Share your coding scheme with another student. Were they able to use it? If they struggled, what were the problems with your coding scheme?

3. **Sentiment analysis**: You and a partner should conduct your own sentiment analysis of an organization using the sentiment analysis categories described in this chapter. Make sure you identify the texts you have used, your coding procedures, and decision rules and provide evidence of intercoder reliability. How well did you do?

4. **Strategic analysis**: Review the data presented in the frequency table in Table 7.1. How would you interpret the sentiment about the organization?

5. **Content audit**: Evaluate the website for your school or workplace. First, conduct a content inventory of each page. Then, for one of the pages, evaluate the page using the categories for a content assessment.

Surveys and Communication Audits

Think about this past week. Were you asked to rate your Uber driver in the app after your ride? Were you asked to go to a website printed on the bottom of your receipt from the grocery store to rate your customer experience? Were you handed a list of questions about your car buying history while waiting for an oil change to be completed? Did you receive an online survey from human resources at your company asking about your work satisfaction? If you had some, or even all, of these experiences in the past week then you know that polls and surveys are very popular tools for research about people's attitudes and opinions. To use polls and surveys effectively, communication professionals should understand how to create polls and surveys that will produce valuable data for strategic decisions. In this chapter, we explain the differences between polls and surveys, discuss types of surveys, and offer advice for effective questions and design. We then discuss the strategic use of surveys when conducting a communication audit.

First, we need to deal with terminology. You may recall from Chapter 2 that a

CHAPTER OUTLINE

◆ Step 1: Identify Your Survey Goals

◆ Step 2: Identify Your Sample

◆ Step 3: Determine the Type of Survey You Will Conduct

◆ Step 4: Determine the Survey Administration Method

◆ Step 5: Follow Best Practices for Writing Questions

◆ Step 6: Make Your Survey Attractive and User Friendly

◆ Step 7: Distribute Your Survey

◆ Step 8: Analyze Your Data

◆ The Strategic Use of Surveys: Communication Audits

◆ Advantages and Limitations of Surveys

survey is a research tool that gathers information about people's attitudes, beliefs, and experiences. Polls and questionnaires are both types of surveys. **Polls** are brief surveys used to assess a small amount of information for immediate use with little to no analysis. Polls are best used to learn more about an isolated opinion, belief, or behavior without wanting to know more about the causes of those attitudes and behaviors or how those attitudes influence behavior (Michaelson & Stacks, 2017). For example, many television stations conduct polls by asking a question and directing viewers to text 1 for yes and 2 for no. **Questionnaires** present a respondent with a list of pre-set questions (usually about their opinions, behavior, or experiences) to answer. They vary in size and length and are typically used to assess multiple pieces of information that require more in-depth analysis. Questionnaires are best used to research not just people's attitudes, beliefs, and behaviors but also *why* they may think or behave as they do and how those attitudes and behaviors may relate to other attitudes and behaviors (Michaelson & Stacks, 2017). If you wanted to learn more about your customers' opinions about the trustworthiness of various social media platforms, then you would develop a survey to find out. Despite the differences between polls and questionnaires, we will use the term *survey* throughout the chapter to indicate that we are talking about all methods that ask respondents to report on how they think or feel. There are eight steps for conducting a survey, which are detailed in Box 8.1.

BOX 8.1

The Steps for Conducting a Survey

Step 1   Identify your survey goals

Step 2   Identify your sample

Step 3   Determine the type of survey you will conduct

Step 4   Decide on the survey administration method

Step 5   Follow best practices for writing questions

Step 6   Make your survey attractive and user-friendly

Step 7   Distribute your survey

Step 8   Analyze your data

Step 1: Identify Your Survey Goals

Surveys are one of the most commonly used methods for researching communication, and that is because they are an ideal tool for a wide variety of research questions. Surveys allow you to investigate the nature of communication, they allow you to compare individuals' or groups' communication practices, and they allow you to relate communication to other variables such as attitudes, beliefs, or other experiences. In Chapter 2, we discussed the process of identifying your research objectives and creating specific research questions and hypotheses to guide your research. This process should be employed before you begin your survey project so that you know exactly what you want to find out by conducting your survey.

As you consider the specific goals of your survey project, keep a word of warning in mind. Despite the ubiquity of using surveys to study communication issues, conducting a survey is usually not the best way to study actual behavior. When seeking to study actual behavior, an observation is the ideal method because it provides an objective measure of what was actually said or done. By their very nature, surveys can only gather information about people's perceptions of their own and others' behaviors. In other words, survey respondents can tell you how they think they behave, which is not the same as how they actually behave. Metts, Sprecher, and Cupach (1991) caution researchers that when using surveys about communication behavior people are more likely to remember the "gist" of the communication rather than actual details, they are more likely to report on verbal rather than nonverbal messages, they are more likely to report on their own messages as compared to the messages of conversational partners, and they are more likely to report the presence or absence of behavior rather than the actual frequency of behavior. For those reasons, using survey data to draw conclusions about actual rather than perceived communication is problematic.

Step 2: Identify Your Sample

Once you have determined what you will be studying you next have to determine who you will study. Chapter 4 provides a detailed description of the nature and types of samples. As you might recall, a *population* refers to all people who have a desired characteristic. In developing your survey, you need to consider the population you are seeking to complete your survey. Who are they? How might you find them? Will you conduct a census or use a sample? If using a sample, will you be using a probability (random) sample or a nonprobability (nonrandom) sample? Something we did not talk a lot about in the sampling chapter are **incentives**, which are a form of "payment" to motivate people to complete a survey or take part in research. Incentives can take the form of cash, gift cards, coupons, or merchandise, but they can also take nonmonetary forms. Many college instructors offer extra credit for student completion of surveys, for example. Research suggests that prepaid incentives increase survey completion more than promised incentives (i.e., you can receive an incentive upon completion of the survey), that small incentives given to every survey respondent work better than the chance to win a larger incentive in a drawing or sweepstakes, and that money is a stronger incentive than other forms of payment (Mercer et al., 2015).

Step 3: Determine the Type of Survey You Will Conduct

Are you interested in studying people's thoughts, feelings, or perceptions at a single point in time, or are you interested in how these things might change over time? Knowing the answer to that question will influence the type of survey you conduct. Survey designs can take the form of either a cross-sectional survey or a longitudinal survey. A **cross-sectional survey** is collected one time with the goal of describing the data captured as the entire basis for the study. Imagine that you took a family photo. From that family photo, you could likely describe a great deal about the family: demographic information (racial background, age, sex, etc.), what they are wearing, where they are, how they seem to relate to one another. In many ways, a cross-sectional survey is like that one family photo; it allows you to learn a great deal about people's opinions, experiences, and beliefs at that one point in time.

Now imagine that instead of just one family photo, the family had a photo taken at the same spot each year, such as at an annual family reunion picnic, over a period of several years. From these annual family photos, you could learn all of the information you did from one single family photo, but you could also learn about changes over time: You could make observations about how people age, how the way the family members relate to one another seems to change, how fashion choices have changed, and about additions to—and losses of—family members depicted in the photos. **Longitudinal surveys** are like that collection of annual family photos. Longitudinal surveys are surveys that are administered at more than one point in time with the goal of comparing the data over that time period.

You may learn different things about the same topic depending on whether you choose a cross-sectional or longitudinal survey design for your project. For example, Shklovski, Kraut, and Rainie (2004) wanted to know more about the relationships among channels used to communicate with family members (by phone, visiting in person, and online) over time. They compared results from cross-sectional and longitudinal surveys on the topic. Cross-sectional survey results suggested that communicating with a family member online enhanced the likelihood that you would also phone and visit with that family member (Shklovski et al., 2004). However, longitudinal survey results painted a different picture: The more a person communicated with family members online the likelihood of visiting that family member decreased over time and the more a person phoned a family member the likelihood of vising that family member increased over time (Shklovski et al., 2004). Thus, it is important to remember that what you learn from a cross-sectional survey may not reflect the whole story you would learn from repeated data collection and comparisons.

There are three types of longitudinal surveys. **Trend longitudinal survey** designs gather a sample that meets the inclusion criteria for the survey from the population each time the survey is being administered. For a trend longitudinal survey project, the inclusion criteria will remain the same each time data is collected, but people who were eligible to take the study at one time the survey was administered may or may not be eligible the next time it is administered. With a trend longitudinal survey design, it is possible but not necessary for the exact same participant to take the survey more than once over the course of the project. For an example of a trend longitudinal survey design, imagine that the National Communication Association (NCA) wanted to track the skills and knowledge of communication majors. NCA may create a survey to measure these student outcomes and administer it to a sample of 10,000 students in May of each year. This is a trend longitudinal survey because the inclusion criteria (must be a communication major) remains the same each time the data is collected, but it is possible that people who change majors may or may not be eligible each time the survey is administered. Further, it is possible that any given student may or may not be selected for the sample multiple times.

A **cohort longitudinal survey** design involves administering the survey multiple times to an unchanging group of potential participants. In other words, if a person is eligible for a cohort longitudinal survey once then they will always be eligible, and vice versa. However, like with a trend longitudinal study, this doesn't mean that the same person will complete the survey multiple times. To continue with the NCA and communication major student outcomes example, imagine that NCA recommended a new curriculum for communication majors and wanted to track the success of that new curriculum over time. If the new curriculum was introduced in 2015, then it would make sense to only include communication majors who began their major after 2015 in the sample. "Communication major starting in 2015 or later" is an including criteria that means any student that was a major before 2015 will never be eligible for the study and any student who was a communication major after 2015 will always be eligible for the study, whether or not they actually participate multiple times.

Lastly, a **panel longitudinal survey** design administers a survey to the exact same group of participants at multiple points in time. In other words, the sample that is gathered for the first time the survey is performed will be the only group of people that are eligible for the survey again. If NCA were to gather a sample of 10,000 first-year communication majors for the student outcomes survey and then return to only that group of 10,000 for the next 3 years to complete the survey again, then NCA would have performed a panel longitudinal survey.

While it may seem that because you can learn more over time from a longitudinal survey design that this type of project is the best way to go, that may not always be the case. Rather, it is important to consider the goals of your project in relation to the benefits and limitations of each type of survey design. If you can address the goals of your research project with information about what people have experienced or how they think or feel without wanting to make comparisons about changes in those experiences, thoughts, and feelings over time, then a cross-sectional survey is a good choice. If you desire to compare trends in your data over time within the same research project, then a longitudinal survey design is appropriate.

Step 4: Determine the Survey Administration Method

After deciding which type of survey design is best for your research project, it is important to consider the type of survey administration that will best fit the goals of your research. Contemporary professional communication research tends to use one of three methods of survey administration: face to face, by mail, and online. Face-to-face surveys can either be administered by the researcher, or they might be self-administered, which means that the respondent completes the survey without assistance of the researcher.

Two particular issues associated with survey administration should be noted. First, the administration method you choose impacts the likely response rate. The response rate is the ratio of those who complete the survey versus those who were asked to complete the survey. The higher the response rate, the more likely the results will be representative of the population. Second, researchers must be aware of the social desirability bias; research also has shown that when taking face-to-face surveys, participants are more likely to skew their answers toward responses they perceive as socially desirable (what people "should" answer) than they would when taking an

TABLE 8.1   Advantages and Disadvantages of Different Survey Administration Techniques

Face to face	**Advantages** ◆ High response rate ◆ High-quality responses **Disadvantages** ◆ Social desirability bias ◆ Inconvenience for participants ◆ High costs (researcher time, printing costs, data entry costs)
Mail	**Advantages** ◆ Participants can complete when they want to ◆ Highest response rate **Disadvantages** ◆ Lengthy process to distribute and receive completed surveys ◆ Money needed for incentives, printing, postage, and data entry
Online	**Advantages** ◆ Inexpensive ◆ Quick to create, distribute, and collect responses **Disadvantages** ◆ Low response rates ◆ Poor quality responses

online survey (Duffy et al., 2005). Table 8.1 provides an overview of the advantages and disadvantages of each method of administration.

Step 5: Follow Best Practices for Writing Questions

Effective surveys require careful question writing. When creating a survey, it is important to remember that your participants are far less interested and motivated about the research project than you are.

Thus, a survey should be constructed with ease of participant use in mind. If a participant finds a survey to be difficult to understand, taxing to answer, confusing, insulting, or too long, they will simply stop taking it or (worse!) provide any answer to a question just to get it done.

In general, there are two types of questions that you might use on a survey. Open-ended questions are those that ask a question and allow the respondent to answer in their own words. Closed-ended questions are those that include both the question and the possible responses from a pre-set list for the respondent to use to represent their answer. A good default for effective surveys is to try to avoid open-ended questions because they take longer for a respondent to answer and the data generated by open-ended questions will require additional analysis steps for you. Open-ended questions should be used only to collect qualitative data in which the participants' own words are of interest (such as when you want to use exact quotes from respondents or learn more about their language choices) or when the focus of the investigation is so new that developing effective closed-ended questions is problematic.

When writing closed-ended questions, there are a number of different formats—or scales—that you might use. A scale is a measurement tool that allows researchers to assign numbers to the variables they are measuring in the survey question. Table 8.2 provides an overview of the five most common scales used in professional communication research: Likert scales, frequency scales, forced ranking scales, fixed sum scales, and semantic differential scales.

There are a few rules of thumb for each of these scale types. First, when using a Likert scale, there should always be an uneven number of response options, as you want to be able to capture a neutral attitude. Typically, Likert scales use five or seven response options. Second, you want to start with disagreement and move to agreement in the response options. This is because the responses are translated to numbers in data analysis, and you want higher numbers to reflect a more positive attitude. Finally, make sure that every response is written out. Respondents might not know what "5" means, but they do know what "strongly agree" means. You can add the numbers later when you are analyzing the data.

TABLE 8.2   Types of Scales

Likert scales

The question is actually phrased as a statement, and respondents indicate their agreement with the statement. Ideal method for measuring attitudes. Provides an interval measurement.

Example: I am satisfied with the customer service I received.

Strongly disagree   Disagree   Neither agree nor disagree   Agree   Strongly

Frequency scales

Used to provide a relative measurement of how often something occurs. Provides an interval measurement.

Example: I ask my professor for assistance when I am unsure of how to complete an assignment.

Never   Rarely   Sometimes   Fairly often   Almost always

Forced ranking

Used to measure preferences. Provides an ordinal measurement.

Example: Please rank the following menu items from 1 = your favorite and 5 = your least favorite.

_____ *Apple pie*

_____ *Chocolate cake*

_____ *Ice cream sundae*

_____ *Cheesecake*

_____ *Strawberry shortcake*

Fixed sum

Gives respondents a number of points that can be distributed as they wish. Allows respondents to provide more nuance to preferences. Produces a ratio measurement.

Example: You have 100 points to distribute among the following items. Indicate your relative preference by giving more points to your most preferred item and giving the least points (or no points at all) to your least preferred item.

_____ *Apple pie*

_____ *Chocolate cake*

_____ *Ice cream sundae*

_____ *Cheesecake*

_____ *Strawberry shortcake*

100 TOTAL POINTS

(continued)

TABLE 8.2 Types of Scales *(continued)*

Semantic differential

Ideal method to measure subjective meanings for things. Two opposite adjectives are presented, and respondents indicate which of the adjectives represents their interpretation best. It is an interval measurement.

Example: Please indicate how you feel about the Springport brand.

Modern	____ ____ ____ ____ ____	*Old fashioned*
Unreliable	____ ____ ____ ____ ____	*Reliable*
Friendly	____ ____ ____ ____ ____	*Unfriendly*
Unsuccessful	____ ____ ____ ____ ____	*Successful*

Turning to frequency, the ideal way of measuring frequency is by measuring **absolute frequency**. What we mean by this is that you ask people to specify an exact number. For example, you might ask people how many hours they spent on Netflix in the past week, or how many days a week they usually work from home. The reason this is the ideal way to measure frequency goes back to the levels of measurement we introduced in Chapter 3: You should always use the highest level of measurement you can, and absolute frequency is considered a ratio measurement. However, there are occasions in which people would not be able to recall the absolute frequency of something. In those cases, a measure of **relative frequency** is appropriate. By the way, be careful of "always" and "never" unless they are actual options. You are better off listing "almost always" or "almost never."

Next, many researchers are interested in asking people to indicate preferences. However, there are several cautions associated with forced ranking scales. First, the list from which people should be asked to rank should be relatively small, typically five or fewer items. Quite simply, respondents find ranking more than five items to be difficult. Second, forced ranking results in ordinal data, which makes data analysis quite complicated. Unless you have statistics expertise, you might consider getting the same data in a different fashion. For example, fixed sum scales provide similar sorts of data, and because they provide ratio data they are easier to analyze. The problem with fixed sum scales, however, is that they are demanding on participants and are dependent of respondents' basic math ability.

Finally, a semantic differential scale is ideal for uncovering individuals' meanings for the object or person being evaluated. The challenge with a semantic differential scale is the selection of the adjective pairs, not only which adjective pairs to use, but how many to use. Osgood (1952), who originated the scale, originally provided a set of possible adjective pairs that could be used. However, researchers often craft their own adjective pairs to better match the goals of their studies. It is important that the adjective pairs used in semantic differential scales represent the opposing aspects of the concept. For example, if you were creating a semantic differential scale about how someone felt after an interaction, you would want to use pairs like "nervous-calm" and "happy-sad" because each word in the pair represents opposite feelings. You would want to avoid using pairs such as "happy-confused" or "happy-angry" because those pairs are not opposing ends of the same emotional experience.

Beyond the selection of which scale formats to use, writing effective survey questions can also be challenging. Whenever possible, we encourage researchers to use established measurements; there is no reason to reinvent the wheel! You can find existing questions and information about their use, reliability and validity through a literature search or in sourcebooks, such as the *Communication Research Measures* sourcebook series published by Routledge. However, if it is necessary to create your own survey questions, there are a number of do's and don'ts that will help you to develop quality survey questions. Tables 8.3 and 8.4 provide a summary of these best practices.

Step 6: Make Your Survey Attractive and User Friendly

The effectiveness of your survey is also dependent on how appealing your potential participants find your survey. The more attractive your survey looks, the more likely it is that your participants will complete it. Survey attractiveness depends on the survey appearing uncluttered,

TABLE 8.3   Best Practices for Survey Questions: Do's

Survey Do's	
Ask about only limited or recent events	People have very little recall over a long period of time, and they tend to just guess rather than provide specific information. *Wrong: How many hours do you spend streaming video?* *Better: How many hours did you spend streaming video in the last week?*
Make choices exhaustive	All possible responses should be included, providing respondents with the option of "other" in case the response options don't match the respondent's experience. *Example: Which internet browser are you using?* _____ *Chrome* _____ *Explorer* _____ *Firefox* _____ *Safari* _____ *Other (please specify)_____*
Make choices mutually exclusive	The respondent should be able to select only one answer. *Wrong: How many cups of tea do you drink in a day?* *1–3* *3–6* *6 or more* *Better: How many cups of tea do you drink in a day?* *0* *1–3* *4–6* *more than 6*
Match stems and scales	Make sure that the possible responses to a question (the scale) make sense given the phrasing of a question (the stem). *Wrong: When you watch a series on Netflix, how often do you binge watch the entire series?* *Strongly agree Agree Neutral Disagree Strongly disagree* *Better: When you watch a series on Netflix, how often do you binge watch the entire series?* *Never Occasionally Often Very often Always*
Include more than one question per concept	Important concepts should be addressed by more than one question to have a "back-up" question for each concept and to improve the quality of data for statistical comparison. *Example: I feel confident in my ability to give an effective presentation.* *Strongly agree Agree Neutral Disagree Strongly disagree* *I believe I can present successfully.* *Strongly agree Agree Neutral Disagree Strongly disagree*

TABLE 8.4 Best Practices for Survey Questions: Don'ts

Survey Don'ts	
Double-barreled questions	Questions that ask two things in the same question. *Example: How would you rate the quality of our product and our customer service?* Why this is a problem: What if you loved the product but hated the service?
Extremes/Absolutes	Ideally your response categories include extremes (strongly agree) or absolutes (always, never). Do not include them in the question as well. *Example: I found the training session very informative.* Why this is a problem: What if you found the session only moderately informative? Do you agree with the statement or disagree with the statement?
Incomplete questions	Make sure comparative questions include the full comparison. *Example: I believe more money should be spent on higher education.* Why this is a problem: More than what? More than is currently spent? More than is spent on prisons?
Leading and loaded questions	Make sure your question doesn't lead people to a particular point of view or presume that there is only one "correct" answer. *Example: Do you think the unnecessary soda tax is working?* Why this is a problem: The word "unnecessary" leads people to a particular way of thinking about the tax.
Vague questions	Try to be as precise as possible. *Example: Where do you like to shop?* Why this is a problem: Shop for what? Groceries? Clothing? Be as specific as possible.
Yes/No questions	Yes/No questions provide very limited information. *Example: Was this service easy to use? Yes/No* Why this is a problem: Unless there are follow-up questions, what if it was sort of easy but you had a few issues?

using an easily readable font, using page breaks to create question groupings that are not too large or too small, and making sure your survey (if online) looks good on computer and mobile modalities. Templates provided by online survey tools can be especially helpful in creating attractive, inviting, and user-friendly surveys.

One major consideration when putting your survey together is including information about informed consent. Remember from Chapter 5 that one of the ethical guidelines for research is that research participants have a free choice about whether they take part in the research or not. In the ethics chapter we also talked about informed consent when using an anonymous survey; researchers may be given permission to include all elements of the informed consent information at the beginning of the survey but not be required to have the participant sign a consent form if there are minimal risks to participants. If your study has been granted this permission, the informed consent information should be the first thing that appears on the survey, with instructions for how the participant might opt out of the study.

In addition, you should limit the number of questions asked on your survey. It's tempting to ask anything and everything that occurs to you but remember that shorter is better. Only the most motivated respondent will spend longer than 10 minutes completing a survey. Each question should have clear purpose associated with answering your research question(s). The more questions you have, the less likely it is that a respondent will complete the entire survey.

Finally, it's helpful to think of your survey as a conversation between you and the respondent. In a conversation, it is common to start with small talk before moving on to more serious topics. In a survey, it is helpful to present simple and easy-to-answer questions first and build into more complex questions as the survey progresses. In a conversation, you generally move from less personal to more personal topics as you continue to talk. The same should be true of a well-constructed survey. It is advisable to start with less personal questions and move to more personal questions as the survey progresses. The flow of an effective survey should build the respondents' comfort with answering questions as the survey progresses.

Step 7: Distribute Your Survey

You are almost ready to actually distribute your survey. There is one final step you should undertake before doing so, however. The best way to know if your survey questions are effective is to pretest them. Ideally, pretests would be performed with members of the target population taking the survey and providing feedback about the questions. Catching and eliminating any mistakes or difficulties with questions before you begin your data collection is the best way to ensure that your survey or poll will generate useful data. Once you are certain that respondents understand what you are asking of them, you are ready to reach out to your respondents, put the survey in the mail, or post the URL link.

Step 8: Analyze Your Data

Much like you need to develop a code book when conducting a content analysis, before analyzing your survey data you should annotate your survey. Using a blank copy of the survey, you should indicate what variable each question is measuring and the level of measurement being used. This will assist you when you are analyzing the data. Also, before you actually analyze your data, you should assess any scales that you have used for reliability. Recall from Chapter 3 that *reliability* means that the scale is consistently measuring a variable. Most often the reliability of a survey is determined by *Cronbach's alpha*, a measure of internal reliability. Finally, open-ended survey questions will be analyzed using qualitative methods, and closed-ended survey questions are analyzed using quantitative methods. More details about these types of analyses are in Chapter 11.

The Strategic Use of Surveys: Communication Audits

One of the most common ways that professional communicators use surveys is through conducting a communication audit. A **communication audit** is an examination of an organization's "entire communication environment" including communication between organizational members (internal communication); communication between the organization and stakeholders such as customers, the government, and the public (external communication); and the cultural, legal, and economic conditions in which the organization operates (Hart et al., 2015, p. 290). The goals of a communication audit are to provide an organization with an assessment of its strengths and weaknesses, as well as detailed information about how it is communicating well and how communication could be improved (Hart et al., 2015).

Although many communication audits will require the development of specific surveys to fit the specific audit needs of an organization, there are also some reliable and widely used communication audit surveys available. Perhaps the most well-known instrument for communication audits is the ICA Communication Audit, which includes a survey instrument that focuses on organizational internal communication (Downs, 1988; Goldhaber, 2002). Research has shown that organizations that made changes based on recommendations derived from use of the ICA Communication Audit had improvements in communication effectiveness as well as employee satisfaction and morale (Hargie et al., 2002).

Another communication audit survey is the Communication Satisfaction Questionnaire (CSQ) (Downs & Hazen, 1977). The CSQ is wider in scope than the survey included in the ICA Communication Audit and assesses eight dimensions: communication climate, supervisory communication, organizational integration, media quality, horizontal/informal/coworker communication, corporate information, and personal feedback and subordinate communication (Downs & Hazen, 1977).

Finally, the Organizational Communication Scale (Roberts & O'Reilly, 1974) addresses additional internal communication factors including information gatekeeping and information overload.

How, then, should you choose an existing communication audit survey? Clampitt (2009) suggests carefully weighing the audit survey characteristics (dimensions measured, how long it takes to complete, does it include open-ended or close-ended questions) against the goals and limitations of your specific communication audit needs. It is also helpful to examine reports from completed communication audits of organizations similar to yours (many of these can be found online) to compare what they were able to learn from the instruments they used to what your own goals are. Whether you use an existing survey instrument or create your own, surveys are in integral part of any communication audit.

Advantages and Limitations of Surveys

Surveys and polls are useful tools to gather data to inform strategic decision making in professional communication. Polls allow for quick and relatively easy gathering of small amounts of information from a large number of people. This information can be critical in a strategic decision-making process. While survey designs and administration forms each have their own pluses and minuses, surveys are a great way to collect information about people's opinions, behaviors, and experiences because surveys are a relatively low-cost way to engage in data collection with a large sample. A significant advantage of surveys is their adaptability. Surveys can be created to be administered in a variety of formats, perhaps most significantly online. Online surveys provide the ability to reach a large number of people spread across a diverse geographic area quickly without spending a lot of resources, and popular online survey tools offer templates and assistance in creating efficient and attractive surveys.

Surveys and polls also have disadvantages. Surveys and polls rely on participant self-reporting of their opinions, behaviors, and experiences. With the self-report nature of survey and poll data comes the possibility that data may be inaccurate because participants skew their answers to be more socially desirable or participants do not correctly remember their behavior or experiences. Further, because surveys and polls are used so often, people may be reluctant to take yet another survey or poll or may not fully pay attention to how they are answering the surveys and polls they do take. It should also be noted that the quality of survey and poll questions is key: Poor questions produce poor data, and there is no way for a researcher to edit, clarify, or adjust the questions once a respondent has begun the survey or poll.

Chapter Summary

This chapter discusses the strategic use of surveys and polls in professional communication. After explaining the difference between polls and surveys, we talked about the essential nature of surveys, which are to understand people's attitudes, beliefs, and experiences. Although surveys are also used to study people's behaviors, the reality is that we can only measure perceptions of behaviors using surveys, not actual behaviors. We talked about the differences between cross-sectional surveys and longitudinal surveys, as well as the strengths and limitations of different survey administration methods. Next, we identified best practices for survey questions, which included the different types of scales, as well as do's and don'ts for writing questions. We then talked about how to make your survey attractive and user friendly to enhance response rates. We introduced the strategic use of surveys in the form of communication audits, which provide a way for organizations to assess the quality of communication within the organization. We concluded the chapter by identifying the advantages and limitations of the survey method.

PRACTICE ACTIVITIES

1. **News polls:** Do a Google video search on a poll about a particular topic. For example, you might search for polls about a political race, polls about current issues (e.g., student loan debt, climate change, immigration, and so forth). Look at the results of the polls of different news organizations. Are the results similar? What can you conclude about the use of polls in the news media?

2. **Evaluate survey administration formats:** In this chapter we talked about the three different methods of survey administration (face to face, mail, and online). Create and conduct a survey to find out what people in your network think about these three methods. For example, you might ask how likely they would be to complete the survey using that format, how easy they find that sort of survey administration, or

how honest they are likely to be when completing a survey using that type of administration.

3. **Constructing closed-ended questions:** Keep the best practices for survey and poll question creation in mind. For each of the following open-ended questions, construct a closed-ended question that could address the same topic in a poll or survey:

a. How well do your coworkers communicate with each other?

b. How do you feel about violence in children's television programs?

c. What is your main reason for text messaging?

d. What is your level of job satisfaction?

e. How often do you click through links within advertisements you see on social media?

4. **Practicing using different scales:** Try writing the same question using each of five different scales we introduced in this chapter (Likert, relative frequency, forced ranking, fixed sum, and semantic differential). The focus for each of the variations should be on coworker communication.

Likert

Relative frequency

Forced ranking

Fixed sum

Semantic differential

5. **Survey and poll question best practices:** Each of the items that follow was written for a survey but violates one of the best practices for creating survey and poll questions. For each item, (a) identify which

best practices is violated by the item and (b) rewrite the item following the advice from the best practices:

a. How would you rate the speed and accuracy of your work? (circle a response)

Excellent   Good   Fair   Poor

b. People grow up in different types of families. What type of family did you grow up in? (circle a response)

   i. Mom as single parent

   ii. Dad as single parent

   III. Both Mom and Dad in same house

c. My boss is very competent. (circle a response)

Strongly disagree   Disagree   Not sure   Agree   Strongly agree

d. How much do you spend on entertainment?

e. Please describe how you and your coworkers feel about the company's social media use policy.

f. *Game of Thrones* is one of the most popular TV shows of all time. How much do you enjoy watching *Game of Thrones*? (circle response)

Do not enjoy   Somewhat enjoy   Enjoy   Enjoy very much

g. How many hours of sleep do you get on an average night?

___ None

___ 1–3 hours

___ 3–6 hours

___ 6–9 hours

___ over 9 hours

Individual Interviews and Focus Groups

In Chapter 8 we introduced you to communication audits, which are a research tool used by organizations in order to assess the strengths and weaknesses of their communication efforts. We introduced communication audits in the survey chapter because there are a number of well-respected questionnaires designed for communication audits. However, you might recall that questionnaires are only one type of survey. In general, a *survey* is a research tool that gathers information about people's attitudes, beliefs, and experiences by asking questions. Questionnaires are a written form of a survey. In this chapter we talk about the oral form of a survey: an interview.

Communication audits might center on internal communication, external communication, or both. One important communication activity is corporate social responsibility (CSR), which is planned efforts that demonstrate that the organization is socially responsible. Typically, CSR efforts include philanthropy, environmental efforts, ethical labor practices, and volunteering (Schooley, 2019). Although engaging in CSR activity is worthwhile, the reality is that

CHAPTER OUTLINE

◆ Step 1: Formulate Your Research Questions

◆ Step 2: Decide on Your Interview Structure

◆ Step 3: Develop Your Question Route

◆ Step 4: Manage Logistics

◆ Step 5: Conduct Interviews

◆ Step 6: Transcribe and Analyze Your Data

◆ The Strategic Use of Interviews: Focus Groups

◆ Advantages and Limitations of Interviews

many organizations engage in CSR because it improves perceptions of their brand. But, does it work? In general, yes. But how about individual organizations' CSR efforts? One way to find out is to interview important stakeholders about their perceptions of the organization's CSR efforts. Green and Pelozza (2014) did just that; they conducted interviews to learn about consumer perceptions of CSR. They found that consumers had fewer expectations for small organizations to engage in CSR, but that they trusted smaller organizations' CSR more. Conversely, consumers had higher expectations for large firms to engage in CSR but they did not trust that this behavior demonstrated genuine social commitment. Their results provide an important context for evaluating CSR.

In this chapter we identify the steps for conducting interviews as a formal research method (see Box 9.1). We identify the strengths and weakness of different types of interviews, including how structured the interview is and how and where the interview takes place. We conclude the chapter with one important type of interview for strategic communication practice: focus groups.

BOX 9.1

The Steps for Conducting an Interview

Step 1   Formulate your research question(s)

Step 2   Decide on your interview structure

Step 3   Develop your question route

Step 4   Manage logistics

Step 5   Conduct interviews

Step 6   Transcribe and analyze data

Step 1: Formulate Your Research Questions

Throughout this book we have reiterated the importance of developing a strong research question, since the question(s) you develop dictate the methods that you use. Interview research designs are most appropriate when you want to gather qualitative data about your topic (qualitative data analysis will be discussed in Chapter 11). The best way to think about an interview as a formal research method is as a systematic conversation between the participant and the researcher that is recorded for the purposes of gathering data. The conversation is systematic because the direction of the conversation is planned so that you can answer your research question. In Chapter 2 we described five different goals for conducting strategic research: monitoring the environment, identifying opportunities, diagnosing problems, selecting a course of action, and evaluating the course of action. Interviews are an effective technique to accomplish any and all of these goals. Accordingly, virtually any question about people's attitudes or experiences can be researched through an interview.

Step 2: Decide on Your Interview Structure

Much like other research methods, there is more than one way to conduct an interview. Accordingly, one of your first steps is to decide on the level of standardization for your interviews. Standardization refers to the amount of similarity you will have in the questions and question pattern for each interview. Generally, there are three possible levels of standardization: standardized, unstructured, and semi-standardized. Standardized interviews (also known as structured interviews) are those that ask the exact same questions in the exact same order from interview to interview. A standardized interview is the most restrictive type and does not allow for any variation in questioning based on what participants have responded, even to ask for response clarification or to probe for more detailed explanations. In this way, a standardized interview is very similar to assisting a participant in completing a questionnaire. Because they do not allow for responsiveness to participants' answers, structured interviews are not commonly used in strategic communication research.

Unstructured interviews are the opposite of standardized interviews. Unstructured interviews are those that do not have a question plan that is carried over from interview to interview; rather, questions are generated individually for each interview and are very responsive to the answers given by participants. While responsiveness to participants' answers can be helpful in an interview, unstructured interviews are also rarely used in strategic communication research because the lack of consistency across interviews makes analyzing data and drawing conclusions from these interviews very difficult.

The most commonly used type of interview in strategic communication research is the semi-standardized interview (also known as a semi-structured interview). Semi-standardized interviews use a planned set of questions and question pattern from interview to interview, but also allow for some responsiveness to what participants have said in the interview, usually in the form of possible follow-up questions, probes for additional information or clarity, and slight changes to question order. Semi-standardized interviews may offer a researcher the "Goldilocks" solution of an interview that is well planned but also allows for some flexibility when needed.

Step 3: Develop Your Question Route

Assuming you have chosen a semi-standardized interview, the next step is to create a question route that will result in an effective interview. Ideally, an interview should be a comfortable, but controlled, conversation about the research topic. A question route (also known as an interview guide) is like a map of the interview created to guide the interviewer when conducting the interview. A question route is organized by types of questions, starting with the least important and moving on to more important questions as the interview progresses. The question route should provide interview participants the chance to "break the ice" with short, easy topical questions early in the interview and then warm to the key, most important questions that require more detailed answers later.

An **opening question** begins the interview and serves as an ice breaker to get the participant talking. An opening question may be related to the topic of the research, but often it is about basic participant demographics such as where they are from or what position they hold in the organization. Data from response to opening questions may or may not be included in analysis. Usually only one or two opening questions is included in an interview.

Introductory questions are the first to get the participants thinking about the interview topic. Introductory questions should be topical, but not require very detailed answers because they are just introducing the topic at hand. Again, data from introductory questions may or may not be used in the analysis. As with opening questions, there should be just one or two introductory questions.

Next, **transition questions** form a bridge from questions that require little detail in response to questions that are the most important and require the most detailed responses in the interview. Responses to transition questions are expected to provide more detail about how participants think about the topic for the purposes of data collection. Once again, there should be just one or two transition questions.

Key questions follow transition questions and are the most important questions to be asked in the interview. The majority of the interview time should be spent discussing key questions and every effort should be made by the interviewer to generate detailed responses to the key questions. Most of the data analysis will also focus on responses to key questions. The number of key questions may vary, but usually range from between five to eight.

The final questions in an interview question route are the **ending questions**. Ending questions serve to wrap up the interview and usually allow participants to reflect on previous answers and clarify, expand, or correct them and/or add any additional information about the topic that was not covered previously in the interview. A summary of the question route can be found in Table 9.1.

In addition to planning a question route, you must also plan the interview questions themselves. Keep in mind that interviews rely on open-ended questions that are designed to generate detailed, qualitative data about your topic. Much of the advice for effective

TABLE 9.1   Interview Question Route

Opening questions	Serves as an ice breaker. Typically a single question.
Introductory questions	Introduces the research topic. No more than one to two questions.
Transition questions	Marks the transition to more important questions on the topic. No more than one to two questions.
Key questions	Most important questions about the topic in the interview; should be the main focus of the interview.
Ending questions	Concludes interview with final questions.

questionnaire questions discussed in Chapter 8 also applies to writing effective interview questions. Kruger and Casey (2015) offer the additional advice for creating useful interview questions:

◆ Ask participants to think back on their thoughts and experiences but not to predict the future

◆ Avoid asking "why" (which can make people feel defensive and assumes a rational reason for a thought or behavior), and instead ask about what prompted them to make a decision or what factors they liked/disliked about something

◆ Make sure questions sound conversational

◆ Be cautious about giving examples in a question because they can limit participants' thinking to things that are only like the example

Step 4: Manage Logistics

Conducting successful interviews requires careful logistical planning. In this section, we will discuss keys to deciding who should participate in your interviews, where you should conduct your interviews, and how you should ensure your interviews' overall success.

Who

The first step in this planning is to decide who your participants should be. Sampling logic and techniques for interviews are the same as for other research designs involving human participants (for a review, see Chapter 4). When thinking about how many participants are needed for an interview study, you should follow the principles for determining sample size for qualitative studies discussed in Chapter 4.

Where

In Chapter 8, we discussed various formats for questionnaire administration. Like questionnaires, interviews may also be conducted in various "locations," each with advantages and disadvantages to consider. **Face-to-face interviews** are conducted in person, with the interviewer and interviewee meeting in person. In face-to-face interviews, conversations are free from the interruptions of faulty technology and can easily become comfortable with the use of competent interpersonal communication techniques such as appropriate eye contact, friendly nonverbal communication, and easier understanding of people's responses because both verbal and nonverbal communication cues are accessible. However, face-to-face interviews also have disadvantages. One significant disadvantage of face-to-face interviews is the need for people to meet in person to conduct the interview. Face-to-face interviews cannot take place with geographically distant participants unless the interviewer travels to various locations to conduct the interviews. Another disadvantage of face-to-face interviews is the physical space needed to conduct the interview. For example, is the topic of the study one that could be comfortably discussed in a coffee shop where others might overhear or is a more private location needed?

Interviews by telephone are another interview administration option. Telephone interviews have the advantage of reaching people who are not in the same geographic location and may be less expensive than face-to-face interviews because rental space is not needed.

Telephone interviews are also recorded easily. However, telephone interviews are disadvantaged by several factors. First, many of the nonverbal cues that may help a face-to-face interview are not available over the phone. Second, participants who are on the phone in a location remote from the person conducting the interview may be distracted by things in their environment, such as dogs barking, people entering the room, and so on. Further, telephone interviews are vulnerable to technical glitches with the phone line or conference call. Anyone who has ever participated in a conference call will also know the inherent difficulties that arise in conversational flow in these calls. For this reason, Kruger and Casey (2015) recommend using fewer overall questions (no more than eight total) and interviews of a shorter duration (no more than 60 minutes) when conducting telephone interviews.

There are also many online tools that could be used to conduct interviews. Online instant messaging tools may be used for interviews. Text-based online interviews have the advantage of being able to reach people who are not geographically close with little expense. Text-based online interviews may also make it possible to shield the identities of the participants with the use of anonymous online handles (Fox, 2017). As Lannutti (2017) points out, another advantage of text-based online interviews is that transcription of the interview is not needed because the entire interview is already text. Disadvantages of text-based online interviewing include vulnerabilities to technical glitches and issues with the flow of the interaction because of the time it takes for people to read the text and type a response. Nonverbal cues are also lost in text-based online interviews. Finally, online text-based interviews require not only access to and comfort with the technology, but the quality of the interaction and data depend greatly on participant literacy level.

Another set of tools that may be used for interviews are video-based online platforms. There are many online video platforms that will host a conversation between two or more people and are appropriate for interviewing. Like telephone and text-based online interviews, online video interviews have the advantage of being able to reach people who are not geographically close for little to no expense. Online video interviews are also easily recorded through the hosting platforms. Importantly, online video interviews may allow for some of the nonverbal advantages lost in other non-in-person interview administration formats. While seeing each other online is not quite the same as seeing each other in person, it can be more similar than different. Hanna and Mwale (2017) point out that online video interviews can create the feeling of a private conversation while using a tool that is readily available to the public. However, online video interviews are vulnerable to glitches in technology and require both the interviewer and the participants to have access to and be familiar with how to use the technology.

When

After deciding what type of "location" you want to use to administer your interview, it is important to decide on the best time to conduct your interview. When to hold your interviews is largely dependent on the topic of your study, the resources and limitations of your particular research situation, and the make-up of your sample. It is important to try to balance the ideal to reach your project goal against the realistic situation you find yourself in. For example, you may want to interview employees at an organization. While ideally you might like to conduct your interview during working hours, the limitations of people's schedules may mean that your best option is to conduct interviews outside of working hours. Keep in mind that you will be conducting multiple individual interviews, so you will have to balance scheduling each interview against the desired overall timeline for the project, with leaving plenty of time for data analysis and reporting.

It is also important to consider how long your interview should last. Interview length should be determined with your research goals and limitations in mind. There are no set rules about how long interviews should last. Generally, individual interviews last between 30 minutes to 1 hour.

How

Although we have been describing the general order of steps in the interview process, it should be noted that some steps may be completed at the same time. For example, you may be continuing the process of identifying and recruiting participants while starting to develop your question route and questions. Further, data analysis is likely to begin after a set of initial interviews are completed to help determine if you have reached saturation and can stop collecting data.

Step 5: Conduct Interviews

Once you have developed your questioning route and decided on the logistics of your interviews you can begin conducting your interviews. Conducting interviews requires excellent communication skill. According to Tracy (2013), effective interviewers are knowledgeable about the topic and the participant, gentle and forgiving, sensitive to nuance, keen observers, open-minded, able to probe when warranted, attentive, and able to clarify and extend respondents' answers. At the beginning of this chapter we described an interview as a form of conversation; skilled interviewers are excellent conversationalists.

Step 6: Transcribe and Analyze Your Data

Because interviews are an oral form of a survey, the data you collect will likely need to be recorded. As we discussed in the section on managing logistics, generally these audio (or video) data will need to be transcribed in order to complete your analysis. Transcribing data can be very tedious, but it is an important step before analyzing your data. If you rely only on your recordings as your data source it can be challenging to pick up on all of the nuances of a response, and it limits your ability to organize information. In fact, you are generally limited to manual analysis of your data if you fail to transcribe your data, which may in fact add time to the data analysis process. Chapter 11 provides details about conducting a qualitative data analysis.

The Strategic Use of Interviews: Focus Groups

A focus group interview is a conversation about a research topic among multiple participants, led by a facilitator from the research team. While both individual interviews and focus group interviews can be effective in gathering rich description about people's opinions, beliefs, experiences, and behaviors, there are important differences between individual interviews and focus group interviews that play a part in determining which design is best for your research project. See Table 9.2 for a summary of the differences between individual interviews and focus group interviews.

Focus group research has a variety of strategic applications in professional communication. For example, focus groups are a popular tool within marketing communication. Marketing professionals rely on focus group data to help them better understand consumers' perceptions of products or potential products, motivations for consumer behavior, and customer satisfaction with services. Focus groups can also be useful with internal communication applications. For example, focus groups are a popular way to assess internal communication needs, employee perceptions and satisfaction, internal communication planning and goal setting, and training needs and success rates. Finally, focus groups have external communication applications as well. Focus groups may be useful in assessing public and stakeholder

TABLE 9.2 Differences Between Individual Interviews and Focus Groups

	Individual interview	**Focus group interview**
Topic sensitivity	Appropriate for sensitive topics	Not appropriate for sensitive topics
Interview depth	In-depth discussion per participant possible	In-depth discussion per participant not possible
Logistics	Does not require participants to gather at same place and time; requires significant time and resources	Requires participants to gather at same place and time; may require less significant time and resources
Self-disclosure effects	No helpful effect from self-disclosure of others	Helpful effect from self-disclosure of others possible

perceptions of the organization, assessing the success of public relations campaigns, and helping to gain information to inform SWOT analyses.

An important factor that determines whether an individual interview or a focus group interview is best for your research project is the sensitivity of the research topic. Sensitive topics that may make people concerned about their privacy or feel vulnerable are not appropriate for a focus group discussion among many people but can be addressed carefully in an individual interview. Relatedly the desired depth of the interview is another important factor to consider when deciding between an individual or focus group interview format. If you desire to have very in-depth discussions with each participant, this is possible in individual interviews but not in focus group interviews.

Logistical factors may also help you determine whether to choose an individual or focus group interview format. If it is possible to gather the participants together in the same place at the same time, then a focus group is an option. If not, then individual interviews may be the only choice you have to gather the data. Focus groups offer the opportunity to collect data from a number of people more efficiently than do individual interviews. Imagine you wanted to interview a sample of 30 people. With individual interviews, an interview must be set up, conducted, transcribed, and analyzed for each of the 30 participants, which may require a significant amount of time and resources. The same number of people may be interviewed (and the data transcribed and analyzed) in three focus groups of 10 people in significantly less time and possibly using fewer resources.

The final, and perhaps most important, factor in deciding whether to use an individual or focus group interview format has to do with the dynamics of a focus group discussion and how those dynamics affect the quality of the data you collect. The very nature of the group discussion may lead participants to share their thoughts more frequently and in more detail than in an individual interview; plus, hearing what others in the focus group think may stimulate participants' own thinking about the topic in ways that would not happen when speaking with an interviewer one on one. Why would this happen? Well-conducted focus groups produce high-quality data if they provide participants with a comfortable, judgement-free atmosphere that encourages them to self-disclose. **Self-disclosure** is simply the sharing of information about the self with others (Wheeless, 1976). A long-standing finding in communication is that when someone self-discloses information to you, this self-disclosure encourages you to self-disclose in return (Derlega et al., 1973). Further, Jourard (1964) found that people tended to self-disclose more when talking with others who were similar to them in some way. Thus, Kruger and Casey (2015) suggest that ideal focus groups will be formed of people with something in common (even if they are strangers), such as an interest in sustainable farming or all having young children, and that this commonality should be pointed out to the group at the beginning of the session to encourage self-disclosure.

Logistics of Focus Groups

The logistics of focus groups can be more complicated than the logistics of individual interviews. First, in addition to determining how many people you need in your overall sample, you will also have to determine how many people you will include per focus group and, relatedly, how many focus groups to conduct as part of your study. Most focus group studies require more than one focus group to be conducted before your data has reached saturation. Kruger and Casey (2015) recommend an ideal focus group size of 10 to 12 people per group for marketing research and five to eight people per focus group for noncommercial research. In most cases, focus groups of less than five people are not an efficient use of resources. You'll also want to be careful about trying to have an about equal number of people per focus group in your study overall. You can imagine that a person who participated in a focus group of 5 people will have a lot more time to talk during the session than will a person who participated in a focus group of 10 people. When you combine your data from the multiple focus groups for analysis, this may result in the opinions of the person in the small group to seem more important in the final analysis than the opinions of the person in the larger group just because the smaller group person got to say more.

Also, it is usually helpful to group people who have something in common together in a focus group. However, you may want to be careful about what that commonality is. Caution should be taken in grouping people by common demographic factors because this may limit the diversity in responses to your questions. Instead, focus on commonalities in other areas such as profession, interests, and so on. Finally, you will need to consider whether you want your focus group members to already know each other before the focus group. In some situations, such as coworkers, it may not be possible or even desirable to form a focus group of strangers. In other situations, participants knowing each other well may threaten the focus group because people may judge each other's answers, devolve into inside jokes, or not take the session seriously. Whether or not you want participants to know each other should be determined by the topic of your study and the limitations of the situation in which you are collecting your data.

Focus Group Facilitation

The quality of focus group research greatly depends on the skills of the focus group facilitator. You may decide to facilitate the focus groups needed for your project yourself, have another research team member facilitate, or hire a professional facilitator. When picking a facilitator, you should look for someone with excellent communication skills, who can be open to hearing what participants have to say, can be respectful to participants, who understands the research topic, and who participants are likely to identify with in some way (Kruger & Casey, 2015). No matter who facilitates the focus groups, there are important tasks for the facilitator to complete before the focus groups, skills the facilitator will need during the focus group, and potential issues the facilitator should be prepared to address at various times throughout the focus group process.

The job of the focus group facilitator begins well before any focus group interview. The facilitator should prepare for the focus group ahead of time by learning about the topic of the research and familiarizing themselves with the question route and questions. A focus group facilitator guide like the one in Box 9.2 should be prepared, usually with the input of the facilitator. This facilitator guide should include not only the questions and question route, but also include any introduction information you want the facilitator to use in the focus group and suggested amounts of time the facilitator should spend on each group of questions. The facilitator should be familiar enough with the facilitator guide that he or she can follow it without reading it even though the guide will be available to him or her during the focus group.

BOX 9.2
Sample Focus Group Facilitator Guide

Client: La Salle University Department of Communication Graduate Program

Research Question: What are students' perceptions of the graduate program at La Salle University?

Facilitation Guide:

Ground rules: Thank you all for coming today. I'm Jodie, and I will be leading our discussion about the MA program in Strategic Communication at La Salle University. You were asked to participate in this discussion because you are all current students in the program, and we want to know what you think of the program. We'll use the information we discuss today to improve the program. Before we start, I want to just lay out some ground rules for our discussion:

First, I would like us all to promise that anything that anyone says today will be kept between us. Please don't discuss what we talked about beyond our conversation today. I'm hoping that will make everyone feel comfortable giving honest responses to the questions. I'd also like us to keep in mind that it's best that only one person talk at a time. I'm really interested in hearing what everyone has to say, but we only have about 90 minutes for our discussion. So, I may have to steer the conversation back on track occasionally so that everyone can say what they think in response to a question. Also, you will notice there are video cameras recording the conversation. The cameras are here so that I can make sure I catch everything that is said. The people who hired me, faculty of La Salle University, will not be shown the video, but they will get a transcript

---

(continued)

of our conversation with all names removed. Also, people at La Salle University will not be told the names of who participated in the discussion. Instead, they will just be given some basic information about you, like your year in the program.

◆ Opening question (5 minutes)
What is your name? (this will be removed for the transcript later; don't worry) and where are you from?

◆ Introductory question (5 minutes)
How long have you been a student in the MA program in Strategic Communication at La Salle University?

◆ Transition questions (10 to 15 minutes)

Now that we have some background, I'd like you to consider your current educational goals:
What factors made you decide to continue your education at the graduate level?
What obstacles did you think you might encounter by pursuing a graduate degree?
How did you find out about La Salle University?

◆ Key questions (30 minutes)
What factors lead you to choose an MA in Strategic Communication?
What factors led you to choose La Salle University for your MA?
What do you think is most beneficial about the MA program in Strategic Communication at La Salle University (Possible probe: Can you tell us more about that)?
What do you think should be changed with regard to the MA program in Strategic Communication at La Salle University (Possible probe: Can you tell us more about that)?

◆ Ending question (8 to 10 minutes)
Thinking about what we have talked about today, is there anything you would like to clarify?
Are there any additional comments relevant to the graduate program that you would like to mention before we end?

Additionally, the facilitator and the rest of the researchers should agree on how the focus group is being recorded. Ideally, video and/or audio recordings would be used during the focus group. However, it should be decided ahead of time whether the facilitator is also expected to take notes during the focus group. If notes are being relied on to capture the focus group data, then it is advisable to have an additional member of the research team observe the focus group to also record notes. The facilitator and the rest of the research team should also agree on how the facilitator will handle potential issues that may occur during the focus group process (more on this next). When they arrive at the focus group sessions but before the session starts, the facilitator should check that all aspects of the focus group set-up, including chair placement and recording systems, are as they should be. The facilitator will also greet and engage in small talk with focus group participants as they gather before the sessions start. The facilitator may be responsible for confirming informed consent (see Chapter 5) for each participant before the session begins.

During the focus groups the facilitator will need to employ excellent communication skills. These communication skills will help the facilitator establish a rapport with the participants, control the flow of the discussion, and draw out rich and descriptive responses from the participants. There are a few specific communication skills that are especially important when facilitating a focus group:

◆ **Pause.** Effective focus group facilitators are skilled in knowing how long to allow a pause in the discussion so that participants may gather their thoughts while not allowing a pause to eat up too much time or stop the flow of the discussion. Kruger and Casey (2015) recommend a 5-second pause as the ideal amount of time to allow after questions or between comments before stimulating the discussion further.

◆ **Postpone comments.** The focus group facilitator needs to stick as closely as possible to the question route. However, a participant may start to discuss some aspect of the research topic that is going to be addressed later in the focus group too early. A skilled facilitator knows how to show appreciation for the untimely comments but keep on track at the same time. Usually, this is done by thanking the participant for their comment but asking them to please come back to it later. When the appropriate point in the question route for the comment does come, a skilled facilitator will remember to encourage the postponed participant to comment at that point.

- ◆ **Probe.** The goal for focus group data is rich, detailed descriptions. Effective focus group moderators are skilled at asking for more detail in a welcoming, nonthreatening way. Having some useful probing phrases at the ready (such as "tell us more" and "can you give us an example?") is helpful to focus group moderators (Kruger & Casey, 2015).

- ◆ **Nonverbal cues.** As discussed, nonverbal cues can be key in helping a focus group facilitator control the flow of the discussion. A skilled facilitator not only monitors the nonverbal cues of the participants to see who wants to talk or who is becoming disengaged and needs to be reconnected with, but also uses his or her own nonverbal cues, including gestures, head nodding, eye contact, and leaning forward to assist in discussion turn taking and engagement.

- ◆ Keep a **participant focus.** The job of the focus group facilitator is to make sure the data reflects the participants' opinions, beliefs, experiences, and behaviors. Therefore, any time spent discussing the facilitator's opinions, beliefs, experiences, and behaviors is wasted time. Plus, knowing what the facilitator thinks could lead participants to modify their own responses to match that of the facilitator. If a participant asks what the facilitator thinks about the topic, the facilitator should deflect the question in a friendly way by saying things such as "Oh, we are really here to see what you think, not me" or "It's much more important to know what you think than what I think."

- ◆ **Neutrality.** The focus group facilitator wants to be friendly and lead a comfortable discussion, but caution should be taken with comments that praise the participants. As mentioned, there is always the danger of the facilitator "leading" participant responses if the participant senses there is a "right" answer and adjusts their response accordingly. Because of this, a facilitator should be careful to remain neutral about the participants' comments. Kruger and Casey (2015) warn that even short comments like "that's great" after a participant response may be leading.

Although ideal interview lengths are between 30 minutes and an hour, conducting a focus group generally takes quite longer. With focus groups, you are hoping for a length of time that allows for all participants to speak in detail about the topic but not too long that it becomes burdensome and tiring for participants. Focus group length usually ranges between 1 and 2 hours, with 90 minutes being generally accepted as the ideal focus group length.

Focus Group Problems

Skilled focus group facilitators should have a plan in place for common potential issues and the ability to think on their feet to address completely unexpected problems. Potential problems may occur at any point during the focus group facilitation process, so we will discuss some common issues at various points in the process.

Before the focus group begins, the facilitator may have problems related to participant attendance. Even the best efforts to recruit participants and schedule focus groups may result in too few participants showing up to the focus group. In coordination with the research team, a focus group facilitator should have a minimum number of acceptable participants in mind and a plan for rescheduling or canceling focus groups with too few people. It is also possible that unexpected people may arrive to participate in the focus group. This may be especially likely to occur when there is an incentive for participation in the focus group being offered. Again, a plan should be in place about whether to include these would-be participants in the focus group, schedule them for a future focus group, or explain to them why they are not able to participate in the research.

During the focus group, facilitators may be faced with difficult participants. At times, the communication styles of focus group participants may pose a challenge to the success of the focus group. When such challenges arise, it is the job of the focus group facilitator to manage these potentially troublesome participants in a way that does not throw the discussion off track and allows for meaningful participation from the challenging and non-challenging group members alike. Some participants may try to dominate the conversation because they believe themselves to be experts on the topic or just because they like to take control of their interactions. With these dominant participants, it is best to allow their comments but also ask the group if they have different opinions and invite others to join in the conversation with comments like "let's hear from someone else on this, too." Shy participants are reluctant to say very much during the focus group. Facilitators should be careful to invite shy participants to speak without seeming threating or demanding. Simply calling on a shy person by saying "What do you think?" may be effective. Another type of potentially problematic participant is one who takes a long time to get to their point. With these participants, helping them to get their point across more efficiently by paraphrasing what they have said is often helpful.

Advantages and Limitations of Interviews

Although we have discussed some of the advantages and disadvantages of various formats for conducting interviews, it is also important to consider the advantages and limitations of interview research methods overall. As a reminder, interview methods are useful for collecting qualitative data that provides rich description of people's opinions, beliefs, experiences, and behaviors. As such, interview research methods allow you to delve deeper into a topic than a qualitative survey would. Interview methods also provide room to ask for clarification and follow-up information from a participant. Interview research designs can also be inexpensive.

There are, however, potential limitations to interview research designs to consider. Beyond the disadvantages of various interview administration formats we discussed, interview methods are limited in that they rely on participants' self-report of their thoughts and behavior. These self-reports may be inaccurate due to faulty recall or answers being skewed to seem more socially desirable or more in line with what the participant perceives to be the researchers' desired responses. Further, Kruger and Casey (2015) warn that people tend to rationalize reasons for their behavior that are often inaccurate simply because human nature precludes us from always understanding why we behave the way we do. For this reason, Kruger and Casey (2015) recommend pairing interview methods with direct observation research methods if the study depends on accurate data about participant behavior and behavior motivations. Another potential problem with interview methods is that people may be reluctant, especially in a focus group, to respond with "I don't know" and may instead invent an answer (Kruger & Casey, 2015). Thus, it is important to make sure interview participants understand that not having an answer to a question is acceptable.

Chapter Summary

This chapter focused on interview research methods. We discussed each of the stages of conducting an interview, including developing your research question, choosing a level of interview standardization for your research project, and developing an effective questioning route. We also discussed the logistics of conducting interviews, including the advantages and disadvantages of several interview administration formats. Because of their popularity in strategic communication, we highlighted the use of focus groups as a form of an interview. We explained the similarities and differences between individual interviews and focus group interviews, including how the nature of self-disclosure is a driving factor in focus group interviews. We also discussed focus group facilitation skills and potential problems with focus groups. We concluded the chapter with a discussion of the advantages and limitations of interview research methods overall.

PRACTICE ACTIVITIES

1. **Create questions and a question route:** Create questions and a question route for an individual interview to address a research question

of interest to you. Make sure to include all of the required types of questions, and make sure you label each question.

2. **Conduct an interview:** Practice conducting an interview with a friend as the interviewee. Be sure to record the interview. After the interview, review it to identify strengths of the interview and aspects of the interview that could be improved.

3. **Evaluate an interview article:** Find a research article that uses an interview research methodology. What did you learn about interviews from reading the study? What do you think were the strengths and weaknesses of the way the researcher(s) conducted the study?

4. **Create a focus group facilitator guide:** Using the focus group facilitator guide in Box 9.2, create your own focus group facilitator guide to address a research question of interest to you.

5. **Practice conducting a focus group:** Using the focus group facilitator guide in Box 9.2, or the one you created in practice activity 4, actually conduct a focus group with your classmates. To do so, decide on what focus group administration format you wish to use and make any needed adjustment to your facilitator guide needed for the format. Decide who will practice being the facilitator and who will practice being participants. Conduct and record the focus group. Use the recording to review the focus group and identify what went well, what could be improved, and why.

Experiments and A/B Studies

I magine you are a communication professional working for a start-up company. One of your first tasks is to develop the logo for the company. Easy, right? Pick a font, type the company name, and maybe throw in some clip art. Or, search "designing a logo" online and check out the companies that promise to design you a killer logo for free. It shouldn't surprise you that it isn't really that simple—nor should it be. Park, Eisingerich, Pol, and Park (2013) have found that logos not only create brand identification, but they also influence brand commitment and company revenue. Creating a logo is an important business decision, and it should involve research.

What do we know about logos? The results of numerous studies give us a number of best practices associated with designing a logo. For example, we know that the shape of the logo will influence how people view the nature of your company. Jiang, Gorn, Galli, and Chattopadhyay (2016) found that circular logos evoke a feeling of softness and that angular logos produce a perception of hardness. Thus, if your start-up is in the human services industry, you probably want to create a round logo, but if you are selling SUVs you probably want an angular logo.

Similarly, consumers make judgments about your brand based on whether your logo uses all uppercase letters, all lowercase letters, or a combination of the two. Xu, Chen, and Liu (2017) found that people who viewed logos with all uppercase letters (such as VISA, HONDA, or CNN) perceive those companies as strong and authoritative. When they view logos with a mix of upper and lowercase (such as Southwest Airlines) or all lowercase letters (such as amazon) people perceived the brand as friendlier. When designing a logo, you must think about what sort of perception you want to foster.

The color of a logo matters, too, but it is not as simple as focusing on customers' preferred colors. Bottomley and Doyle (2006) found that the nature of the product or service influences consumers' perceptions of the appropriateness of the color of a logo; they found that consumers preferred colors like blue or gray for "functional" products or services such as tires or a law firm, but they preferred colors like red or yellow for "sensory" products and services such as perfume or a restaurant. Not only does the type of product or service matter, so does the strength of the brand. Sundar and Noseworthy (2014) found that consumers preferred the logo to appear high on the packaging for powerful brands (i.e., those that consumers are familiar with and that have a strong market share), but they prefer the logo to appear low on the package for less powerful brands. Finally, how straightforward should the logo be? Research indicates that the answer to this question is not very straightforward at all. van Grinsven and Das (2016) found that simple logos had a positive effect on brand awareness in the short term, but that there were more positive attitudes toward complex logos in the long term.

How have we learned this information about logos? From experiments. Each of the studies mentioned studied the effect of aspects of logo design on people's perceptions of the logo, brand, and company. You may recall from Chapter 2 that an **experiment** is the *only* way you can determine cause and effect. For this reason, the research requires a set of quite different steps than other research methods. In this chapter, we will discuss the steps involved in conducting an experiment, which are listed in Box 10.1. We introduce the strategic use of experiments in the professional world: A/B studies. We conclude the chapter with the advantages and limitations of the experimental method.

BOX 10.1

The Steps for Conducting an Experiment

Step 1   Articulate your research question(s) or hypotheses

Step 2   Consider manipulation and control

Step 3   Operationalize your variables

Step 4   Determine the location of the experiment

Step 5   Select your research design

Step 6   Conduct your experiment

Step 1: Determine Your Research Question and/or Hypothesis

You should recognize by now that the first step for every research method we have described has been to determine your research question (RQ). This is because the purpose of conducting research is to answer a question; if you don't have a specific research question, you shouldn't be conducting research. However, you likely noticed that in this chapter we added the possibility of posing a hypothesis (H) to begin the research process. You may recall from Chapter 2 that hypotheses and research questions guide research, but a hypothesis makes a prediction about the relationship between variables while a research question simply asks if there is a relationship between variables. Because of the possibility of determining cause and effect, when conducting an experiment, you may find yourself making a prediction (hypothesis).

Another essential difference between experiments and other research methods has to do with the variables in your RQ/H. In Chapter 3 we talked about two types of variables: *independent* variables (the presumed cause) and *dependent* variables (the presumed effect). Because the goal of an experiment is to determine cause and effect, the researcher must be able to articulate which variable in the RQ/H is the independent variable and which is the dependent variable prior to developing the study. In other methods, it might be possible to not identify independent and dependent variables at all or to not do so until data analysis. However, when conducting an experiment, you cannot even begin the research process unless you have established which variable is the independent variable and which is the dependent variable.

To illustrate, in the case of developing a new brand logo, the design of the logo would be the independent variable, and customer perceptions of the logo would be the dependent variable. Possible values of the independent variable might be the shape, color, or text choices used in the logo. Possible values of the dependent variable might range from positive to negative evaluations, or to judgments that range from appropriate to inappropriate, or even perceptions of the brand that range from strong to weak. Knowing this allows the researcher to move forward with designing the experiment.

Step 2: Consider Manipulation and Control

There are two important concepts that allow us to determine cause and effect through the experimental method: manipulation of the independent variable and control over additional influences. **Manipulation of the independent variable** refers to the researcher's ability to determine the levels of the independent variable that participants are exposed to. In the case of the logo design that we have been talking about, manipulation involves exposing some participants to one design (level 1 of the independent variable) and exposing other participants to a different design (level 2 of the independent variable). Then the researcher carefully measures the dependent variable(s), which in this example may be how positive the participants felt about the logo and how appropriate participants found the logo to be. The researcher will then look for differences in the dependent variable for each logo design type. In this case, the researcher will feel confident that any differences in participants' evaluation will be because of the manipulation of different design aspects of the two logos.

Manipulation in experiments usually breaks up participants into different groups. As in the logo study example, some participants were exposed to logo 1 and some were exposed to logo 2, creating two groups of participants. But how should participants be assigned to different experimental groups? Random assignment to groups is one of the most important aspects of an experimental design. Random assignment means that each participant has an equal chance of being assigned to any group in the experiment.

Typically, there are at least two groups in an experiment. The control group is the group of participants who experiences no change from their existing experience. For example, if we were testing new logo designs and were interested in how different design aspects might influence perceptions of the organization, it could be possible that the control group is shown no logo at all before their perceptions of the organization are measured. In medical experiments, the control group sometimes receives a placebo, which gives the impression of receiving a treatment, but participants are not in fact experiencing the independent variable (in this case, the drug). In contrast to the control group, the treatment group is the group that does experience the variation in the independent variable; they see the new logo designs, or in the case of the medical experiment, they take the new drug.

We have mentioned control groups, but we have not yet discussed the second important element of experimental designs: control over additional influences. Control over additional influences means ensuring there are no extraneous or confounding variables. An extraneous variable is a variable that is not a part of the study that has the potential to affect the results of the study. They can be associated with the situation, the participants, or the researcher. Examples of extraneous variables might be the setting of the experiment (e.g., some participants are seated in a comfortable room and others are in an uncomfortable room), the nature of the participants (e.g., some participants have just completed a full work day and others have not), or the researchers themselves (e.g., the instructions given by one researcher may be different than the instructions given by a different researcher).

There are also potential **confounding variables**, which are variables that are related to the independent variable but are not a part of the study. For example, if the lighting of the room influences how people perceive the colors of the logos, this would be a confounding variable, or if some of the participants were color-blind this too could influence how the logo is perceived. A very important confounding variable to control is **experimenter bias**, which occurs when the researcher's preferences influence the experimental outcome. For example, if the researcher subconsciously exhibits a preference for one of the logos, this could bias the participants' responses to be more positive toward the logo the researcher preferred.

Step 3: Operationalize Your Variables

The next step in an experiment is to identify how you are going to measure your variables, a process known as **operationalization.** One of the things that often confuses novices to research methods is that what makes something an experiment has more to do with manipulation and control than it does with actual measurement. After all, what makes something an observation is that the researcher observes naturally occurring behavior (in person or online). What makes something a content analysis is that the researcher classifies messages. What makes something a survey (whether a poll, question-naire, interview, or focus group) is that the researcher asks people questions about their attitudes, beliefs, or experiences. However, the variables of an experiment can be measured through any one of these other methods; you might measure variables in an experiment by observations, variations in messages, or the completion of a survey.

Let's go back to our example of whether differences in logos cause different perceptions of the brand. The independent variable is characteristics of the logo. Your independent variable is being operationalized by different qualities or elements of the logo, just like in a content analysis. Your dependent variable is perceptions of the brand—and the only way to determine people's perceptions is to ask them, which is what you do when you conduct a survey. So, even though this is an experimental study, the actual things being assessed are message characteristics and responses to a survey.

Consider a different example. Mau, Steinmann, and Schramm-Klein (2016) conducted an experiment to find out how the location of supermarket promotional displays affects purchasing behaviors. Their independent variable was the location of the display, with the levels of the independent variable being a congruent location (the display was close to the store shelf for the product) or an incongruent location (the display not being located near the store shelf for the product). The dependent variable was the number of purchases of the product. They used observations to measure their dependent variable. They found that people purchased significantly more of the product when the promotional display was located near the product shelf.

In sum, there are many different techniques that researchers can use to operationalize the variables being measured in an experiment. For that reason, researchers need to carefully consider the conceptual fit of their measurements when conducting an experiment.

Step 4: Determine the Location of Your Experiment

The fourth step in conducting an experiment is to determine where your experiment will take place. Regarding the location of your experiment, there are three types of experiments. Laboratory experiments take place in a research setting. That is, research participants are brought to a location that is unfamiliar to them and that is set up with the tools for the experiment. In professional communication research, these tools might be a two-way mirror, microphones, cameras, and computers. Field experiments, on the other hand, take place in an environment that is natural to the participants. Typically, it is some public place such as a shopping mall, a park, or a college campus. Remember the study of promotional displays we just talked about? That experiment took place in a supermarket. One increasingly common form of experiments is online experiments, which combine some of the elements of a laboratory experiment with elements of field experiments. Like a laboratory experiment, in an online experiment the researcher carefully develops the elements of the study and how the participants are exposed to the variables of concern. And, like a field experiment, the participants take part in the study while in their own natural environment.

To illustrate the use of online experiments, Hecht, Martin, Donnelly, Larson, and Sweetser (2017) were interested in testing perceptions of reporter credibility in video news releases. They simulated a public relations crisis that involved a cruise ship fire that required U.S. Naval assistance. Hecht and colleagues (2017) created five different video news releases, varying whether the reporter in the video worked for the cruise company or the Navy, and whether the reporter wore a uniform or other professional clothing. They randomly sent one of the five videos to media professionals online and asked the professionals to indicate how likely they would be to use the news release and how credible they found the reporter. Their results found that regardless of whether the Naval personnel wore their uniform, the media professionals viewed members of the military as more credible than the cruise ship official. However, the media professionals indicated that they were unlikely to use the video release regardless of the affiliation and apparel of the simulated reporter.

It should come as no surprise that researchers have more control in laboratory experiments than other forms of experiments. This means that they have increased internal validity, or an increased likelihood that any changes in the dependent variable are caused by the independent variable. When you are in an environment that is not under the researcher's direct control (as is the case with field or online experiments) the chances of extraneous and confounding variables are increased. After all, the sights, sounds, smells, and activities of real-life environments are not under anyone's direct control. On the other hand, field experiments have increased external validity, which is the extent to which results of an experiment will hold true in other environments, with other people, and over time. In fact, it is the very inability of a researcher to carefully control elements in a field experiment that increases their external validity. Interestingly, despite their increasing popularity, online experiments are relatively weak in both internal and external validity. Table 10.1 provides an overview of the specific threats to validity associated with experimental research.

TABLE 10.1 Threats to Validity

Threats to Internal Validity	
History	A real-life event occurs during the course of the experiment that might affect the result of the study. Imagine that you are studying perceptions of workplace violence, and during the study a workplace shooting occurs at another company and there is substantial news coverage. The real-life event might influence people's scores on a posttest irrespective of exposure to the independent variable.
Instrumentation	The way that the dependent variable is measured might change. For example, imagine that after a training session on sexual harassment research participants are interviewed about their perceptions of sexual harassment in the workplace. Male interviewers and female interviewers might receive different responses based on the sex of the interviewer alone.
Location	Where the study takes place might affect the results. Imagine that you are testing perceptions to a training video. One group watches the video in a location that has strong Wi-Fi, but the other group watches the video in a location with poor Wi-Fi, which causes buffering problems while trying to show the video.
Maturation	People naturally change over time. If an experiment takes place over a period of time, changes in the dependent variable might be a function of the natural maturation process. For example, when comparing changes in students' critical thinking skills from before entering university to after completion of university, any improvement might not be due to university instruction at all, but instead be due to natural changes in intellectual development true of all young adults.
Mortality	It is common for people to drop out of a study. However, if more people drop out of a study from one experimental group versus another experimental group, the results might be distorted. Consider a study comparing the effectiveness of online versus in-person corporate training programs. If a lot of the people in the online training session don't complete the training session, leaving only those who are highly motivated to do the training in the online group, the results might be skewed.
Selection	If the two groups are selected versus different methods, then a potential selection threat occurs. Imagine that you are studying perceptions of a new coffee blend. One group of respondents is a judgmental sample (e.g., they are solicited from patrons at a coffee shop) and the other group of respondents are a convenience sample (e.g., they are members of the researcher's friends and family group). The two groups might respond in very different ways simply because of how they were selected.

(continued)

TABLE 10.1   Threats to Validity *(Continued)*

Threats to Internal Validity	
Statistical regression	Statistical regression happens when groups are selected based on having extreme scores and is best understood by thinking about a bell curve—those at the far ends of the bell are likely to move toward the middle over time. To illustrate, imagine that employees who have received the lowest performance evaluations are chosen to take part in skills training. Their subsequent performance evaluations are likely to have improved just because people become more "average" over time.
Testing sensitization	Although using both a pretest and posttest allows for a stronger assertion that the independent variable actually caused the changes in the dependent variable, simply by taking a pretest research participants might change their responses on a posttest: They might "learn" how to answer, for example, or become more aware of the experimental manipulation when it occurs.
Threats to External Validity	
Ecological validity	Because the researcher is able to carefully control the environment in a laboratory study, the results might not hold true in a less controlled setting.
Population validity	If the sample used in the experiment is not representative of the actual population, the results might not be able to generalize to people who did not take part in the study.

Step 5: Select Your Research Design

There are also different types of experiments based on the *way* that the researcher has designed the study. There are three general classes of experimental designs: pre-experimental designs, quasi-experimental designs, and full experimental designs. We will provide a brief overview of these three types of experimental designs. Table 10.2 provides more details about specific experimental designs that fall under each category.

Pre-Experiments

Pre-experimental designs are the simplest form of experimental design. They typically involve only one group, which means that true manipulation and control cannot be achieved. The problem of pre-experimental designs is that causality cannot be guaranteed because there is no formal way to establish whether the measurement of the dependent variable is due to the independent variable or to some other cause. For example, consider the one-group pretest posttest design illustrated in Table 10.2. Imagine that you have one group of people, and you assess their perceptions of workplace violence. You then have the members of the group read about a real case of

TABLE 10.2 Experimental Designs

Pre-experimental designs	**One-shot case study design**
	There is only one nonrandom group, which experiences the variation in the independent variable, and then the dependent variable is measured.
	X O
	One group pretest-posttest design
	There is only one nonrandom group, and the dependent variable is measured both before and after the variation in the independent variable.
	O X O
	Static group comparison
	There are two nonrandom groups. One is exposed to the independent variable, the other is not. The dependent variable is measured in both groups.
	X O O
Quasi-experimental designs	**Nonequivalent control group design**
	Although there are two groups, the researcher was not able to randomly assign people into groups.
	O X O O O

(continued)

TABLE 10.2 Experimental Designs *(continued)*

Quasi-experimental designs *(continued)*	**Matched pretest-posttest group**
	The groups are not randomly assigned; instead, the researcher makes sure that the two groups are similar (i.e., matched) in important ways. O X O O O
	Time series design
	Used when there are existing measurements of the dependent variable over a regular period of time; after the change in the independent variable, the same measure of the dependent variable is used over time. O O O X O O O
Experimental designs	**Pretest-posttest control group design**
	Participants are randomly assigned to groups and both groups are tested before and after being exposed to the independent variable. RO X O RO O
	Posttest-only control group design
	When pretests are not appropriate, the researcher randomly assigns participants to groups and takes only one measure of the dependent variable. R X O R O
	Solomon four design
	This combines the previous two designs, which controls for both testing sensitization and effects of extraneous variables. Participants are randomly assigned to groups. RO X O RO O R X O R O

Note: R means the random assignment to a group; O means a measurement of the dependent variable; X means exposure to the independent variable.

workplace violence, and then ask them again about their perceptions of workplace violence. How do you know that any changes in perceptions of workplace violence are due to the case you had the participants read? Perhaps the pretest measurement itself sensitized people to issues of workplace violence. Or, perhaps a current example of workplace violence appeared on the news between the pretest and the posttest. For that reason, pre-experimental designs are particularly vulnerable to internal and external validity concerns.

Quasi-Experiments

There are three possible reasons why an experimental design would be considered quasi-experimental, or partially experimental. The first reason is that the researcher is unable to randomly assign people into groups. To illustrate, perhaps the researcher was interested in how a shift in an organizational policy might affect people's satisfaction with a workplace. However, the two groups that are used are existing work groups. That is, one group consists of members of the accounting group and the other group consists of members of the marketing group. These groups already exist; the researcher does not have the ability to randomly shift someone's department.

The second reason an experimental design might be considered quasi-experimental is because the researcher wants to carefully match the two groups based on issues that might affect the experiment. For example, the researcher might seek to make sure that the two groups have the same number of men and women, or the same number of years of service to the organization, or the same general salary level. This type of matching might make the two groups more equivalent in some ways, but the matching itself prevents the two groups from being randomly assigned.

The final reason an experimental design is considered quasi-experimental is because the researcher is studying only one existing group. In the case of a time series design, the researcher has access to existing data that have been collected over time. Consider an organization that has a strong mission and asks employees to assess the extent to which the organization is living its mission on a yearly basis. These data are preexisting measurements of the dependent variable. The organization then conducts enhanced training on living the mission, and the results of annual survey after the training are compared to the results prior to the training.

Full Experiments

A **full experiment** is one that maximizes both manipulation and control and is therefore considered the most rigorous type of formal research. In order to accomplish this, the researcher must randomly assign participants to each experimental group. Ideally, there is both a **pretest** and a **posttest**, which allows researchers to measure a change from baseline. In addition, in full experiments there is a control group that does not experience a change in the independent variable—for example, they aren't exposed to any new information in our hypothetical workplace violence study. In this way, researchers know that any changes in the measurement of the dependent variable are due to the independent variable and nothing else.

Step 6: Conduct Your Experiment

After so much planning, the final step is to conduct the experiment. Like other methods, we recommend that you pilot the experiment so that your data are as strong as they can be. Remember that your actual measurements in an experiment typically mirror those from other methods, so test your method of observation, the classification of your messages, or the ease and understanding of your survey. In addition, carefully consider the threats to internal and external validity we presented. Carefully consider the timing and location of the study to minimize any possible extraneous or confounding variables.

The Strategic Use of Experiments: A/B Testing

As we indicated in Chapter 2, experiments are not frequently used in public relations or organizational communication research. They are much more common in marketing communications, and one of the most important tools in a marketing professional's research repertoire is A/B testing. **A/B testing** is a type of marketing experiment in which participants are exposed to two versions of a digital marketing initiative: two versions of an online advertisement, for example, or two versions of a website landing page. Major companies like Microsoft, Amazon, and Booking.com make frequent use of A/B testing, with estimates that each organization conducts more than 10,000 A/B tests annually (Kohavi & Thomke, 2017).

If you understand the concept of experimental control, it is relatively easy to understand the nature and purpose of A/B testing. The "A" version of a digital message is the control: It is the current version used by an organization. The "B" version is the treatment, or the variation in the message that is considered the independent variable. As real users visit the site, they are randomly shown either the A version of the message or the B version of the message. The dependent variable is what the user does after seeing the message. Possible dependent variables might be click-through rates (recall from Chapter 6 that a click-through rate is how frequently people click on a "call to action" button) or actual sales figures.

Consider the following example. Humana, a U.S. health insurance company, conducted several A/B tests of their website homepage (Pun, n.d.). In one test, the company tested changes in their homepage banner, which is the information on the website that is visible without scrolling. Their original banner (the A option) had quite a bit of text information and a subtle call-to-action button. They created a new banner (the B option) that limited the amount of text and had a bolder call to action. The results found an increase of 433% more clicks on the call to action with the B variation (Pun, n.d.). They then tested the text on the call-to-action button. The original A version read "Get Started Now." The B version read "Shop Medicare Plans." The B version lead to a 192% increase in clicks.

As you can see with the example, typically A/B tests are focused on only *one* element of the Web page. That is, the researchers might change just the headline, or the images, or the layout, or the call to action. The focus on changing just one element achieves the control element essential to conducting an experiment; if more than one element is changed, the researchers cannot determine which specific variation caused the change in consumer behavior. Of course, nothing prevents an organization from conducting multiple A/B tests. The organization might first determine which headline is more appealing, and then test the layout, and so on.

Calling these types of experiments an A/B test implies that only the control version and one alternative version of the digital message is used, but in reality, there can be any number of variations tested. An organization can actually conduct an A/B/C/D/E test. What is essential is that there is a control version, and that each iteration changes the same element in some way. There might be four different layouts tested, or four different placements of the call-to-action button.

A/B tests don't work for everyone. Typically, these tests require a large number of active users of an organization's digital media (Kohavi & Thomke, 2017). As such, they are more effective for large organizations with established Web traffic. Birkett (2019) suggests that you need at least 1,000 discrete visitors to a Web page in order to collect enough data to make effective decisions. A/B tests also take time. Birkett (2019) recommends that A/B tests run over a minimum of 2 weeks. Moreover, they aren't always successful. Kohavi and Thomke (2017) estimate that only about 10–20% of A/B tests conducted at major organizations demonstrate positive effects. At Microsoft, they say, about one-third of the A/B tests they conduct have neutral effects, and another one-third have negative effects. Finally, both reliability and validity are important research concerns. Kohavi and Thomke (2017) recommend conducting occasional A/A tests, which simulates a form of split-half reliability. Moreover, if there are no statistical differences between the two groups, it also suggests that there are limited threats to internal validity.

Advantages and Limitations of Experiments

As should be clear by now, the major advantage of conducting an experiment is that it is the only method that allows a determination of cause and effect. In addition, the methods themselves are relatively straightforward; the most difficult part of conducting an experiment is making sure that the operationalization of the variables is reliable and valid. Finally, because of the control and precision that are involved, experiments are relatively easy to replicate, which is an essential part of the scientific method.

The major liability of experiments is that they are artificial, and therefore results might not be generalizable to real-life situations. We described internal and external validity earlier in the chapter, and one of the major challenges of experimental research is that there is a trade-off between the two types of validity: The more a researcher emphasizes internal validity, the greater the threats to external validity and vice versa. Experiments can also be costly, both in terms of time and money, making them a less appealing option in some professional settings. Finally, although experiments are very good at establishing the nature of the relationship between the independent and the dependent variable, they are not as useful in determining *why* the relationship exists.

Chapter Summary

This chapter provided an overview of the most rigorous of formal research techniques, the experiment. An experiment is the only way that researchers can determine cause and effect. We described the essential elements of what constitutes an experiment: manipulation and control. We differentiated between laboratory experiments, which occur in a setting specifically designed to conduct experiments, field experiments, which occur in a natural setting, and online experiments, which combine the other two. We differentiated between internal validity, or elements of how an experiment was conducted that might threaten the accuracy of the results, and external validity, which refers to how the nature of manipulation and control might influence the accuracy of the results for different people in different settings. We identified three categories of experimental designs, which range from the least controlled to the most controlled: pre-experiments, quasi experiments, and full experiments. Finally, we talked about one particular type of experiment that is conducted by marketing communication professionals: A/B testing. We concluded the chapter by identifying the advantages and limitations of using experiments in professional communication research.

PRACTICE ACTIVITIES

1. **Conduct an experiment:** Conduct a pretest posttest experiment about company logos. Design a "fake" logo for a real organization. Do a pretest on people's perceptions of the organization, then show one group the company's actual logo and the second group the logo you created. Then, conduct your posttest of people's perceptions of the company. Was there a difference in the pretest and posttest perceptions? Did this difference depend on which logo the group viewed?

2. **Organizational cases:** Search "marketing experiments" online. You will find a large number of links to real-life case studies. Choose one of the cases and examine what was done. Was it a pre-experiment, quasi-experiment or full experiment? What experimental design was used? Do you see any threats to validity?

3. **Threats to validity:** Identify the threats to validity in the following examples:

   a. A researcher decides to try a new research methods curriculum in the Strategic Communication program and plans to compare exam scores from the old curriculum with the new curriculum. However, students using the new curriculum have access to the instructor's PowerPoint slides, and those using the old curriculum did not have that access.

   b. A researcher wants to compare student's perceptions of the textbook across two different classes. Almost 20% of the students were absent in the morning class, but no one was absent in the afternoon class.

c. In a study investigating sex differences in leadership styles, male and female interviewers get different results.

d. A study of perceptions of violence on television administers a pretest and a posttest to both the participants who viewed the violent program and those who did not see the violent program.

e. A researcher compares the effects of weekly individual and group counseling sessions on the improvement of financial literacy. The individual counseling sessions are at the participant's home, and the group counseling sessions are in a classroom.

f. Employees who scored at the bottom 10% of an information literacy scale are selected for a personal enrichment program. The program includes lectures, weekly social activities, and free meals. They score substantially higher 6 months later.

4. **Experimental designs:** Identify the experimental design in each of the following studies:

a. A marketing agency does a lot of e-mail marketing for their clients. They want to find out if the sender name on the e-mail influences the rate of opening the e-mail. They create two versions of an e-mail, one that has the marketing agency name as the sender, and a second that has the name of a specific member of the marketing agency as the sender. They randomly select who receives the e-mail with the company name and who receives the e-mail with the specific person's name. They determine that 292 more people opened the e-mail when a specific person's name was listed as the sender rather than the marketing agency name.

b. An insurance company wants to find out if providing an incentive for joining a health club will decrease health care costs. They select 200 members and match them to a second group of 200 members that has similar health expenditures. The health insurance company offers to subsidize the health club costs of the first group, and then 1 year later they compare the expenditures of the two groups.

c. A consumer products company wants to investigate whether allowing select employees to work from home will negatively impact employee engagement. They allow members of the corporate communications staff to work from home but require members of the Human Resources department to work in the office over the period of 1 month. They then ask members of the two groups to fill out an employee engagement survey.

d. A nonprofit agency wants to increase awareness of the services they provide to new mothers. The agency uses public record to identify recent births and sends a survey to all new mothers to assess how much they know about their agency. They then send a package of materials about the agency's services to everyone on the list, and 3 months later they resend the survey to everyone on the list to compare their awareness of the agency's services after receiving the promotional materials.

e. The training and development department of a pharmaceutical company wants to investigate the efficacy of using online training modules. They assess all employee's knowledge of quality management procedures. They then randomly assign half of the employees to attend an in-person training session about quality management and half of the employees to complete a Web training session on quality management. At the completion of the training session each employee is again assessed on their knowledge of quality management procedures.

5. **A/B testing case studies:** Search "A/B test case studies" online. Review at least five different examples and create a list of best practices for website designs. Then look at a website you use often. Are they following the best practices?

PART III

Creating a Research Product

11

Analyzing Data

The majority of this book has focused on the ways that data, or sources of information, may be collected. This chapter shows you the next step in the research process, which is analyzing the data you have collected in order to develop or assess communication strategy. The choices you make for the analysis of your data should be guided by your research questions and overall goals for your project. To remind you, there are three different goals of research questions: to *describe* communication, to *compare* communication, and to *relate* communication to some other variable. You need to know which of these three things your research question is asking in order to make the appropriate data analysis decisions. In this chapter, we discuss foundational ideas related to the analysis of qualitative and quantitative data. We will begin our discussion of data analysis with qualitative data and then move on to the analysis of quantitative data.

Analyzing Qualitative Data

As we have discussed previously, the goal of qualitative data collection is to provide rich description of people's opinions, beliefs, experiences, and behaviors related to the topic of your research project. In this book, we have described various methods of collecting qualitative data including observations, surveys, interviews, and focus groups. Qualitative data takes the form of quotes, texts, and narratives that must then be analyzed to show themes and patterns that address your research questions. Corbin and Strauss (2008) urge researchers analyzing qualitative data to try to capture as much of the complexity of the data as possible in the analysis while still producing a report that makes the usefulness of the data regarding the research question clear. With this advice in mind, we will explain steps to follow when analyzing qualitative data. The qualitative data analysis steps we will discuss can be generally described as **thematic analysis**, an umbrella term used to refer to qualitative data analysis processes performed with the goal of identifying patterns of meaning, or themes, within the data. Other forms of qualitative data analysis can be found in Tracy (2013).

There are many ways of performing thematic analysis. The thematic analysis steps here represent the way your authors generally approach thematic analysis and are largely informed by Clarke and Braun (2016) and Corbin and Strauss (2008). A summary of thematic analysis steps can be found in Box 11.1.

BOX 11.1

Thematic Analysis Steps

Step 1   Organize and Prepare Your Data

Step 2   Immerse Yourself in the Data

Step 3   Identify Themes

Step 4   Confirm your Analysis

Step 1: Organize and Prepare Your Data

There are several forms that your qualitative data might take. If you have conducted an observation, your data might be in the form of *field notes*. If you have conducted a qualitative survey, you have *written answers to open-ended questions*. If you have conducted an interview or focus group, you have *recordings* of people's responses. If your data was audio or video recorded, you will likely need to transcribe your data before beginning the first step of qualitative data analysis. The first step in the qualitative data analysis process is organize the information you have collected (Tracy, 2013). There are several different ways you might organize this information. First, you might organize your information **chronologically**, which means that you put the data in order of when you collected it. As an example, you might have separate transcriptions for the first focus group you conducted, the second focus group you conducted, and so forth. Alternatively, you might organize your data by **source**, which means that you organize your data around the specific person or place that provided the information. If you have conducted interviews, for example, you might have separate files for each person you interviewed. Finally, you might organize your data around specific **prompts**. So, you might create a file of all responses to a particular question.

Another consideration when organizing and preparing your data is to consider whether you will manually analyze the data or employ the software to aid you in analysis. Because qualitative research is an inherently subjective process (i.e., it is grounded in the interpretations of the researcher), most people automatically assume that the researcher him- or herself will manually analyze the data. As Tracy (2013) says, manual data analysis can sometimes resemble an arts and crafts project, including color coding, white boards, glue sticks, and vision boards. At its heart, manual coding involves sorting pieces of information in a 3D space. However, there is also computer assisted qualitative data analysis (CAQDS). In short, CAQDS involves using a software package that identifies patterns in your data set. Note that these programs don't actually analyze the data; their real benefit is in their ability to store, code, sort, and query your data (Tracy, 2013). Think of it like the "find" function of your word processing software; it helps you to locate elements in your text.

Step 2: Immerse Yourself in the Data

Next, you need to make sure you are very familiar with the entire data set. This involves reading and rereading the entire data set several times. This data familiarization stage is important even if you were directly involved in collecting the data so that you can orient yourself to the content and immerse yourself into the details provided in the data. After becoming familiar with the data, the researcher begins to code the data. **Coding** involves identifying and labeling features in the data that are relevant to addressing your research question (Clarke & Braun, 2016). We talked a bit about coding in content analysis, and you might remember that there are deductive and inductive coding schemes. **Deductive coding** involves using preexisting (usually from previously completed research) sets of codes and themes to see if they also describe your data well. **Inductive coding** does not involve preexisting codes and themes; rather, the codes and themes are entirely generated by the content of the data on hand. Deductive coding allows easy comparisons between the data you have collected and previous data while inductive coding is useful when there is not a lot of previous research on your topic or you don't want to be influenced by previous research on the topic. If you are coding deductively, then the preexisting list of codes and themes will guide you in the rest of your data coding process; essentially, you will try to duplicate what was done in previous research. If you are using inductive coding, then you will engage in the rest of the thematic analysis steps we describe.

You might also recall from the content analysis chapter that another important aspect of coding is to identify your **unit of analysis**. A unit of analysis is the part of data you will use in your coding. Each unit of analysis is a "case" to be coded. For example, if a participant answered an open-ended survey question to produce your data, you must decide which parts of what the participant wrote constitutes a "unit" for your coding process. You could opt to include the entire response as one "unit," you could treat each individual thought expressed in the response as a "unit," or you could even identify key words, such as adjectives to describe a product, as "units." Previous research on the topic as well as your specific research goals and limitations should inform the determination of units of analysis.

After identifying all units of analysis in your data set, you should code the data by labeling each unit of analysis with a descriptive label that identifies what is important about that unit of analysis for answering your research question. Clarke and Braun (2016) point out that, depending on the research project, codes may vary in level of interpretation and abstraction. Some codes are simply brief summaries of what a participant has said ("dislikes the schedule"), while others may point out more abstract concepts reflected in the data ("lack of trust in the process"). Coding is often an iterative process that requires going over and coding the data multiple times, refining the coding each time.

Step 3: Identify Themes

When using qualitative data, a researcher is looking for patterns. A theme is an identified pattern in the coding that provides information to address the research question. Themes are identified after the coding is complete by looking for meaningful patterns among the codes. Corbin and Strauss (2008) recommend engaging in constant comparisons when trying to identify themes. To engage in a constant comparison process, a researcher examines each code to see if it should be grouped together with other codes in a theme. If the code is similar enough to other codes, then it contributes to a theme with the similar codes. If the code does not seem to belong in a group with the codes already organized into themes, the code forms the basis of a new theme. This constant comparison process is continued until all codes are organized into themes. During the formation of themes, you should also make note of any piece of the data that could serve as a good example of that theme. These exemplars will be useful in both reporting your findings to help explain the meaning of your themes and to give your audience useful examples of the data.

If your research question was solely to describe communication, the identification of themes is sufficient to answer your research question. However, your research question might have sought to make a comparison. For example, your research question might have been something like "Are there differences in the perceptions of supervisors and frontline workers on the quality of internal communication?" In this case, you would do separate analyses based on the respondent's level in the organizational hierarchy. Ideally, you should conduct two different thematic analyses, one for each group. Separate analyses will allow for differing perspectives to emerge. If you seek themes that exist in the entire data set, important differences in perspective might be overlooked.

Finally, your research question might have sought to identify relationships between elements. Thus, you would seek to determine if there are relationships among the themes. To illustrate, Kopaneva (2019) was interested in how employees identify with organizational mission and vision statements. She identified 12 themes that emerged through her interviews with employees. However, she recognized that these individual themes could be organized into two overarching themes: Some of the individual themes served to drive employee identification with the mission, and other individual themes reflected restraining forces. The most important aspect of identifying relationships among your themes is to be able to tell the story of the data set so that you can explain to your audience what you found and why what you found is important, meaningful, and/or useful in addressing your strategic communication goals.

Step 4: Confirm the Analysis

Qualitative research is fundamentally different from quantitative research. Chapter 3 focused on measurement; in that chapter we talked about the scientific method and the importance of *reliability* (consistency of the measurement) and *validity* (accuracy of the measurement). However, these concepts are not useful ways to judge the value of qualitative research. Instead, strong qualitative research allows for **naturalistic generalization**, which means that readers of the research are able to apply the study's findings to their own situation (Tracy, 2013). In addition, it is important to make sure that the themes garnered from your analysis match the intended meaning of the data sources. A popular method of data confirmation is called **member checking**. Member checking involves presenting the process and results of your data analysis to some participants to make sure the results of the analysis are consistent with what they meant when the data were collected (Charmaz, 2006). Other forms of analysis confirmation may involve asking experts on your topic to review your data and your analysis to make sure you have fairly represented the data. Confirming your analysis helps to ensure the quality of your project and to build confidence in your findings.

After confirming the analysis, you are ready to report your data to your audience. Writing and presenting research reports will be discussed in Chapter 12. Although there are multiple approaches to the analysis of qualitative data that may be taken, we believe that communication professionals will find these thematic analysis steps described useful. Next, we turn to the analysis of quantitative data.

Analyzing Quantitative Data

Like qualitative data analysis, quantitative data analysis is largely about finding meaningful patterns among the data to address your research question. Unlike qualitative data analysis, quantitative data analysis examines patterns in the data using statistical tests. It is beyond the scope of this book to discuss and explain all statistical tests that may be used to address strategic communication questions. Table 11.1 provides a summary of some of the most common statistical tests used in strategic communication research. Because statistics involves its own language of sorts, Table 11.2 lists some of the most common symbols and abbreviations used when using statistics. In this section, we will discuss the foundational ideas behind common statistical reasoning and how they may be used in professional communication applications.

As we reiterated when talking about qualitative data analysis, the first step is to understand what your research question is asking: Is it seeking to describe communication, to compare groups on their communication, or to seek to relate communication to some other variable? All three types of research questions will start with descriptive statistics. However, there are additional techniques necessary for research questions centering on comparisons or relationships.

TABLE 11.1 Common Statistical Tests

t-test ANOVA MANOVA	All test to see if there are differences between groups (a nominal variable) on an interval or ratio variable (e.g., to see if men or women are more likely to be aggressive). t-tests can only compare dichotomous groups on one DV; ANOVA can compare more than two groups on one DV; MANOVA compares more than one independent variable n more than one dependent variable, looking for both interaction effects and main effects.
Chi-square 2	Tests to see if there are differences in groups but is used when both variables are nominal level (e.g., to see if there are more men or women are physically abusive versus psychologically abusive). Uses a cross-tabulation or contingency table to look for differences between expected and observed frequencies.
Correlation (Pearson correlation)	Tests to see the relationship between two interval or ratio variables. Positive correlations indicate the more of one variable, the more of the other. Negative correlations indicate the more of one variable, the less of another.
Multiple regression	Used to determine how much of one variable can be predicted by a set of other variables. For example, which of five possible independent variables (IVs) (amount of studying, amount of brown nosing, intelligence, luck, and class attendance) or combination of these five IVs best predict a class grade (the dependent variable)?
Factor analysis	Used to determine if there are underlying "structures" (called factors) in a measurement. For example, you develop a scale to measure love, and you do a factor analysis and determine there are two factors: passionate love and companionate love.

It may be useful to review the information about levels of measurement discussed in Chapter 3 as you move through this section.

Descriptive Statistics

Descriptive statistics provide general information about the data you have collected. Descriptive statistics are a way to provide a statistical summary of your data to your audience (Baxter & Babbie, 2004). The most basic type of descriptive statistical is a **frequency distribution**. A frequency distribution, which we introduced to you in the content analysis section, simply counts how often a value occurred among the

TABLE 11.2   Common Statistical Abbreviations and Symbols

Symbol	Meaning
α (alpha)	A measure of reliability. Should be at least .70 to be considered acceptable.
β (beta)	A standardized score in a regression equation. It allows you to compare the relative impact of independent variables on the dependent variable, the higher the beta, the more effect that variable has.
df	Degrees of freedom. It is an indicator of sample size, usually expressed as two numbers (1, 365). The higher the degree of freedom, the "easier" to find significant differences.
F	The statistic you compute when doing an ANOVA or MANOVA.
M	The mean, or average.
Mdn	The median, or value at the midpoint of the frequency distribution.
N	The number of objects/people in the sample.
n	The number of objects/people in a subset of the sample.
p	Probability value. Used as a measure of significance. p should be .05 or smaller (e.g., .01, .001) for a statistical test to be considered significant.
R	Indicator of the relationship between two variables (i.e., a correlation). Capital R is used for the relationship between multiple variables.
r^2	Coefficient of determination. In short, it tells you how much of the variance of one variable is explained by another variable (e.g., SAT scores explain 22% of college GPA).
SD	Standard deviation. A measure of the dispersion of the scores. The more spread out the scores, the higher the sd.
t	The statistic calculated for a t-test.
z	A standard score. If two measures have different scales (i.e., one is 1–5, and the other is 1–7), you can translate them into z scores so you can make a better comparison.

responses to an item. They are most useful for describing nominal data, or data that simply classifies information. For example, if you were collecting demographic data about your participants' relational status, then the frequency distribution will tell you how many (and what percentage) of your participants responded that they were single, engaged, married, divorced, or "other" in response to your question about relationship status. Frequency distributions not only provide a useful summary of the data, but they can also be used as a first step in helping you to organize your data for comparisons. If you wanted to compare your participants' responses to further questions by their relational status, you would use the information from the frequency distribution to know how to separate your responses into groups for single, engaged, married, divorced, and "other" participants.

If you have interval or ratio data, you should use a measure of central tendency as your descriptive statistic. Central tendency statistics give you information about the typical values in your data. There are three different measures of central tendency. The mode is the value that occurs most frequently among the responses to an item. As such, the mode is useful for all levels of measurement discussed in Chapter 3 (nominal, ordinal, interval, and ratio data). The mode is the only measure of central tendency that is useful for nominal data (such as the relationship status measure that we just discussed). However, if there are no responses repeated in your data, then there will be no mode. You can imagine this happening if you asked people to provide their age and none of your participants were the same age.

The median is the middle value among your responses. Because the median is identified as the middle value among the responses, it is useful in transforming data into two categories. For example, if you were to measure people's listening skills on an aptitude test with possible scores ranging from 1 to 10, the median would be the middle value among the scores you collected. If the median were 6, then you could group the participants who scored less than 6 as "low" in listening skills and all of those who scored 6 and higher as "high" in listening skills.

You are probably already familiar with the most common type of central tendency statistic, the mean. The mean is the mathematical average of the responses to a question. To calculate a mean, you add together all of the responses and then divide that number by the total number of responses you had. The mean can only be calculated for interval and ratio data. Remember when we advised you to always use the highest level of measurement you can? That is, if you can use a ratio measurement, you should; if you can't, the next best is interval, then ordinal, then nominal. We made this recommendation because the mean is used as the basis for almost all statistical tests. Being able to calculate the mean gives you much more statistical choice.

A measure of central tendency is only one type of descriptive statistic. A second important descriptive statistic is a measure of the dispersion of your data, or the range of the values of your data. Data with wide dispersion have values spread across a large range (think 1 to 100) while data with a narrower dispersion have values spread across a much small range (think 1 to 10). The simplest summary of data dispersion is the range. Range identifies the lowest value and the highest value in your data. Another useful indication of dispersion is the standard deviation. The standard deviation tells you about the variability in your data by indicating how close the values are to the mean. Smaller standard deviations indicate that most of the values in your data are closer to the mean; larger standard deviations indicate that the values in your data are more spread out from the mean. The more variation you have in your values, the larger the standard deviation will be. For example, if you measured how many hours your participants spend steaming videos, your average may be 2 hours per day. If your standard deviation was 10 minutes, then you would know that most of your participants spend about the same amount of time (around 2 hours per day) streaming videos. If your standard deviation was 1 hour, you would know that your participants differ from each other a great deal in the amount of time they spend steaming videos.

Differences Between Groups

If your research question seeks to compare groups, there are specific statistical techniques you need to use. If all of your data are nominal data, you must conduct a chi-square test for independence. The chi-square test tells you if the data is distributed into groups independently or if the groups are a significant association among the groups in your data (they are not independent). Imagine that you had collected data about the effectiveness of political advertisements and you wanted to see if the sex of your participants (male, female, other) was significantly associated with the political party affiliation of your participants (Democrat, Independent, Republican). A chi-square test would tell you if participant sex was related to participant political affiliation.

The data summaries provided by the descriptive statistics give an overall idea of the data, but even more information may be generated by statistical tests for the differences between groups. Often, a strategic communication research question will call for a comparison of some qualities by participant groups such as those based on sex, age, occupation, and so on. To address these questions, it is necessary to organize the responses by the desired grouping and compare the values of the data among the groups. Statistics that compare groups are testing not just to see if there is a difference among the groups, but rather to see if there is a **statistically significant difference** among the groups. A statistically significant result is one that is more likely than the result that would happen by chance. Statistical significance involves a standard known as the **p-value**, which represents the possibility that the relationship identified by the statistical test could occur by chance. Usually, a p-value of .05 (5%) is considered the standard for statistical significance.

Another common comparison between two groups is the **t-test**. A t-test is used to determine if there is a statistically significant difference in the means of two groups. For example, if you wanted to know if your female customers reported higher customer satisfaction than your male customers, you would use a t-test to compare the mean customer satisfaction scores for both groups. T-tests are a very useful analysis, but they are limited to comparisons between only two groups. If you wanted to see if there were statistically significant differences among the customer satisfaction scores for three or more groups (such as young adult customers, middle-aged customers, and senior citizen customers), then you would use a test known as **analysis of variance** (ANOVA). Analyses of variance can become larger as more variables are added to delineate groups and consider multiple outcome variables simultaneously and can grow into complex model testing.

Tests of Relationships

A third type of statistical comparison is based on seeking relationships between variables, often known as **correlation-based tests**.

The idea behind this set of tests it that the variables are influencing each other in real life and the tests indicated this influence exists when they are statistically significant. However, caution must be taken when applying this idea. It is possible for two variables to be significantly correlated without having an influence on each other, known as a **spurious correlation**. A spurious correlation may occur because of coincidence or, more likely, because of the influence of a third but unidentified variable. While spurious correlations can be fascinating and entertaining (go to tylervigen.com for some fun examples), they should not be used to inform strategic decision making. Careful attention to the previous research on a topic and the use of theory to inform research questions help protect against falling into the trap of making decisions based on spurious correlations.

Correlation-based tests are meant to compare relationships between interval and/or ratio-level data. Imagine you have a research question that asks, "What is the relationship between customer satisfaction and commitment to our brand?" To collect data, you have customers complete a survey that asks about how happy they are with your brand's customer service and asks about how committed they are to your brand. To answer your research question, you need to find out the relationship between customer satisfaction and brand commitment. One easy way to visualize this is through an XY graph (Figure 11.1 provides an example). Each individual respondent's score on customer satisfaction would be located along the X axis, and their score for brand commitment would be located on the Y axis—you then actually plot where the two meet. This is done for every single respondent you have, culminating in a graph with the same number of plot points as number of respondents in your study. You can then interpret the plot.

A **positive correlation** is one in which the values of the related variables move in the same increasing or decreasing direction. On our XY graph, it is when the imaginary line that connects the plot points you have made goes up and to the right, as it does in Figure 11.1. If two variables are positively correlated, the first variable will increase in value as the second variable also increases in value, *or* the first variable will decrease in value as the second variable also decreased in value.

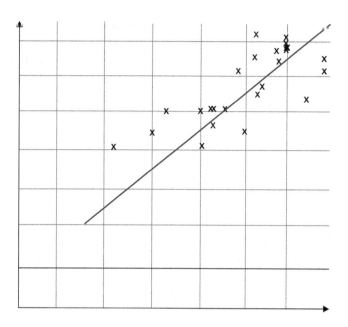

FIGURE 11.1 Example of an XY Graph

A **negative correlation** is one in which the related variables move in opposite directions of each other. On our XY graph, the imaginary line that connects the plot points would start high and move down and to the right. If two variables are negatively correlated, one variable is increasing in value while the other variable is decreasing in value. Examples of both positive and negative correlations were found by Landay, Harms, and Crede (2018) in their meta-analysis of the relationship between psychopathy and corporate leadership. In reviewing over 92 studies on psychopathy and leadership, Landay and colleagues (2018) found a significant positive correlation between psychopathic tendencies and leadership emergence. In other words, people who had greater psychopathic tendencies also were more likely to emerge as leaders in the corporate world. Landay and colleagues (2018) also found a significant negative correlation between psychopathic tendencies and leadership effectiveness. In other words, as level of leader psychopathy increased, level of leadership effectiveness decreased. So, if you think your boss is a psychopath and not very good at leadership, the data suggests you may be right!

Although the XY graph is a simple visual illustration of how we can determine correlations, in general researchers use a statistic called a **Pearson correlation** as a measure of the relationship between two variables. The resulting number of a Pearson correlation ranges from –1.0 to +1.0. Anything close to zero indicates that there is no significant relationship between the two variables. Scores approaching +1.0 indicate a strong, positive correlation. Scores approaching –1.0 indicate a strong, negative correlation. So, scores between .20 to .40 (whether positive or negative) can be interpreted as small to moderate relationships, scores between .40 and .70 can be considered moderate to substantial relationships, and scores higher than .70 are considered strong relationships.

Correlations are the basis of other relationship tests as well. Regression models are predictive tests that examine the influence of a variable or variables on another variable or group of variables. Like analysis of variance models, regression models can become complex. Regression models are useful in determining not just whether some variables influence others, but the relative strength of the influence of variables on others. For example, Mikkelson, Hesse, and Sloan (2017) wanted to test the influence of various aspects of the way that supervisors may communicate with employees (affection/involvement, dominance, formality, etc.) on a set of employee outcomes (job satisfaction, motivation, organizational commitment) and used regression modeling to do so. Mikkelson and colleagues (2017) were able to use regression to examine the relative influence of their supervisor communication variables on their employee outcomes variables and found that three supervisor communication variables (affection/involvement, similarity/depth, and composure) had the strongest influence on employee outcomes.

We have discussed the foundational ideas behind statistical reasoning that can be used to analyze quantitative data in strategic communication. We encourage you to explore more about statistical reasoning and tests that may be relevant to your specific research projects. One source is Wrench, Thomas-Maddox, Richmond, and McCroskey (2016), who describe more advanced statistical techniques. In addition, please see the *Publication Manual of the American Psychological Association*, seventh edition (American Psychological Association, 2019) for more information on how to report statistical tests.

Chapter Summary

This chapter has discussed foundational procedures for the analysis of qualitative and quantitative data. We discussed a process for the analysis of qualitative data known as thematic analysis. The steps for conducting a thematic analysis include organizing and preparing your data, immersing yourself in the data, identifying themes, and confirming the analysis. We also discussed several types of statistical tests used in the analysis of quantitative data. Descriptive statistics are fundamental for all types of research questions and include a frequency distribution, measures of central tendency, and measures of data distribution. We discussed statistical tests for significant differences among groups and relationships among variables.

PRACTICE ACTIVITIES

1. **Recognize variations in themes:** Collect approximately 10 objects that have something in common (e.g., 10 books, or 10 T-shirts, or 10 items in your refrigerator). Try to find at least three different ways you can classify the items. For example, you might classify them in terms of size, or color, or content, or any of many other ways. Consider what this means for thematic analysis and the importance of confirming the analysis.

2. **Practice thematic analysis:** For this activity, you can use qualitative data you may have collected as part of an activity you did earlier in the book. If you have not already collected qualitative data, you should go to Amazon.com and select a product with a large amount of customer reviews and use these reviews as your data. Formulate a research question you would like to address. Following the steps for thematic analysis described in this chapter, analyze your data to address your research question.

3. **Confirmation of thematic analysis:** Find a research article that uses thematic analysis of qualitative data. Identify key decisions the authors made at each step of thematic analysis. How do you think these deci-

sions affected the findings? Identify any steps the authors took in their thematic analysis that were different than the steps described in this chapter. Did they provide any evidence of confirming their themes?

4. **Interpret quantitative data analysis:** Find a research article that analyzes quantitative data. In your own words, explain the statistical tests that were performed and the findings derived from those tests.

5. **Practice basic statistics:** There is a small data set listed below. Which statistical analyses should you use to answer each research question? What are the answers to each research question?

   You have surveyed 25 people. The data are listed. Answer each of the research questions:

   RQ1: How positive are people toward Product X?

   RQ2: Do men or women view Product X more favorably?

   RQ3: Is there an interaction effect between sex and marital status on views of Product X?

   RQ4: What is the relationship between a person's religiosity and their views of Product X?

   Information about the data:

   Column A: Marital status

   　1 = Married

   　2 = Unmarried

   Column B: Sex

   　1 = Male

2 = Female

Columns C–F: Items measuring views of Product X

1 = Strongly disagree (very negative), 7 = Strongly agree (very positive)

Columns G–I: Religiosity

1 = not at all religious, 7 = very religious

M/D	Sex	Feel 1	Feel 2	Feel 3	Feel 4	Rel 1	Rel 2	Rel 3
1	2	7	6	5	6	7	6	7
1	2	6	5	6	6	6	7	6
2	2	6	4	4	6	5	4	4
2	2	5	4	4	4	5	5	4
1	1	7	6	5	6	7	6	7
1	1	7	7	6	7	6	6	6
2	1	4	5	5	5	7	6	5
1	2	3	3	3	4	4	6	5
1	2	7	6	7	6	6	5	5
2	1	6	6	6	6	7	7	6
2	1	5	6	6	7	7	7	7
2	1	4	4	4	4	4	4	4
1	2	5	5	6	6	6	6	5
1	2	2	4	3	3	4	4	5
1	2	4	4	5	4	5	5	5
2	1	6	6	6	6	7	6	7
2	1	7	7	7	6	6	6	7
1	1	6	6	6	5	7	6	7
1	1	4	5	4	5	5	5	5
2	2	5	5	5	6	5	5	6
2	2	4	4	5	3	5	5	5
2	2	5	6	5	5	7	7	7
2	1	2	2	3	2	4	4	4
2	1	4	4	5	4	5	5	5
2	1	6	6	6	5	6	7	6

Writing and Presenting the Research Report

In order to demonstrate communication competence, professional communicators must strive for both effectiveness and appropriateness. **Effectiveness** means achieving your goals. Accordingly, when seeking to communicate the results of your research, you need to explain what you did, what you found, and what it means so that you can demonstrate that you have met your research goals. **Appropriateness** refers to following standards and meeting expectations. An essential way to demonstrate appropriateness is to adapt your message to your audience. When it comes to writing and presenting the research, this means not only that you need to use language that your readers and listeners can understand, it also means that you need to follow the writing and speaking conventions for your audience. In this chapter, we will talk about the differences in how to present your research for an academic audience versus a professional audience. We will also provide some best practices for oral research reports, as well as advice for visual aids.

CHAPTER OUTLINE

◆ Writing the Academic Report

◆ Writing the Professional Report

◆ Presenting the Research

◆ Visual Aids

Writing the Academic Report

The best way to think about academic research is as an ongoing scholarly dialogue. When you are engaged in a dialogue, you need to use the language in which all of the participants are fluent—you shouldn't launch into Spanish if all of the participants are native speakers of English. We say this because the academic style can be considered a type of language that has its own rules, terms, and ways of understanding the world. In the academic discipline of communication, especially among those scholars who conduct the sorts of research that inform professional communication, the language that is used is that of the American Psychological Association (APA), which provides a specific structure for how to report primary research. We

TABLE 12.1 Sections of an Academic Paper Using APA Style

Section	Components
Title page	Page header
	Title
	Authors (in order of importance)
	Professional affiliations
Abstract	Summary of the research in 150–250 words
	Key words
Introduction	Introduction to the paper
	Research goal(s)
	Literature review and rationale
	Hypotheses and/or research questions
Method	Sample
	Procedure
	Instruments
Results	How results were calculated
	The answer(s) to the RQ(s)
	Support/failure to support H(s)
Discussion	Conclusions
	Implications
	Limitations
	Areas for future research
References	
Tables and figures	

will discuss each of the required sections of a research report using APA, providing not only the rules for how to report the study, but also why those rules exist. Table 12.1 provides an overview of the sections in a research paper using APA style.

First, APA style is very specific in terms of the format of the paper, including the layout and font. Standard paper sizes should be used—in North America the standard size is called "letter" and is 8 1/2 x 11 inches; most of the rest of the world uses a different standard called A4, which is 8.3 x 11.7 inches. All margins should be set at 1 inch, and the font should be 12-point Times New Roman. There should also be a **page header** at the top of every page, which includes what is a called a **running head** at the top left side of the paper, and the page number on the top right side of the paper. A running head is a short-ened version of the title of the paper, and it is in all capital letters.

The first section of the paper is the **title page**. Centered in the middle of the paper should be the title of the study, with the names of the authors and their professional affiliations immediately after the title. The titles of academic papers are often complex and involve both a main title and a subtitle. The main title should indicate not only the general topic of the study, but also the major variables used in the study. Very often, the main title is followed by a colon, after which some additional details are offered. Consider the following academic paper title:

Public Perceptions of Organizational Social Media Use:
A Uses and Gratifications Approach

The main title indicates that the two variables of concern are *organizational social media* and *public perceptions*. The subtitle indicates the name of the theory used to frame the research. Although the title isn't flashy, potential readers have a very clear sense of what the research is about without actually having to read the study.

The second part of an academic research paper appears on the second page. It is an **abstract**, or summary, of the research. An abstract should be between 150 and 250 words and should include the focus of the research, including the major variables of interest; the methods used, including an overview of the sample or partici-pants; the results of the study; and a summary of major conclusions.

Immediately after the abstract are between two and four **key words**. The purpose of the abstract is to allow people to get an overview of the study to determine whether they should invest the time and energy to read the entire study. The key words are used for indexing. Whenever you do an internet search, whether it is a search using a general database such as Google or a search using an academic database such as *Communication Source*, the way you find potential results is through the key terms associated with the report. In the case of the study on organizational social media provided earlier, the key terms would likely be *social media, organizational messages, public perceptions*, and *uses and gratifications theory*.

In APA style, the body of the paper begins on page 3 and includes four major sections: the literature review and rationale, the methods section, the results section, and the discussion section. The literature review and rationale section is usually not labeled. The literature review and rationale include four important subsections. First, the writer must provide readers with an **orientation to the problem**. What is the focus of the paper? Typically, this is achieved in just a few sentences. Second, the writer must provide the goal(s) for conducting the research. These goals should link the overall topic of the research to one of the overarching goals for conducting research. In Chapter 2, we described four general goals for conducting professional research: identifying opportunities, diagnosing problems, selecting a course of action, and evaluating the course of action. In an academic paper, these general goals are translated into specific goals. To illustrate, consider these sample goals:

> Given the centrality of communication and lack of evidence-based data in managing school crises, this study identified the challenges school districts experienced on social media and strategies they employ to address social media during crisis events. (Thompson et al., 2017, p. 9)

From this statement, it is clear that the general goal of this research was to diagnose problems, and the specific focus was on diagnosing challenges experienced by school districts during crises. Consider the goals of a second study:

> The present study seeks to provide some answers about the effectiveness of social media as a public relations tool by focusing on the gratifications sought by the public's use of organizational social media efforts, as well as the perceptions they have of organizations that use social media. (Dainton et al., 2014, p. 1)

In this case, the general goal is to evaluate a course of action, with a specific focus on organizational social media use.

The third part of the introduction section is the **literature review**. The literature review provides a synthesis of previous research on the topic. Although literature reviews may be organized by summarizing each published research article one at a time, this is not a preferred organizational scheme. Table 12.2 lists stronger ways of organizing a literature review. Crafting a thorough and articulate literature review is essential in academic research reports. This is where the writer establishes credibility; it demonstrates expertise in the topic of interest and shows the logic behind the purpose for the research itself.

Typically, the research questions (RQs) and/or hypotheses (Hs) appear in the literature review immediately following the previous research about the particular variables that appear in the RQ/H. When there are multiple RQs/Hs, each may be listed as the previous research on the topic has been summarized, or they may appear at the very end of the literature review. In essence, the literature review provides a justification for the specific RQs and Hs that have been formulated, so the conclusion of the literature review marks the end of the justification for the study.

TABLE 12.2   Ways of Organizing a Literature Review

Organizing Scheme	Examples
Historical	The history of organizations' use of social media.
Conceptual	First, what we know about organizational use of social media.
	Second, what we know about why people use social media.
	Third, what we know about public perceptions of organizations.
Theme based	Theme 1: Positive perceptions of organizational social media use.
	Theme 2: Negative perceptions of organizational social media use.
Methodological	Content analyses of organizational social media messages.
	Survey results of perceptions of these social media messages.

Immediately following the literature review is the **method section**, which is identified with a first-level heading (i.e., it is capitalized and centered). The method section describes in detail how the research was conducted. Remember that the scientific method requires precision and replicability. For this reason, it is important that the authors carefully and clearly describe how the research was conducted; if they have done so, subsequent researchers can emulate the methods used to provide evidence that supports (or refutes) the findings of the study. Also note that the method section is always written in past tense, since the research has already been conducted when you write the report.

There are typically three subsections in the method section. The first subsection identifies the **sample**. In the case of a textual analysis (e.g., social media analytics, Web analytics, content analysis, or A/B testing), the universe of texts is described. In the case of a survey, focus group, or experiment, the population is described. Regardless of the method, the researchers then report the sampling frame: the number and nature of the texts/participants, as well as the sampling method used (e.g., random, nonrandom convenience, etc.).

The second subsection is called **procedure**. This section describes the overarching method used (i.e., textual analysis, survey, or experiment) and information about the ethical conduct of the study. If the method was a textual analysis, the procedure section will also include the code book (the coding scheme, coding procedures, and decision rules). If the method was a survey, the procedure section includes the type of survey (paper or online questionnaire, interview, or focus group), the time and location of the survey, and instructions given to the participants. If the method was an experiment, the procedures section describes the experimental design.

The final subsection is called **instrumentation**, and it includes a description of the materials, measures, equipment, or stimuli used in your study. If you are using existing measures or methods, make sure to cite the source that describes the development of the measures/method, evidence for the reliability and validity of the measure/method when it was developed, as well as evidence of reliability and validity in your study. If you have created a new measure or method, then carefully describe how you established reliability and validity.

The method section describes what you did; the next major section of an academic research report is what you found out. Just like with the method section, the **results section** is labeled using a first-level heading. In this section you focus on each individual RQ or H and identify what you determined to be the answer to your question(s) or the support/lack of support for your hypothesis(es), including the techniques used to determine these findings. In the case of qualitative research, your results will typically take the form of themes, which are supported by pulling examples or quotes from your data. In the case of quantitative research, you should describe the statistics used and the results of the statistics. This section should be written so that the reader knows exactly what the answer to research question is, or, in the case of a hypothesis, the extent to which the hypothesis has been supported or failed to receive support.

The final major section of an academic research report is the **discussion section**. The goal of the discussion section is to make sense of the results and to demonstrate how the results of the study contribute to the scholarly dialogue. Researchers should be careful to differentiate between conclusions and implications. **Conclusions** refer to the actual results of the study. **Implications** answer the "so what" question: Why are these results important? One of the essential ways of developing a strong discussion section is to link your conclusions and implications back to the literature you reviewed earlier in your report. To what extent do your results add to, support, or contradict previous findings? Why? How have you added to the knowledge base about the variables you studied?

The final part of the discussion section is a focus on the limitations of your study and areas for future research. There are limitations to every research endeavor. Perhaps the sample is relatively small or is skewed in some way. Your measures might be less reliable than you had anticipated. There may have been some potential threats to internal validity. In short, you should take a critical look at your own research and acknowledge the areas that were not as strong as they might have been. This, too, provides evidence of your expertise. As for areas for future research, we remind you again that all academic research serves as part of the scholarly dialogue about a particular topic. As such, your report should provide some potential ways that dialogue might continue.

Although the discussion section is the last formal section of the paper, APA style requires that immediately following the conclusion to the paper, and starting on the top of the next page, all references that were used in the research should be listed alphabetically. Once again, a first-level heading is used (i.e., the word "References" is centered). Immediately following the references are any tables, charts, or figures. If the research is eventually published, these items will be placed in the text where they belong.

Writing the Professional Report

If a research report is being written for a professional audience, the required structure is a bit different. Certainly, the researcher needs to establish expertise in the writing of the report, but the means

TABLE 12.3 Sections of a Professional Research Report

Section	Components
Executive summary	Background to the problem
	Objectives of the research
	Method of data collection and analysis
	Summary of findings
	Recommendations
Table of contents	
Introduction and problem statement	Background of the problem
	Authorization information
	Research objective(s)
Methodology	Research design
	Research method
Findings	
Conclusions and recommendations	Interpretation of the findings
	Recommendations
	SMART goals
References	
Appendices	Copies of the survey/interview protocol/focus group script
	Details of statistical analyses
	Charts/graphs/figures

for establishing expertise is quite different because academics and professionals "speak" different languages and have different goals for conducting the research. As you might expect, the specific parts needed in a professional research report and the preferred manner of presenting the report might differ depending on the norms for reports for a specific industry or organization. For example, some organizations might prefer that research reports be presented as a series of annotated PowerPoint slides while others will prefer a long-form written report format. We will discuss common aspects of professional reports for communication professionals, but you should always confirm the specific report expectations for each research project. Table 12.3 summarizes the sections of a professional research report.

You will notice that there are some sections that are the same in both professional and academic research reports; both include sections that describe what the researchers did and what they found out as a result of the research. However, the names of the sections are slightly different ("Method versus Methodology," "Results versus Findings") and the way the sections are written is slightly different as well. Academic reports tend to use quite a bit of methodological and statistical terms because the audience (other academics) use the same technical terms. However, when writing professional reports of method and findings you should avoid using too many technical terms about methods and analysis because it is unlikely that the professionals reading the report will all understand that type of jargon.

Similarly, both academic and professional reports put references and tables, charts, and figures at the end of the report (in the case of professional research, these elements are a part of the appendix). One difference is that a copy of the survey, interview protocol, or focus group script is usually included in the appendix of a professional report, whereas they usually don't appear in in an academic report.

One of the most significant elements of a professional research report is the **executive summary**. As the title implies, an executive summary is written so that busy executives can understand the gist of the report without having to read the entire report. The executive summary is much more than the type of abstract that is used in academic research. A general rule of thumb is that the length of the executive summary should be about 10% of the length of the final report. That means the executive summary should be a single page long for a 10-page report, but that it should be 10 pages long for a 100-page report.

The components of an executive summary include the background of the professional situation that necessitated conducting the research, the objectives for the research, the methods used for data collection and analysis, the key findings, and recommendations for action. Indeed, because the ultimate purpose for conducting professional research is to inform decision making, the recommendations themselves should be fully described in the executive summary; they should be written out in their entirety, with a justification made for each recommendation. Obviously, although it appears first in the report, the executive summary can only be written after the rest of the report has been completed.

A second difference between an academic research report and a professional research report is in the justification for the research. The beginning of an academic paper is a literature review because previous research is used as the foundation for a scholarly dialogue. The professional research report, however, starts with a **problem statement**, which is a description of the problem that necessitated the research in the first place. Remember from Chapter 2 that establishing your research objective is an essential part of the research process. These elements should appear in the professional report. Specifically, the problem statement section should include a description of the nature of the problem, a summary of any meetings or discussions that centered on the problem, and any preliminary or secondary research that was used to inform the research project. Authorization information is also included in this section. **Authorization** involves the scope and timing of the research: who will conduct the research, who has approved the research, what the research will and will not entail, and the specific deadline for the final report. Finally, the problem statement should include a clear statement of objectives for the research.

The final difference between academic and professional research reports is in the final section. Because the goal of an academic report is to contribute to the scholarly dialogue, the discussion section links the conclusions and implications of the study to previously published research. However, the goal of a professional report is to assist with decision making. For this reason, the conclusion and recommendations section of the professional research report should include how the results have achieved the objectives of the research. What did the research find, and how does it address the problem that prompted the research? More importantly, what recommendations does the researcher make vis à vis the professional problem? What are the justifications for those recommendations? This section is where the professional researcher establishes expertise. Translating research results to recommended organizational actions, especially in terms of SMART goals, is the ultimate goal of the professional research report.

Presenting the Research

Whether you are conducting research to meet academic or professional goals, there is a good chance that you may need to give an oral presentation to highlight your research project. As we discussed at the beginning of the chapter, an important consideration in skillful communication is to adapt to your audience. This is particularly true for oral presentations; we listen quite differently than we read, which requires organizing your material differently than you would for a written report. In general, successful oral research presentations simplify the content and use a conversational style. Moreover, they include clear supporting visual aids that enhance the presentation.

First, we want to reiterate that the goal of an oral presentation is not to share the entire research report but to highlight only key elements of that report. Remember that audience members will likely receive a copy of the final report so that they can review the details on their own time. An additional consideration is that the goal of a research presentation is likely to be a hybrid between an informative and a persuasive presentation. On the one hand, most of the audience members will know very little about what you did and why you did it, making the presentation resemble a typical informative presentation in structure. However, the goal of professional research is ultimately to guide decision making; as such, you are simultaneously seeking to convince audience members of the value that your research data provide in guiding the problem-solving process.

Part of presenting yourself as an expert on the topic is the careful selection of content. Although the level of detail will vary depending on the expertise of your audience, we recommend focusing on the following content in a research presentation:

◆ First, you should provide an overview of the need for the research, providing the professional context that necessitated conducting the research.

◆ Second, the objectives should be specified.

◆ Third, you should identify the overarching method used, including an overview of the nature of the sample.

◆ Fourth, you should highlight key results, making sure to avoid statistical jargon unless the audience members will understand that jargon or are in a position to judge the quality of the research.

◆ Finally, you should focus on the recommendations that emerge from the research, allowing time for questions about those recommendations.

In addition to the careful selection of content, you need to present your information with confidence in your knowledge of what was done, why it was done, what was found, and what the results mean. An analogy might be the way you explain something you know very well to someone else, like the plot of your favorite book or film, or the recipe for your favorite dish. Rather than writing a script and seeking to memorize it, we encourage you instead to practice simply explaining the research to a friend or colleague who will not be a part of your formal audience. During these practice efforts, encourage people to interrupt and ask questions, as that will most closely simulate what you might expect in a professional presentation.

There are two additional concerns associated with delivery. The first is your speaking rate. If you listen to podcasts or watch TED Talks, the speaking rate is typically quite high: Podcasters typically speak at 150 to 160 words per minute, and the average Ted Talk is at 173 words per minute (Barnard, 2018). However, the ideal speaking rate for a formal presentation should be about 100 to 150 words per minute, which is considerably slower than the speed of normal conversation (Barnard, 2018). Think about it this way: When people need to process complicated information, they need more time to process that information. Listeners often lack the ability or motivation to put effort into understanding the information being presented, placing the onus on the speaker to make it as easy as possible for the listener.

A second major issue in professional research reports is the tendency for audience members to multitask during the presentation. Too often, professionals send e-mails and respond to texts during meetings because they believe that it is the only way to get work done in an era of back-to-back meetings. Yet, the research is consistent: There is no such thing as multitasking. Instead, what happens is that people switch from one task to another very rapidly, resulting in the exertion of increased cognitive energy, as well as an increased likelihood of making mistakes (Napier, 2014). Interestingly, people tend to multitask because of an individual propensity to do so rather than because of any objective measure of busyness. Fuller, Shikaloff, Cullinan, and Harmon (2018) examined the number of hours that managers spent in meetings per week and found no relationship between hours spent in meetings and the likelihood of multitasking during meetings. Some very busy people refrain from multitasking, and others do not. Nevertheless, given the ubiquity of multitasking in meetings, an effective research presentation should be planned in a way to combat multitasking. Don't hand out physical copies of the report while you are speaking; it only tempts people to read rather than listen. Don't put up slides with too much text or elaborate charts or graphs, as people will stop listening to look at that information. In short, set the stage so that people can actually *hear* what you have to say.

Visual Aids

Visual aids can help make sense of complex information and are useful for both the written and oral report. Written reports benefit from the use of tables, charts, and graphs. Figure 12.1 provides examples of these forms of visual aids. A **table** summarizes information using

Table Showing Percentage of Adults Who Use Social Media Platforms by Age				
	18–29	**30–49**	**50–64**	**Over 65**
Facebook	79%	79%	68%	46%
Instagram	67%	47%	23%	8%
Twitter	38%	26%	17%	7%
LinkedIn	28%	37%	24%	11%

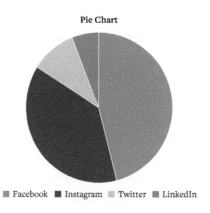

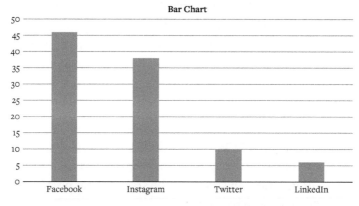

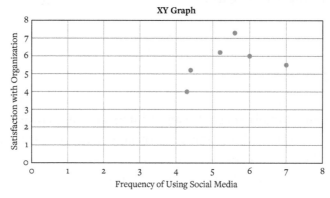

FIGURE 12.1   Forms of Visual Aids

FIGURE 12.1   Forms of Visual Aids *(Continued)*

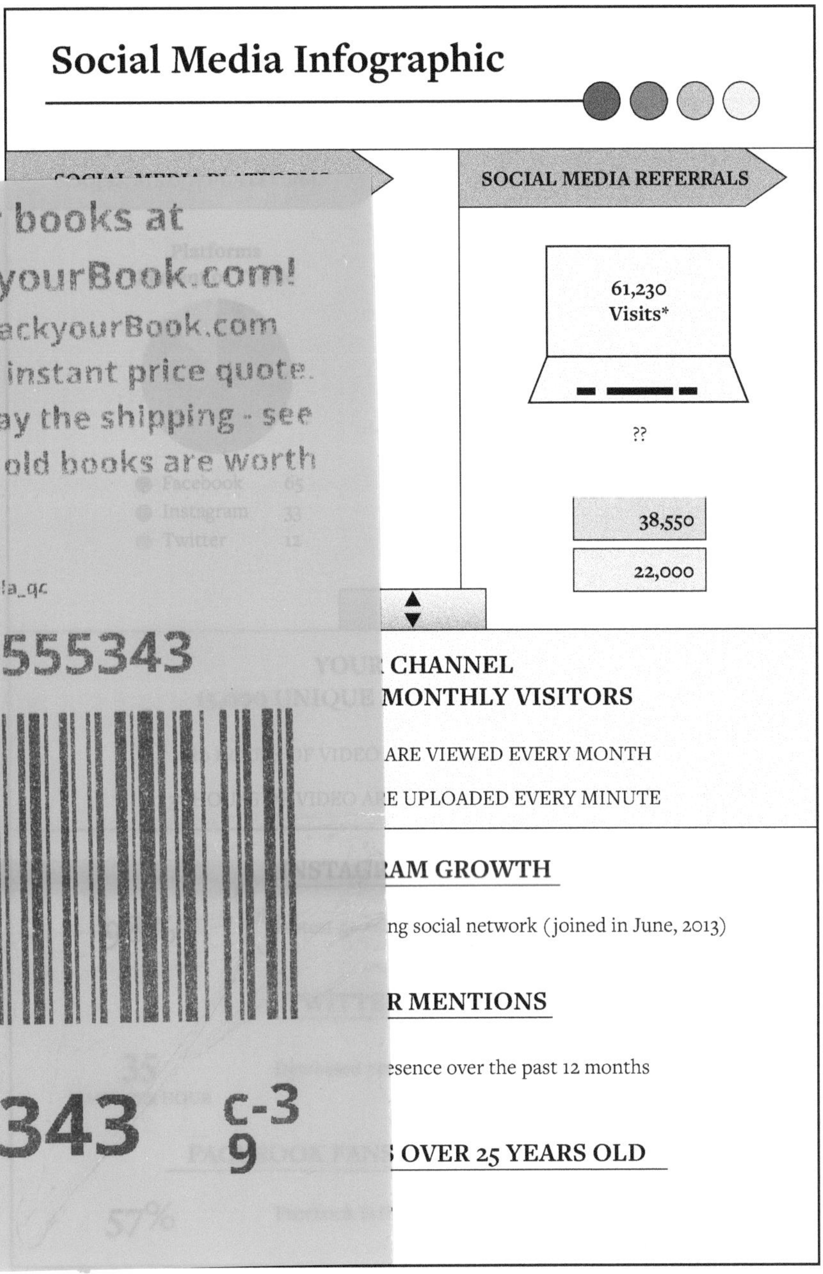

Social Media Infographic

SOCIAL MEDIA PLATFORMS		SOCIAL MEDIA REFERRALS

61,230
Visits*

??

38,550

22,000

CHANNEL

MONTHLY VISITORS

ARE VIEWED EVERY MONTH

UPLOADED EVERY MINUTE

AM GROWTH

ng social network (joined in June, 2013)

R MENTIONS

esence over the past 12 months

OVER 25 YEARS OLD

columns and rows. It is most useful for presenting numerical information. A **chart** translates numerical information into visual form. The most common form of charts are pie charts and bar charts. **Pie charts** show the composition of elements for a nominal variable, such as the percent of an organization's social media traffic by various social media platforms. Although they can be visually interesting, they have been criticized for being less than precise and difficult to interpret (Few, 2007). A **bar chart** demonstrates the same information: The values of nominal data. However, they can be crafted in a way that is much easier for the average viewer to interpret.

A final type of visual aid is a graph. Of interest, all charts are a type of graph, but not all graphs are charts. A **graph** is a mathematical diagram that illustrates the relationship between two variables. The most common form of a graph is an **XY graph**, which has the value of the dependent variable along the vertical axis and the value of the independent variable along the horizontal access. Correlations (see Chapter 11) are based on the relationship that is evident when plotting data on an XY graph. Graphs are particularly useful for showing trends over time. Finally, although rarely used in research reports themselves, infographics are an increasingly popular way to portray data. An **infographic** is a collection of images, charts, and graphs that are designed to communicate complex information in a simple fashion. We include samples of these forms of visual aids in Figure 12.1 (Pew Research Center, 2019).

Pie charts, bar charts, and graphs are also useful visual aids when giving an oral presentation, as they can be imported into Power-Point or other forms of dynamic presentation software. However, we encourage you to follow best practices when putting together your presentation (Verderber et al., 2018). These tips include the following:

◆ Use the same font throughout the presentation. Sans serif fonts are easier to read, text should be at 30-point minimum, and avoid all caps. Keep the size of the font in mind with charts and graphs in particular.

◆ Use a simple slide format, preferably with a light background and dark text. Dark backgrounds with light text can be challenging to read when projected onto a screen in a room that is brightly lit.

◆ Use limited text and visuals. Limit the number of words on a slide, using key words or phrases rather than full sentences. A general rule of thumb is no more than five words per line of text, five lines of text per slide, and five text-heavy slides in a row.

◆ Show one bullet point at a time to keep the audience focused. Avoid distracting transitions.

Chapter Summary

In this chapter, we provided an overview about reporting your research project. We talked about the differences between an academic research paper and a professional research paper. Typically, an academic research paper is written to contribute to the scholarly dialogue about a particular topic. As such, the researcher should establish credibility by demonstrating an understanding of previous research on the topic and should clearly articulate the contributions made to that understanding by the research that she or he has conducted. Professional research is undertaken as a part of the decision-making process, however. For that reason, technical jargon should be avoided. Expertise is established by constructing detailed recommendations grounded in the research findings. For these reasons, the formats for writing the research report vary based on the intended audience. After providing information about the structure of written reports, we provided some guidelines for the oral presentation of research. We concluded the chapter with best practices for the use of visual aids in written and oral research presentations.

PRACTICE ACTIVITIES

1. **Identifying the parts of a study:** Find a current academic research study and identify the following elements:

   a. The citation for the study in APA format

    b. The orientation to the problem

    c. The goal(s) of the study

    d. The major concepts or variables in the study

    e. The RQ(s)/H(s)

    f. The method used

    g. The nature of the sample and the sampling procedure

    h. Evidence for reliability and validity

    i. The techniques used to answer the RQ(s)/test the hypothesis(es)

    j. The answer to the RQs and/or the extent to which the hypothesis(es) were supported

    k. Implications of the research

    l. Limitations of the research

    m. Areas for future research

2. **Researching professional report formats:** Search online for three examples of professional research reports. Identify how the formats for these research reports differ from each other and the degree to which the reports match the parts of a research report described in this chapter (you can use Table 12.3 as a guide). What do you see as the strengths and weaknesses of the professional report formats you examined?

3. **Academic versus professional reports:** Use a current academic study as the foundation for a professional report. That is, use the information in the academic article to create a professional report, using the style of professional research reports.

4. **Research presentation:** Prepare and deliver a 15-minute presentation describing a research article using the techniques for described in this chapter.

5. **Pop culture version of research:** Write a "translation" paper. That is, using an academic research article, write a popular culture article or blog that describes the results of the study using everyday language. In doing so, create an infographic using some element of the study.

Glossary

@ mentions The number of times an organization, brand, product, or service is mentioned on social media using the @ symbol. An indicator of engagement.

A/B testing A type of experiment that involves testing to see which of two options has the stronger or better effect.

Absolute frequency The ideal way of measuring how often someone does something, it asks people to fill in a number representing the number of hours, times, days, and so on they engage in the behavior. A ratio measurement.

Abstract A summary of the research that appears before an academic research paper. Typically, it is between 150 and 250 words long.

Advertising Value Equivalency (AVE) A measure that seeks to quantify the benefit to a client from a public relations campaign.

Advocacy when social media followers provide recommendations or positive reviews of an organization, brand, or its products and services.

Amplification rate The ratio of shares per post as compared to the overall number of viewers. An indicator of engagement.

Analysis of variance (ANOVA) Statistical tests to determine if the means for three or more groups are significantly different.

Anonymity There is no way to connect research data to an individual participant.

Applause rate The number of approvals (e.g., likes, favorites) a post receives in proportion to the total number of followers. A measure of engagement.

Application programming interface (API) A structured channel of access to an application. All social media platforms provide an API that allows users to identify data associated with their account.

Applied research Research conducted to solve a real-world problem.

Appropriateness Following standards and meeting expectations when presenting research.

Assent A child's verbal agreement to take part in a research study.

Audience growth rate The change in the number of followers of an organization's social media channels. A measure of exposure.

Audience insight Information about who the audience is and how they behave.

Authorization The section of a professional research report that indicates the scope and timing of the research: who will conduct the research, who has approved the research, what the research will and will not entail, and the specific deadline for the final report.

Average engagement rate The number of engagement actions (e.g., likes, favorites, shares, comments) a post receives in proportion to the total number of followers.

Bar chart A visual aid that demonstrates the values of nominal data. Preferable to pie charts.

Basic research Research conducted to create or refine a theory.

Belmont Report Summarizes the ethical guidelines for research involving humans. It is the core of the U.S. Department of Health and Human Services regulations for the treatment of research participants.

Beneficence The ethical guideline that researchers must maximize the benefits to participants and minimize risks of harm.

Bounce rate The percentage of visitors who click on a link in a post but who quickly leave the page when they land on it without taking any further action. A measure of preference.

Census Research that includes all members of a population or all messages in a universe.

Central tendency statistics Statistics that provide information about the typical values in the data.

Channel insight Information about which social media channels drive visitors to a website.

Chart A visual aid that translates numerical information into visual form.

Chi-square test for independence Statistical test to determine independence among nominal groups.

Chronological order Putting your qualitative data in the order in which you collected it.

Click-through rate How often people click on a "call to action" link (e.g., subscription link, contact the organization link, etc.). A measure of preference.

Closed-ended questions Survey and poll items that include both the question and the possible responses from a pre-set list for the respondent to use to represent their answer.

Cluster random sampling A probability sampling technique that involves placing the population into groups known as clusters. Rather than individually selecting individuals for the study, the groups or clusters are randomly selected.

Code book A document that includes the coding scheme, coding procedures, and decision rules.

Code of conduct Guidelines for action that provide a way to handle the typical dilemmas faced in a profession.

Coding procedures An explicit set of policies about which types of content should be placed into which categories. Typically involve formal definitions and examples.

Coding scheme The categories used to classify messages.

Coding The process of identifying and labeling features in the data that are relevant to addressing your research question.

Cohort longitudinal survey Survey design in which the survey is administered multiple times to a sample with inclusion criteria that distinguish an unchanging group of potential participants.

Common Rule A set of rules and procedures for studying human participants that governs research conducted by U.S. federal agencies and at all American universities.

Communication audit An examination of an organization's communication environment, including communication between organizational members, communication between the organization and stakeholders, and the cultural, legal, and economic conditions in which the organization operates.

Compare A type of research question that seeks to determine if there are differences between groups.

Competitive analysis A type of latent content analysis that refers to conducting a content analysis both for one's own organization as well as for a competitor. In this way, professional communicators can benchmark how well they are doing relative to competitors.

Complete observer role When it is clear that the researcher is not participating in the activities under investigation.

Complete participant role The people being observed believe that the researcher is simply another person taking part in the activities under observation.

Concept An agreed-on aspect of reality.

Conceptual definition A precise description of the concept.

Conceptual fit How well the operational definition matches the conceptual definition.

Conclusions and recommendations The final section of a professional research report that identifies what the research found, how the findings address the problem that prompted the research, and specific recommendations that have emerged from the research.

Conclusions The actual results of an academic study.

Confidence interval Usually expressed in a percentage, it is an indicator of how likely the results from your sample are likely to match the results if you studied the entire population. The goal is to achieve at least a 95% confidence interval.

Confidentiality The researcher does have identifying information about the participants, but they promise not to share it.

Confounding variables Variables that are related to the independent variable but are not a part of the study.

Constant A concept that does not vary or take on more than one value in the research project.

Constant comparison process A process in which each code is examined to determine if it should be grouped together with other codes in an existing theme or form the basis of a new theme.

Construct validity Comparing the measurement of a concept to other measurements of that concept that have already been shown to be valid.

Content analysis An objective research method that is focused on the content, nature, or structure of messages.

Content analysis A research method that is focused on the content, nature, or structure of messages.

Content assessment When conducting a content audit, it is a determination of the extent to which the content is meeting strategic goals.

Content audit A method for professional communicators to identify and evaluate the nature of an organization's owned media.

Content inventory The first step of a content audit, it involves creating a complete and thorough description of all content being reviewed.

Control group The group of participants who experiences no change. They either maintain the standard experience of the independent variable, a placebo, or have no experience with the independent variable at all.

Control over additional influences The researcher's ability to ensure there are no extraneous or confounding variables in the experiment.

Convenience sampling A nonprobability sampling technique that creates a sample from the most readily available members of the population.

Conversation rate The ratio of comments per post in proportion to the number of followers. A measure of engagement.

Conversion A social media metric that demonstrates the effectiveness of social media content.

Conversion rate The number of visitors who click on a link on a post and then take action on the page as compared to the page's total number of visitors. A measure of engagement.

Correlation-based test A statistical comparison of the relationship between the movement of variable values.

Cost per click The amount paid per individual click on sponsored social media content. A measure of preference.

Count A single number as a metric in Web analytics, such as number of visits or number of sales.

Criterion validity A validity assessment that involves determining how well the scores of a measurement predict the scores on another measurement.

Cross-sectional survey A survey collected at just one time.

Customer satisfaction score A social media metric that identifies what customers think or feel about your organization, brand, product, or service. A measure of advocacy.

Dashboard A single digital interface that displays a variety of distinct social media metrics in order to provide a coherent report of social media activity.

Data Information. Might be quantitative (numbers) or qualitative (words or themes).

Data fabrication When a researcher creates some or all data reported in a research study.

Data falsification Changing or omitting data in order to achieve desired results.

Data protection In order to make sure that research participants are not subjected to any risk, data must be stored in a secure location, and data should be deleted or destroyed at the conclusion of the study.

Debriefing If the research process includes any deception of the participants, researchers are required to discuss the true nature of the study to the participants at the end of the research experience.

Decisional impairment Potential research participants who do not have the mental capacity to make the decision to take part in research. The Common Rule requires these people to be safeguarded.

Decision rules A set of rules for where content should be placed in the case of uncertainty.

Deductive coding A coding process using a preexisting set of codes and themes to see if they also describe your data well.

Deductive coding scheme A coding scheme that has been previously developed and used.

Dependent variable The "effect" variable in a cause-effect relationship.

Describe A type of research question that seeks to identify a current state or condition.

Descriptive statistics Statistics that provide general information about the data.

Digital data analytics A research method that involves examining digital data to make strategic decisions. There are three types of digital data analytics: social media analytics, Web analytics, and data mining.

Directional hypothesis A prediction of the exact nature of the relationship between two variables.

Direct observations The focus is on observing actual behavior.

Discussion section The final part of an academic research report. The goals are to draw conclusions based on the research and link the results to existing understanding of the issue. It should also include a description of any limitations of the research and areas for future research.

Disguised observations When the people being observed are not aware that they are being observed.

Dispersion The range of values in the data.

Effectiveness Achieving your goals for presenting research.

Empirical Verifiable by observation rather than by logic.

Ending questions Questions that wrap up the interview.

Engagement A social media metric that demonstrates how the audience is interacting with social media content.

Environmental scanning The process of monitoring, interpreting, and responding to emerging social, political, organizational, and industry trends.

Equivalent Categories in a coding scheme must operate at the same level of abstraction.

Ethnography A type of observation that involves an in-depth analysis of the communication practices of particular communities or contexts.

Evaluation In the RRIE model, determining whether the objectives were achieved.

Executive report The beginning of a professional research report. It should include the background of the professional situation that necessitated conducting the research; the objectives for the research; the methods used for data collection and analysis; the key findings; and recommendations for action.

Exemplar A part of the data that serves as a representative example of a theme.

Exempt Research that does not require explicit informed consent.

Exhaustive Categories in a coding scheme must be able to capture every unit that is coded.

Exhaustive response categories Response options that capture all possible responses to the question.

Experiment A research method in which the researcher carefully controls the situation and tests to see how changes in one variable might influence changes in another variable.

Experimenter bias When a researcher subconsciously exhibits a preference for value of the independent variable.

Expert jury validity A validity assessment that involves a panel of experts reviewing the measurement and deciding how well they think it will accurately measure the variable it is meant to measure.

Exposure The extent to which an audience has encountered social media content.

External validity The extent to which the results of an experiment will hold true in other environments, other people, and over time.

Extraneous variable A variable that is not a part of the study that has the potential to affect the results of the study. Potential extraneous variables can be associated with the situation, the participants, or the researchers.

Face-to-face survey A survey administered to the participant in person.

Face validity A validity assessment that involves the researcher reviewing the measurement and comparing it to the conceptual definition of the variable being measured to see if the measurement is likely to accurately access the variable.

Face-to-face interviews an interview conducted in person

Field experiment An experiment that takes place in an environment that is natural to the participants.

Field notes Detailed notes that a researcher writes either during or immediately after the observation.

Fixed sum scale A measurement that gives respondents a set number of points to distribute among options, which provides a ratio measurement of preference.

Focus group interview A research method in which multiple participants have a conversation responding to questions developed by the researcher.

Forced ranking scale A measurement that asks people to rank a set number of options; an ordinal scale.

Formal research Systematic collection of information.

Frequency distribution A count of how often a value occurred among the responses to an item.

Frequency scale A type of measurement that asks people how often they engage in a particular behavior in relative terms (e.g., almost never, rarely, sometimes, often, almost always).

Frequency table A chart that identifies each category and the frequency with which content was assigned to that category.

Full experiment The design allows for both manipulation and control and therefore minimizes threats to internal validity.

Goal Broad statements of organizational intent.

Graph A diagram that illustrates the relationship between two variables.

Guideline Statements of action that do not have legal force.

Hawthorne effect Named after observational research in the 1930s, the tendency for people being observed to alter their behavior because they are being observed.

HTTP cookie A small piece of data that is placed on a user's computer by the browser that they are using (also called a Web cookie, a browser cookie, or an internet cookie).

Human data collection The use of trained researchers to observe interaction.

Hypothesis A prediction about the relationship between two factors.

Impact A measurement for the direct effect of a social media message, campaign, or program.

Implementation In the RPIE model, putting the plan into action.

Implications The answer to the "so what" question; why are these results important?

Impressions The number of people who have viewed a social media post. A measure of exposure.

Incentive A form of "payment" to motivate people to complete a survey or take part in research.

Independent variable The "cause" variable in a cause-effect relationship.

Indirect observations Research that centers on the symptoms or effects of the behavior.

Individual interview A one-on-one conversation between the participant and the researcher about the research topic.

Inductive coding A coding process in which codes and themes are entirely generated by the content of the data on hand.

Inductive coding scheme A coding scheme that is developed after an analysis of the texts.

Infographic A collection of images and charts that are designed to communicate complex information in a simple fashion.

Informal research Collection of information involving little control and is highly subjective.

Informed consent Research participants must be presented with sufficient information about the study that they voluntarily agree to take part in.

Institutional Review Board (IRB) The IRB is responsible for approving and monitoring all research that is conducted at an institution that receives U.S. federal funds, either directly or indirectly. Its charge is to make certain that the guidelines set forth in the Belmont Report are followed.

Instrumentation In a research report, description of the materials, measures, equipment or stimuli used in a study.

Intercoder reliability A reliability assessment used when multiple people assess data to ensure a good match between their assessments.

Internal communication A professional function with a goal of facilitating effective communication among organizational members.

Internal reliability A reliability assessment testing whether multiple items used to measure one variable are being answered consistently enough so that all of the items can be considered to be appropriately contributing to the measurement of the variable.

Internal validity The likelihood that any changes in the dependent variable are actually caused by the independent variable.

Interval measurement A level of measurement that allows for rank ordering with the assumption of equal distance between points on the ranking scale.

Interview A formal research method that involves a systematic conversation between the participant and the researcher that is recorded for the purposes of gathering data.

Introductory question Question(s) that are the first to get the participants thinking about the interview topic.

Judgmental sampling A nonprobability sampling technique, also known as purposive sampling, in which a specific group of people is chosen for your sample because of some information you know about them.

Justice The element of the Belmont Report that focuses on the balance of benefit and harm across groups of people.

Key questions The most important questions in the interview.

Keyword insight An analysis of the search terms that drive people to a website.

Key words In an academic paper, a list of three or four terms that are essential to the research project. Appears after the abstract; used for indexing.

Laboratory experiment An experiment that takes place in a research setting. Research participants are brought to a location that is unfamiliar to them that is set up with the tools for the experiment.

Latent content Content that requires interpretation on the part of the researcher.

Likert scale A type of closed-ended question that makes a statement and asks respondents their level of agreement to the statement. Designed to measure attitudes.

Likes The number of likes/favorites a post receives. A measure of engagement.

Literature review A synthesis of previous research on the topic that is a part of an academic research report.

Longitudinal research The ability to study an issue over a period of time.

Longitudinal survey Survey design that collects data at multiple points in time with the goal of comparing trends in your data over time.

Machine learning Algorithms a computer uses in order to improve its performance on a task. Used for supervised and unsupervised computer-assisted coding.

Mail survey A survey that is sent to the participant via the postal service.

Manifest content The observable words, phrases, or images that appear in a text.

Manipulation of the independent variable The researcher's ability to determine the levels of the independent variable that participants are exposed to.

Margin of error How much the results from using a sample are likely to vary from the results of the population.

Marketing communications The development of messages to sell a product, service, or idea.

Mean The mathematical average of the responses to a question.

Measurement A mechanism for observing something using a clear standard.

Measuring social media Determining how well an organization's social media activities are achieving organizational goals.

Mechanical data collection Machines are used to record observations (e.g., computers, audio or video recordings, and so forth).

Median The middle value among your responses.

Member checking Qualitative analysis confirmation technique, which involves presenting the process and results of your data analysis to some participants to make sure the results of the analysis are consistent with what they meant when the data were collected.

Method section The part of an academic research report that describes exactly what was done and how it was done. It typically includes a section on the sample, the procedures, and the instrumentation (including evidence of reliability and validity).

Metric Numeric values assigned to the output or outcomes of social media efforts.

Mode The value that occurs most frequently among the responses to an item.

Monitoring social media Engaging in surveillance of the social media environment and attending to mentions of an organization, its product or services, and its stakeholders.

Multidimensional concept A complex concept that includes several distinct but related elements.

Mutually exclusive In content analysis, each unit should be placed into only one category.

Mutually exclusive response categories Response options that capture the respondent's answer in only one of the possible categories.

National Research Act A 1974 law that details the ethical principles to be followed when conducting research involving human beings.

Naturalistic generalization Readers of qualitative research are able to apply the study's findings to their own situation.

Negative correlation Correlation in which the related variables move in opposite directions of each other.

Neither too broad nor too narrow Criterion for the evaluation of a research question or hypothesis requiring that the research question or hypothesis be neither too expansive nor too trivial.

Net promoter score A measure of advocacy that is derived from asking customers how likely they would be to recommend a product or service.

Network sampling A nonprobability sampling technique that relies on people in the researcher's network to take part in the study.

Neutrality The interviewer/facilitator must be careful to remain neutral so as not to lead the participant(s) to particular responses.

Nominal measurement A level of measurement that allows for placing data into categories.

Non-disguised observations The people being observed are aware that they are being observed.

Nondirectional hypotheses A prediction that two variables are related to each other, but the exact nature of the relationship is unknown.

Nonprobability sampling techniques Sampling techniques that draw a sample from a population without employing random selection.

Nonreactive The focus of the research does not change because it is the focus of research.

Nonverbal cues A skilled interviewer/facilitator will monitor respondents' nonverbal cues and ask for verbal information as warranted.

Objective The part of the planning process that involves the identification of what will be achieved. Should be SMART (specific, measurable, attainable, results oriented, and time specific).

Observation A research technique that involves surveillance of naturally occurring behavior.

Online experiment An experiment that takes place entirely online. It represents a blend of laboratory and field experiments but is associated with a large number of threats to validity.

Online survey A survey that uses the internet to collect data.

Open-ended question Survey and poll items that ask a question and allow the respondent to answer in their own words.

Opening question A question that begins the interview and serves as an ice breaker.

Operational definition Translates the conceptual definition into a measurement tool.

Operationalization The way variables are measured.

Ordinal measurement A level of measurement that allows for the ranking of categories.

Orientation to the problem The section of an academic paper that introduces readers to the topic of the paper. Appears in the introduction section.

Outcomes Results achieved through the use of outputs such as employee engagement, increased customer awareness of product, or more positive evaluations of the organization by the public.

Outputs Specific items or products created such as press releases, employee newsletters, and presentations.

Owned media Content produced and controlled by an organization.

p-value Statistic that represents the possibility that the relationship identified by the statistical test could occur by chance.

Page header Information at the top of every page of an academic research report, which includes a running head at the top left side of the page and the page number on the top right side of the page.

Page quality Metrics about how well a website is meeting viewers' needs.

Panel longitudinal survey Survey design in which a survey is administered to the exact same group of participants at multiple points in time.

Participant focus Skilled interviewers/facilitators refrain from offering their own thoughts or opinions, keeping the focus on the thoughts or feelings of the participants.

Participant observer role When the researcher is simultaneously taking part in the activities being observed and playing a researcher role.

Pause Interviewers/facilitators should provide a sufficient amount of time after asking a question to ensure a respondent will answer.

Pearson correlation A statistical measure of the relationship between two interval and/or ratio variables.

Personally identifiable information Although state and national guides differ, personally identifiable information is information in a data set that is specifically associated with an individual's identity. In order to achieve anonymity, these data must be removed from datasets.

Pie chart A visual aid that shows the composition of elements for a particular variable.

Plagiarism An unethical behavior that involves using another person's words, in whole or in part, without citing the source of the work or using quotation marks; paraphrasing someone else's work without citing the true author; imitating a source's syntax or phrasing; or not including the names of authors who contributed to the document, or, conversely, including the names of people who did not contribute.

Planning The development of communication goals, objectives, strategies, and tactics.

Poll A brief questionnaire used to assess a small amount of information for immediate use with little to no analysis.

Population All people who meet the desired criteria.

Positive correlation A correlation in which the values of the related variables move in the same increasing or decreasing direction.

Postpone Occasionally a respondent will shift to a new focus when answering a question. An effective interviewer/facilitator will acknowledge the comment but refocus the conversation.

Post reach The number of people who have had a social media post on their screens. A measure of exposure.

Posttest The measurement of the dependent variable that occurs after participants are exposed to the independent variable.

Power analysis A process to determine sample size for quantitative research.

Pre-experimental designs The simplest form of experimental design. They typically involve only one group, which means that true manipulation and control cannot be achieved.

Preference A social media goal associated with actions performed as a result of a social media post. Also called influence and conversions.

Pretest A measurement of the dependent variable that occurs before the participants are exposed to the independent variable.

Primary research Research reported directly by the person or group who conducted it.

Probability sample techniques Sampling techniques that use random selection of individuals from the population to form the sample.

Probe Follow-up questions designed to gather additional data.

Problem statement The first part in the body of a professional research report. It includes the nature of the situation that prompted the research, information about authorization, a summary of any preliminary or secondary research that informed the research project, and the objectives for the research.

Procedure A subsection of the methods section in an academic report. The section describes the overarching method used, information about the ethical conduct of the study, and specific details about how the research was conducted.

Prominence analysis A type of latent content analysis that focuses on the nature of an article, including the reputation of the publication and factors associated with the article such as the length of the article and where in the publication the article appears.

Prompt An organizing scheme for qualitative data that puts all answers to a specific question in its own file, creating separate files for each question asked.

Proprietary research Research available only to a select group.

Public relations A strategic communication process that builds mutually beneficial relationships between organizations and their publics.

Public research Research available to all. Often it is scholarly or academic research.

Qualitative Research based on in-depth descriptions that present results in themes and examples.

Quality of coverage A type of latent content analysis that involves measures of sentiment, prominence, and the overall volume of articles generated.

Quantitative Research based on numerical and statistical comparisons of trends, usually using a large sample and precise measurement.

Quasi-experimental designs Considered partially experimental, the researcher either (a) was unable to randomly assign people into groups; (b) was careful to match participants in each group based on an important characteristic; or (c) studied only one group but had multiple measurements before and after the introduction of the independent variable.

Questionnaire A survey tool that presents a respondent with a list of pre-set questions, usually about their opinions, behavior, or experiences, to answer.

Question route A plan for the interview, created to guide the interviewer or focus group facilitator in conducting the interview. Also known as an interview guide.

Quota sampling A nonprobability sampling technique that involves using other nonprobability sampling techniques to create a sample in which subgroups of the population are represented in the sample along desired proportions.

Random assignment Each participant has an equal chance of being assigned to any group in the experiment.

Random selection Process by which every individual in the population has an equal chance of being chosen for the sample.

Range Identifies the lowest value and the highest value in your data.

Ratio measurement A level of measurement with rank ordering with equal distance between points on the scale and real mathematical value assigned to integers.

Regulation A rule developed by a government agency. It must be followed by everyone who does business with the agency.

Relate A type of research question that seeks to determine the relationship between two variables.

Relative frequency A measure that seeks to ascertain the perceived frequency of a behavior. Typically measured with a frequency scale.

Reliability The consistency of measurement.

Representative sample When the group that you study closely matches the larger population or universe. A high-quality sample allows you to generalize your results.

Research The systematic gathering, analysis, and reporting of information.

Research objective A statement that indicates what will be achieved by conducting research and why it is being conducted.

Research question A question referencing what you want to learn as a result of the study. They must be researchable.

Researchable and answerable Criterion for the evaluation of a research question or hypothesis requiring that the question or hypothesis be one that is able to be realistically assessed by the researcher.

Response rate Ratio of people who completed the survey versus those who were asked to complete the survey.

Results section In an academic report, the techniques used to answer a research question or test a hypothesis, as well as the actual answer to the RQ or the extent to which the hypothesis has been supported.

RPIE model A strategic planning model that includes four steps: research, planning, implementation, and evaluation.

Running head A shortened version of the title of the paper that appears on the top left of the header.

Sample A small group of a population that is meant to represent the qualities of the whole population.

Sample The subsection of the methods section that describes the universe or population, the number of participants/texts, a description of the participants/texts, and the sampling method.

Sampling frame A master list that identifies all members of the population.

Saturation The standard for sufficient sample size in qualitative research, which is reached when new data does not provide new information about themes or the connection among themes.

Scale A measurement tool that allows researchers to assign numbers to variables in survey questions; the responses to a question or statement.

Secondary research Research described by a party other than the person or group who conducted it.

Self-administered A survey the participant reads and completes without help from a researcher.

Self-disclosure Communication that shares information about the self with others.

Semantic differential scale A measurement of an individual's subjective meaning of a concept, it involves a series of opposite adjectives and the respondent indicates how closely their perception of the concept is relative to the opposing adjectives.

Semi-standardized interviews Interviews that use a planned set of questions and question pattern across interviews but also allow for some responsiveness to what participants have said in the interview. Also known as semi-structured interviews.

Sentiment analysis A type of latent content analysis that focuses on the valence (positive, negative, or neutral) of a message author's views on the topic of interest. Also called tonality analysis.

Shares A measure of engagement indicated by the number of times a post is reposted by followers.

Simple random sampling A probability sampling technique of randomly selecting individuals for the sample from a master list that identifies all members of the population.

Situational or positional vulnerability Because of the situation involved or a person's role in an organization, an individual might be susceptible to coercion to take part in the study. The Common Rule requires these people to be safeguarded.

SMART objectives Describes guidelines for establishing measurable objectives using the acronym SMART. Each letter signifies a part of the guideline as follows: S = specific, stated in the most simple and clear way possible; M = measurable, you establish a way to provide evidence that the objective was achieved; A = achievable, appropriate given the resources involved—not too challenging, but not too easy, either; R = results focused, focused on the outcomes of an activity, not the activity itself; T = time bound, linked to a specific timeframe.

Snowball sampling A nonprobability sampling technique that relies on participants in the study to identify additional participants to take part in the study.

Social desirability bias Phenomenon that occurs when participants skew their responses away from an accurate answer and toward what they think is in line with social norms.

Social media analytics An organization's ongoing efforts to monitor and measure social media traffic that is related to the organization and its practices.

Social media firehose A data provider that is open access; it provides all of the data that comes from a social media platform.

Social media influencer An individual whose use of social media is associated with a perception of expertise.

Social share of voice A metric that measures all social media activity referencing an organization, brand, product, or service as compared to social media activity of competitors. A measure of exposure.

Source An organizing scheme for qualitative data that places individual sources of data into separate files.

Split-half reliability A reliability assessment in which the researcher randomly divides the items measuring the same concept into two different groups and then compares the correlation between them.

Spurious correlation Occurs when two variables are significantly correlated without actually having an influence on each other.

Standard deviation Statistic that measures the variability in the data by indicating how close the values are to the mean.

Standardization The amount of similarity among the questions and question pattern across interviews.

Standardized interviews Interviews that ask the exact same questions in the exact same order across interviews. Also known as structured interviews.

Statistically significant difference Indicates the result is more likely to occur than it would by chance.

Strategy A coordinated approach to reach an objective. It addresses how an objective will be achieved.

Stratified cluster sampling A probability sampling technique similar to random cluster sampling but that adds a stratification process so that the sample includes proportionate numbers of clusters.

Stratified random sampling A probability sampling method, also known as proportional random sampling, that allows for control over how subgroups of the population are represented within the sample.

Structured observation The researcher uses an observation checklist to collect data.

Supervised learning Computer-assisted coding in which the researcher has been involved with the creation of content categories and their identification.

Survey A research tool that gathers information about people's attitudes, beliefs, and experiences.

Systematic random sampling A probability sampling method that uses a predetermined number (such as every fifth person) to select members of a population to become the sample.

t-test Statistical test used to determine if there is a statistically significant difference in the means of two groups.

Table A visual aid that summarizes information using columns and rows. It is most useful for presenting numerical information.

Tactic Specific activities that will be used to accomplish a strategy.

Test-retest reliability A reliability assessment in which a measure is compared to its own measurement if performed more than once.

Testimonials Any review or endorsement of an organization, brand, product, or service posted on social media. A measure of advocacy.

Text Any written or recorded message.

Text mining A rule-based computer system for identifying attributes based on an established "dictionary" of concepts.

Thematic analysis An umbrella term used to refer to qualitative data analysis processes performed with the goal of identifying patterns of meaning, or themes, within the data.

Theme An identified pattern in the coding that provides information to address the research question.

Third-party cookies Information placed on the computer from a domain other than the one shown on the address bar (see HTTP cookies).

Title page The first page of an academic report. It includes the title, which is centered in the middle of the paper and should be the title of the study, and the names of the authors and their professional affiliations.

Transition questions Questions that form a bridge from questions that require little detail in response to questions that are the most important and require the most detailed responses in the interview.

Treatment group The group that does experience the variation in the independent variable; they are exposed to the new product, idea, or service.

Trend longitudinal survey Survey design that allows for sample inclusion criteria that a participant may become eligible or ineligible for each time the survey is being administered.

Trends Tracking data over time.

Unidimensional concept A concept that has only a single underlying dimension.

Unitizing The process of determining the unit of analysis. Possible units include symbols or words, individuals or roles, time/space, items, or themes.

Unit of analysis The part of data that represents an individual case for coding.

Universe All messages that fit the criteria of interest.

Unobtrusive A research method that does not involve direct contact with people.

Unstructured content Naturally occurring content rather than content in a database. For example, the content available on social media, websites, newspapers, or organizational reports.

Unstructured interviews Interviews that do not have a question plan that is carried over from interview to interview; rather, questions are generated individually for each interview and are very responsive to the answers given by participants.

Unstructured observation The researcher has not predetermined the types of behaviors that will be used for analysis.

Unsupervised learning Computer-assisted coding in which the computer software creates the content categories without input from the researcher.

Validity The truthfulness or accuracy of the measurement.

Value neutral Criterion for the evaluation of a research question or hypothesis requiring that the research question or hypothesis be free from bias based on the researcher's desired outcome for the research.

Values The amount or degrees in which the variable can represented.

Variable A concept that takes on more than one value within the research projcct.

Virality rate The number of people who share a post relative to the number of unique views of that post. A measure of engagement.

Volunteer sampling A nonprobability sampling technique that involves distributing information about your study and asking people who qualify to participate.

Vulnerable populations Groups of people who may not have the ability to make the decision to take part in research.

Web analytics The collection, measurement, analysis, and reporting of internet data for the purpose of understanding and optimizing website usage.

Website crawlers A computer program that scans the internet looking for information, typically for the purpose of indexing content. Also called spiders, spiderbots, crawlers, or bots.

XY graph A mathematical visual aid that has the value of the dependent variable along the vertical axis and the value of the independent variable along the horizontal access.

References

Adams, C., & Telling, G. (April 6, 2017). How many millions could Pepsi's pulled Kendall Jenner ad cost the company? *People*. https://people.com/food/kendall-jenner-pepsi-commercial-company-cost/

Allcott, H., & Gentzkow, M. (2017). Social media and fake news in the 2016 election. *Journal of Economic Perspectives, 31(2)*, 211–236. https://doi.org/10.1257/jep.31.2.211

American Association for Public Opinion Research. (2015, November 30). *The code of professional ethics and practices.*https://www.aapor.org/Standards-Ethics/AAPOR-Code-of-Ethics/AAPOR_Code_Accepted_Version_11302015.aspx

American Psychological Association. (2019). *Publication manual of the American Psychological Association 7th ed.,* APA.

Barnard, D. (2018, January 20). *Average speaking rate and words per minute. Virtual Speech.* https://virtualspeech.com/blog/average-speaking-rate-words-per-minute

Barthel, M., & Mitchell, A. (2017, May 10). *Americans' attitudes about the news media deeply divided along partisan lines.* Pew Research Center. https://www.journalism.org/wp-content/uploads/sites/8/2017/05/PJ_2017.05.10_Media-Attitudes_FINAL.pdf

Baxter, L. A. & Babbie, E. (2004). *The basics of communication research.* Wadsworth.

Bigby, G. (2018, January 25). 35 *Amazing Web analytics tools that rival Google Analytics. Dyno Mapper Newsletter.* https://dynomapper.com/blog/21-sitemaps-and-seo/436-35-amazing-web-analytics-tools-that-rival-google-analytics

Birkett, A. (2019, May 10). *A/B testing guide.* CXL Institute. https://conversionxl.com/blog/ab-testing-guide/

Blanchard, O. (2011). *Social media ROI: Managing and measuring social media efforts in your organization.* Pearson.

Bortree, D. (2003, May). *Human subjects in internet research: Ethical concerns with the study of human communication on the internet.* Paper presented at the conference of the International Communication Association, San Diego, CA.

Bottomley, P. A., & Doyle, J. R. (2006). The interactive effects of colors and products on perceptions of brand logo appropriateness. *Marketing Theory, 6(1)*, 63–83. https://doi.org/10.1177/1470593106061263

Bowen, S. A. & Stacks, D. W. (2013). Toward the establishment of ethical standardization in public relations research, measurement, and evaluation. *Public Relations Journal, 7(3)*, 1–28.

Bowen, S. A., Gilfeather, J., & Rawlins, B. (2012, March 7). *Ethical standards and guidelines for public relations research and measurement.* Institute for Public Relations. https://instituteforpr.org/wp-content/uploads/Ethical-standards-and-guidelines-for-public-relations-research-ver-1.1.pdf

Budak, C., Goel, S., & Rao, J. M. (2016). Fair and balanced? Quantifying media bias through crowdsourced content analysis. *Public Opinion Quarterly, 80(S1)*, 250–271. https://doi.org/10.1093/poq/nfw007

Center for Science in the Public Interest. (2007, April 17). *Quaker agrees to tone down exaggerated health claims on oatmeal: CSPI drops plans to sue.* https://cspinet.org/news/quaker-agrees-tone-down-exaggerated-health-claims-oatmeal-20070417

Charmaz, K. (2006). *Constructing grounded theory: A practical guide through qualitative analysis.* SAGE.

Cho, M., Furey, L. D., & Mohr, T. (2017). Communicating corporate social responsibility on social media: Strategies, stakeholders, and public engagement on corporate Facebook. *Business & Professional Communication Quarterly, 80(1)*, 52–69. https://doi.org/10.1177/2329490616663708

Clampitt, P. G. (2009). The questionnaire approach. In O. Hargie & D. Tourish (Eds.), *Auditing organizational communication: A handbook of research, theory and practice (2nd ed.).* (pp. 55–77). Routledge.

Clark, M., Michel, J., Early, R., & Baltes, B. (2014). Strategies for coping with work stressors and family stressors: Scale development and validation. *Journal of Business & Psychology, 29(4)*, 617–638. https://doi.org/10.1007/s10869-014-9356-7

Clarke, V. & Braun, V. (2016). Thematic analysis. In E. Lyons & A. Coyle, (Eds.), *Analysing qualitative data in psychology (2nd ed.)* (pp. 84–103). SAGE.

College of Physicians of Philadelphia. (2018, January 25). *Do vaccines cause autism? The History of Vaccines.* https://www.historyofvaccines.org/content/articles/do-vaccines-cause-autism

Comcowitch, W. (2015, July 23). *3 case studies of successful PR measurement. Glean.info.* https://glean.info/3-case-studies-of-successful-pr-measurement/

Cooper, D. R., & Schindler, P. S. (2008). *Business research methods (10th ed.)*. McGraw-Hill.

Corbin, J. & Strauss, A. (2008). *Basics of qualitative research: Techniques and procedures for developing grounded theory (3rd ed.)*. SAGE.

Cronbach, L. J. (1951). Coefficient alpha and the internal structure of tests. *Psychometrika, 16(3)*, 297–334.

Dainton, M., Correa, G., Kohr, S., & Taormina, M. (2014). Public perceptions of organizational social media use: A uses and gratifications approach. *Journal of New Communications Research, 5*, 1–29.

Department of Health and Human Services. (2018). *Office for Human Research Protections*. https://www.hhs.gov/ohrp/

Derlega, V., Harris, M. S., & Chaikin, A. L. (1973). Self-disclosure reciprocity, liking and the deviant. *Journal of Experimental Social Psychology, 9(4)*, 277–284. https://doi.org/10.1016/0022-1031(73)90065-6

Dewey, C. (2014, July 1). 9 answers about Facebook's creepy emotional-manipulations experiment. *Washington Post*. https://www.washingtonpost.com/news/the-intersect/wp/2014/07/01/9-answers-about-facebooks-creepy-emotional-manipulation-experiment/?noredirect=on&utm_term=.04e7748e4845

Dixon, S., & Quirke, L. (2018). What's the harm? The coverage of ethics and harm avoidance in research methods textbooks. *Teaching Sociology, 46(1)*, 12–24. https://doi.org/10.1177/0092055X17711230

Downs, C. W. (1988). *Communication audits*. Scott, Foresman.

Downs, C. W. & Hazen, M. D. (1977). A factor analytic study of communication satisfaction. *Journal of Business Communication, 14(3)*, 63–73. https://doi.org/10.1177/002194367701400306

Driver, S. (2018, April 17). Guide to social media analytics. *Business News Daily*, https://www.businessnewsdaily.com/10694-understanding-social-media-analytics.html

Droms, C. (2013). Take it back: The impact of dynamic consumer goals in return and exchange interactions. *Services Marketing Quarterly, 34(1)*, 67–85. https://doi.org/10.1080/15332969.2013.739944

Duffy, B., Smith, K., Terhanian, G. & Bremer, J. (2005). Comparing data from face-to-face and online surveys. *International Journal of Market Research, 47(6)*, 615–639. https://doi.org/10.1177/147078530504700602

Eisenmann, M., O'Neil, J., & Geddes, D. (2015). An examination of the validity, reliability and best practices related to the standards for traditional media. *Research Journal of the Institute of Public Relations, 2(1)*, 1–28. https://

instituteforpr.org/wp-content/uploads/Eisenmann_ONeil_Geddes_
REVISIONS_V2_01_07_2015.pdf

Facebook. (n.d.). *Community standards enforcement report.* https://transpar-
ency.facebook.com/community-standards-enforcement

Few, S. (2007, August). *Save the pies for dessert. Perceptual Edge.* http://www.
perceptualedge.com/articles/08-21-07.pdf

Finneman, T., & Thomas, R. J. (2018). A family of falsehoods: Deception, media
hoaxes and fake news. *Newspaper Research Journal, 39*(3), 350–361. https://
doi.org/10.1177/0739532918796228

Fleming, J. (2018, November 11). How the Flyers created Gritty, the internet's most beloved mascot. *Adweek.* https://www.adweek.com/creativity/
how-the-flyers-created-gritty-the-internets-most-beloved-mascot/

Fox, F. (2017). Meeting in virtual spaces: Conducting online focus groups. In V.
Braun, V. Clarke, & D. Gray (Eds.). *Collecting qualitative data: A practical guide
to textual, media and virtual techniques.* (pp. 275–299). Cambridge University
Press.

Franz, T. M. (2012). *Group dynamics and team interventions: Understanding and
improving team performance.* Wiley.

Frederick, D. (2016, September 16). KLM wants Americans to know it's an airline,
not a radio station. *PR Week.* https://www.prweek.com/article/1409221/
klm-wants-americans-know-its-airline-not-radio-station

Fuller, R., Shikaloff, N., Cullinan, R., & Harmon, S. (2018, January 25). If you multitask during meetings, your team will, too. *Harvard Business Review.* https://
hbr.org/2018/01/if-you-multitask-during-meetings-your-team-will-too

Gallup. (2017). *State of the American workplace.* https://www.gallup.com/work-
place/238085/state-american-workplace-report-2017.aspx

Gallup. (n.d.) *Gallup Daily: U.S. Employee Engagement.* https://news.gallup.com/
poll/180404/gallup-daily-employee-engagement.aspx

Gewirtz, P. (1996). On "I know it when I see it." *Yale Law Journal, 105,*
1023–1047.

Goldhaber, G. M. (2002). Communication audits in the age of the internet. *Management Communication Quarterly, 15*(3), 451–457. https://doi.
org/10.1177/0893318902153007

Green, T., & Peloza, J. (2014). How do consumers infer corporate social responsibility? The role of organisation size. *Journal of Consumer Behaviour, 13*(4),
282–293. https://doi.org/10.1002/cb.1466

Hanna, P. & Mwale, S. (2017). "I'm not *with* you, yet I am ...": Virtual face-to-face interviews. In V. Braun, V. Clarke, & D. Gray (Eds.). *Collecting qualitative data: A practical guide to textual, media and virtual techniques.* (pp. 256–274). Cambridge University Press.

Hargie, O., Tourish, D., & Wilson, N. (2002). Communication audits and the effects of increased information: A follow-up study. *Journal of Business Communication, 39(4)*, 414–436. https://doi.org/10.1177/002194360203900402

Hart, C., Vroman, M., & Stulz, K. (2015). Experiential, collaborative and team projects: Communication audits in the MBA communication classroom. *American Journal of Business Education, 8(4)*, 289–306. https://doi.org/10.19030/ajbe.v8i4.9423

Hecht, R. D., Martin, F., Donnelly, T., Larson, M., & Sweetser, K. D. (2017). Will you run it? A gatekeeping experiment examining credibility, branding, and affiliation within information subsidies. *Public Relations Review, 43(4)*, 738–749. https://doi.org/10.1016/j.pubrev.2017.07.006

Heckathorn, D. D. & Cameron, C. J. (2017). Network sampling: From snowball and multiplicity to respondent-driven sampling. *Annual Review of Sociology, 43*, 101–119.

Henningfield, J. E., Rose, C. A., & Zeller, M. (2006). Tobacco industry litigation position on addiction: Continued dependence on past views. *Tobacco Control, 15*, iv27–iv36.

Holsapple, C., Hsaio, S., & Pakath, R. (2014). *Business social media analytics: Definition, benefits, and challenges.* Paper presented at the Twentieth Americas Conference on Information Systems, Savannah, GA. https://pdfs.semanticscholar.org/d7d7/1ec49476e54a350e9091087345dcd3d7866c.pdf

Horner, J., & Minifie, F. D. (2011). Research ethics I: Responsible conduct of research (RCR)—Historical and contemporary issues pertaining to human and animal experimentation. *Journal of Speech, Language & Hearing Research, 54(1)*, S303–S329. https://doi.org/10.1044/1092-4388(2010/09-0265)

Hu, Y., Manikonda, L., & Kambhampati, S. (2014). *What we Instagram: A first analysis of Instagram photo content and user types. Proceedings of the Eighth International Association for the Advancement of Artificial Intelligence Conference on Weblogs and Social Media.* https://www.aaai.org/ocs/index.php/ICWSM/ICWSM14/paper/viewFile/8118/8087

Hutchinson, A. (2017, August 23). *Consumer expectations rising on social customer care* [*report*]. *Social Media Today.* https://www.socialmediatoday.com/social-business/consumer-expectations-rising-social-customer-care-report

Infsoft. (2017). *Analysis of consumer behavior in a supermarket* [White Paper EN 2018-04]. https://cdn.infsoft.com/www/images/solutions/basics/whitepaper/infsoft-Whitepaper-EN-Indoor-Positioning_download.pdf

International Association for the Measurement and Evaluation of Communication (AMEC). (2019). AMEC's Social Media Measurement Framework User Guide. https://www.social-media-measurement-framework.org/

International Association of Business Communicators. (2018). *IABC code of ethics for professional communicators.* https://www.iabc.com/about-us/purpose/code-of-ethics/

Jeffries-Fox, B. (2003). *A discussion of advertising value equivalency* [*White paper*]. Institute for Public Relations Commission on PR Measurement and Evaluation, https://instituteforpr.org/advertising-value-equivalency-3/

Jiang, Y., Gorn, G. J., Galli, M., & Chattopadhyay, A. (2016). Does your company have the right logo? How and why circular- and angular-logo shapes influence brand attribute judgments. *Journal of Consumer Research, 42*(5), 709–726. https://doi.org/10.1093/jcr/ucv049

John, L. K., Kim, T., & Barasz, K. (2018). Ads that don't overstep. *Harvard Business Review, 96,* 62–69. https://www.hbs.edu/faculty/Pages/item.aspx?num=53707

Jones, C. (2009a, August 3). *Content analysis: A practical approach. UX Matters.* https://www.uxmatters.com/mt/archives/2009/08/content-analysis-a-practical-approach.php

Jones, C. (2009b, April 13). *Toward content quality. UX Matters.* https://www.uxmatters.com/mt/archives/2009/04/toward-content-quality.php

Jones, J. M. (2017). *In U.S., 10.2% of LGBT adults now married to same-sex spouse.* Gallup. https://news.gallup.com/poll/212702/lgbt-adults-married-sex-spouse.aspx

Jourard, S. M. (1964). *The transparent self.* D. Van Nostrand.

Keyton, J. (2015). *Communication research: Asking questions, finding answers* (*4th ed.*). McGraw-Hill.

King, N. (May 31, 2019). *Ava DuVernay hopes you hear "the heartbeat of the boys" in Central Park 5. National Public Radio.* https://www.npr.org/2019/05/31/727329700/ava-duvernay-hopes-you-hear-the-heartbeat-of-the-boys-in-central-park-5

Kohavi, R., & Thomke, S. (2017). The surprising power of online experiments. *Harvard Business Review.* https://hbr.org/2017/09/the-surprising-power-of-online-experiments

Kopaneva, I. M. (2019). Left in the dust: Employee constructions of mission and vision ownership. *International Journal of Business Communication, 56(1),* 122–145. https://doi.org/10.1177/2329488415604457

Kruger, R. A. & Casey, M. A. (2015). *Focus groups: A practical guide for applied research (5th ed.).* SAGE.

Lacy, S., Watson, B. R., Riffe, D., & Lovejoy, J. (2015). Issues and best practices in content analysis. *Communication Studies Faculty Publications and Presentations, 8.* https://pilotscholars.up.edu/cgi/viewcontent.cgi?article=1011&context=cst_facpubs

Landay, K., Harms, P. D., & Crede, M. (2018). Shall we serve the dark lords? A meta-analytic review of psychopathy and leadership. *Journal of Applied Psychology, 104(1),* 183–196. https://doi.org/10.1037/apl0000357

Lannutti, P. J. (2014). *Experiencing same-sex marriage: Individuals, couples, and social networks.* Peter Lang.

Lannutti, P. J. (2017). A productive chat: Instant Messenger interviewing. In V. Braun, V. Clarke, & D. Gray (Eds.). *Collecting qualitative data: A practical guide to textual, media and virtual techniques.* (pp. 235–255). Cambridge University Press.

Lauzen, M. M. (1995). Toward a model of environmental scanning. *Journal of Public Relations Research, 7(3),* 187–203.

Lieb, R. (2015, February 16). *How to conduct a content audit. Marketing Land.* https://marketingland.com/conduct-content-audit-117781

Liu, X., Burns, A. C., & Hou, Y. (2017). An investigation of brand-related user-generated content on Twitter. *Journal of Advertising, 46(2),* 236–247. https://doi.org/10.1080/00913367.2017.1297273

Lombard, M., Snyder-Duch, J., & Bracken, C. C. (2002). Content analysis in mass communication: Assessment and reporting of intercoder reliability. *Human Communication Research, 28(4),* 587–604. https://doi.org/10.1111/j.1468-2958.2002.tb00826.x

Luttrell, R. (2016). *Social media: How to engage, share, and connect (2nd ed.).* Rowman & Littlefield.

Madden, N. (2010, March 4). Soy-sauce flavored Kit Kats? In Japan they're no. 1. *AdAge.* https://adage.com/article/global-news/marketing-nestle-flavors-kit-kat-japan-markets/142461/

Madden, P. (2018, September 25). Flyers new Gritty mascot: Why it works. *Philadelphia Business Journal.* https://www.bizjournals.com/philadelphia/news/2018/09/25/flyers-new-gritty-mascot-pr-branding-success.html

Maine Public (2018, November). *Strategic plan 2019–2023.* https://www.strategicplan.mainepublic.org/

Malhotra, N. K., & Peterson, M. (2006). *Basic marketing research: A decision making approach (2nd ed.).* Pearson.

Mau, G., Steinmann, S., & Schramm-Klein, H. (2016). In the right place: The in-store location of promotional displays can alter shoppers' attention and buying decision. *AMA Winter Educators' Conference Proceedings, 27,* K-19–K-20. http://www.proceedings.com/30524.html

Mercer, A., Caporosa, A., Cantor, D., & Townsend, R. (2015). Monetary incentives and response rates in household surveys. *Public Opinion Quarterly, 79(1),* 105–129. https://doi.org/10.1093/poq/nfu059

Merriam-Webster Dictionary. (n.d.a.) *Time.* https://www.merriam-webster.com/dictionary/time

Merriam-Webster Dictionary. (n.d.b) *Edible.* https://www.merriam-webster.com/dictionary/edible

Metts, S., Sprecher, S., & Cupach, W. R. (1991). Retrospective self-reports. In B. M. Montgomery & S. Duck (Eds.), *Studying interpersonal interaction* (p. 162–178). Guilford Press.

Meyersohn, N. (2018, September 6). *Barnes & Noble is overrun with problems. CNN Business.* Https://money.cnn.com/2018/09/06/news/companies/barnes-and-noble-books-amazon/index.html

Michaelson, D. & Stacks, D.W. (2017). *A professional and practitioner's guide to public relations research, measurement, and evaluation (3rd ed.).* Business Expert Press.

Mikkelson, A. C., Hesse, C. & Sloan, D. (2017). Relational communication messages and employee outcomes in supervisor/employee relationships. *Communication Reports, 30(3),* 142–156. https://doi.org/10.1080/08934215.2017.1300677

Milliman, R. E. (1982). Using background music to affect the behavior of supermarket shoppers. *Journal of Marketing, 46(3),* 86–91. https://doi.org/10.2307/1251706

Moodie, C. (2018). Adult smokers' perceptions of cigarette pack inserts promoting cessation: A focus group study. *Tobacco Control, 27,* 72–77. https://doi.org/10.1136/tobaccocontrol-2016-053372

Moon, R. (2018). Getting into living rooms: NGO media relations work as strategic practice. *Journalism, 19(7)*, 1011–1026. https://doi.org/10.1177/1464884917691542

Napier, N. K. (2014, May 12). *The myth of multitasking. Psychology Today.* https://www.psychologytoday.com/us/blog/creativity-without-borders/201405/the-myth-multitasking

Newman, N., & Fletcher, R. (2017). *Bias, bullshit, and lies: Audience perspectives on low trust in the media. Reuters Institute for the Study of Journalism.* https://reutersinstitute.politics.ox.ac.uk/sites/default/files/2017-11/Nic%20Newman%20and%20Richard%20Fletcher%20-%20Bias%2C%20Bullshit%20and%20Lies%20-%20Report.pdf

Ohlheiser, A. (2017, April 11). The full timeline of how social media turned United into the biggest story in the country. *Washington Post.* https://www.washingtonpost.com/news/the-intersect/wp/2017/04/11/the-full-timeline-of-how-social-media-turned-united-into-the-biggest-story-in-the-country/?utm_term=.2164a74404e1

Olson, P. (2009, September 2). A Twitterati calls out Whirlpool. *Forbes.* https://www.forbes.com/2009/09/02/twitter-dooce-maytag-markets-equities-whirlpool.html#178d386d45b6

Oracle. (2015, January). *A new perspective on Millennials: Segmenting a generation for actionable insights for consumer goods companies and retailers.* http://www.oracle.com/us/industries/consumer/interbrand-cg-retail-cx-wp-2400662.pdf

Osgood, C. E. (1952). The nature and measurement of meaning. *Psychological Bulletin, 49(3)*, 197–237. https://doi.org/10.1037/h0055737

Park, C. W., Eisingerich, A. B., Pol, G., & Park, J. W. (2013). The role of brand logos in firm performance. *Journal of Business Research, 66(2)*, 180–187. https://doi.org/10.1016/j.jbusres.2012.07.011

Pew Research Center (2018). *Human coding of news media.* http://www.pewresearch.org/methods/about-content-analysis/human-coding-of-news-media/

Pew Research Center. (2019, April 9). *Use of different online platforms by demographic groups.* https://www.pewresearch.org/fact-tank/2019/04/10/share-of-u-s-adults-using-social-media-including-facebook-is-mostly-unchanged-since-2018/ft_19-04-10_socialmedia2019_useofdifferent/

Pinsker, J. (April 8, 2017). How on earth does an ad like Pepsi's get approved? *The Atlantic*. https://www.theatlantic.com/business/archive/2017/04/pepsi-kendall-jenner-ad-how/522423/

Pratt, S. (1988, May 12). Claims in oatmeal ads exaggerated, group says. *Chicago Tribune*. https://www.chicagotribune.com/news/ct-xpm-1988-05-12-8803160439-story.html

Public Relations Society of America. (2019). *About public relations*. https://www.prsa.org/about/all-about-pr

Pun, H. (n.d.). *Here are 10 fascinating A/B tests that will blow your mind*. Design for Founders. https://www.designforfounders.com/ab-testing-examples/

Quick, J. D., & Larson, H. (2018, February 28). The vaccine-autism myth started 20 years ago. Here's why it still endures today. *Time*. http://time.com/5175704/andrew-wakefield-vaccine-autism/

Roberts, K. H., & O'Reilly, C. A. (1974). Measuring organizational communication. *Journal of Applied Psychology, 59*(3), 321–326. https://doi.org/10.1037/h0036660

Rockland, D. B. (2015, October). *Barcelona Principles 2.0: What's new and what's out*. Public Relations Tactics. http://apps.prsa.org/Intelligence/Tactics/Articles/view/11220/1116/Barcelona_Principles_2_0_What_s_New_and_What_s_Not#.W75BfHtKiUk

Rockland, D. B. (2015, October). *Barcelona Principles 2.0: What's new and what's out*. Public Relations Tactics. http://apps.prsa.org/Intelligence/Tactics/Articles/view/11220/1116/Barcelona_Principles_2_0_What_s_New_and_What_s_Not#.W75BfHtKiUk

Rojas, J. P. F. (December 27, 2017). Tesco faces anger over 'rancid' Christmas turkeys. *Sky News*. https://news.sky.com/story/tesco-faces-anger-over-rancid-christmas-turkeys-11185871

Rupp, R. (2015, June 14). Surviving the sneaky psychology of supermarkets. *National Geographic*. https://www.nationalgeographic.com/people-and-culture/food/the-plate/2015/06/15/surviving-the-sneaky-psychology-of-supermarkets/

Saunders, B., Sim, J., Kingstone, T., Baker, S., Waterfield, J., Bartlam, B., Burroughs, H. & Jinks, C. (2018). Saturation in qualitative research: Exploring its conceptualization and operationalization. *Quality and Quantity, 52*(4), 1892–1907. https://doi.org/10.1007%2Fs11135-017-0574-8

Scharkow, M. (2011, May). *Online content analysis using supervised machine learning—An empirical evaluation.* Paper presented at the annual conference of the International Communication Association, Boston, MA.

Schooley, S. (2019, April 22). What is corporate social responsibility? *Business News Daily.* https://www.businessnewsdaily.com/4679-corporate-social-responsibility.html

Schulz, E. J. (2018, March 27). *How did this happen? Behind Heineken Light's "lighter is better ad campaign." Ad Age.* https://adage.com/article/cmo-strategy/heineken-light-s-lighter-ad-mistake/312887

Schumann, C., Bowman, N. D., & Schultheiss, D. (2016). The quality of video games: Subjective quality assessments as predictors of self-reported presences in first-person shooter and role-playing games. *Journal of Broadcasting and Electronic Media, 60(4),* 547–566. https://doi.org/10.1080/08838151.2016.1234473

Schwartz, H. A., & Ungar, L. H. (2015). Data-driven content analysis of social media: A systematic overview of automated methods. *Annals of the American Academy of Political and Social Science, 659(1),* 78–94. https://doi.org/10.1177/0002716215569197

Shen, H., Jaing, H., Jin, Y. & Sha, B. (2015). Practitioners' work-life conflict: A PRSA survey. *Public Relations Review, 41,* 415–421. https://doi.org/10.1016/j.pubrev.2015.07.011

Shklovski, I., Kraut, R. & Rainie, L. (2004). The internet and social participation: Contrasting cross-section and longitudinal analyses. *Journal of Computer-Mediated Communication, 10(1),* https://doi.org/10.1111/j.1083-6101.2004.tb00226.x

Sinickas, A. D. (2003). *What you should know about research.* https://www.sinicom.com/resources/publications/what-you-should-know-about-research/

Smith, Y. (2014). Rethinking decision making: An ethnographic study of worker agency in crisis intervention. *Social Service Review, 88(3),* 407–442. https://doi.org/10.1086/677846

Stacks, D. W. (2002). *A primer of public relations research.* Guilford.

Stacks, D. W. (2016). *A primer of public relations research (3rd ed.).* Guilford.

Steffan, J. E., Fassler, E.A., Reardon, K. J., & Egilman, D. S. (2018). Grave fraudulence in medical device research: A narrative review of the PIN seeding study for the Pinnacle hip replacement system. *Accountability in Research, 25(1),* 37–66. https://doi.org/10.1080/08989621.2017.1405259

Stewart, C. (2014, July 2). *Avoiding unethical market research decisions. Market Research.com.* https://blog.marketresearch.com/avoiding-unethical-market-research-decisions

Sundar, A., & Noseworthy, T. (2014). Place the logo high or low? Using conceptual metaphors of power in packaging design. *Journal of Marketing, 78(5),* 138–151. https://doi.org/10.1509/jm.13.0253

Swant, M. (2018, May 15). A breakdown of all the offensive content Facebook removed in the first quarter of 2018. *Adweek.* https://www.adweek.com/digital/a-breakdown-of-all-the-offensive-content-facebook-removed-in-the-first-quarter-of-2018/

Thompson, B., Mazer, J. P., Payne, H. J., Jerome, A. M., Kirby, E. G., & Pfohl, W. (2017). Social media and active shooter events: A school crisis communication challenge. *Qualitative Research Reports in Communication, 18(1),* 8–17. https://doi.org/10.1080/17459435.2016.1247111

Tracy, S. J. (2013). *Qualitative research methods: Collecting evidence, crafting analysis, communicating impact.* Wiley-Blackwell.

Turnbull, S., & Wheeler, C. (2016). Exploring advertiser's expectations of advertising agency services. *Journal of Marketing Communications, 22(6),* 587–601. https://doi.org/10.1080/13527266.2014.920902

United States Department of Labor. (n.d.). *Occupational outlook handbook.* https://www.bls.gov/ooh/media-and-communication/public-relations-specialists.htm

Vallor, S., & Rewak, W. J. (2018). *An introduction to data ethics.* Markkula Center for Applied Ethics, Santa Carlita University. https://www.scu.edu/media/ethics-center/technology-ethics/IntroToDataEthics.pdf

van Grinsven, B., & Das, E. (2016). Logo design in marketing communications: Brand logo complexity moderates exposure effects on brand recognition and brand attitude. *Journal of Marketing Communications, 22(3),* 256–270. https://doi.org/10.1080/13527266.2013.866593

Verderber, R.F., Sellinow, D. D., & Verderber, K. S. (2018). *Speak.* Cengage.

Vraga, E., Bode, L., & Troller-Renfree, S. (2016). Beyond self-reports: Using eye tracking to measure topic and style differences in attention to social media content. *Communication Methods & Measures, 10(2–3),* 149–164.

Walters, C. (2011, June 10). Taking a closer look at benefits the Wegmans way. *Rochester Business Journal.* http://www.hrworks-inc.com/article/taking-closer-look-benefits-wegmans-way

Warner, J. (2018, March 12). *7 Definitions of employee engagement. Decision-wise.* https://decision-wise.com/7-definitions-of-employee-engagement/

Wheeless, L. R. (1976). Self-disclosure and interpersonal solidarity: Measurement, validation, and relationships. *Human Communication Research, 3(1),* 47–61.

Wiedmaier, B. (2017). Statistical power analysis. In M. Allen (Ed.), *The SAGE encyclopedia of communication research methods.* (pp. 1676–1677). SAGE.

Wilhite, T. (2017, September 26). *How to calculate the required number of observations. Bizfluent.* https://bizfluent.com/how-8148011-calculate-required-number-observations.html

Wilson, L. J. & Ogden, J. D. (2016). *Strategic communications planning for public relations and marketing* (6th ed.). Kendall Hunt.

Wrench, J. S., Thomas-Maddox, C., Richmond, V. P., & McCroskey, J. C. (2016). *Quantitative research methods for communication: A hands-on approach.* Oxford University Press.

Xu, X., Chen, R., & Liu, M. W. (2017). The effects of uppercase and lowercase wordmarks on brand perceptions. *Marketing Letters: A Journal of Research in Marketing, 28(3),* 449–460. https://doi.org/10.1007/s11002-016-9415-0

Young, B., & Musyi, K. (2018, April 11). Facebook's scandal forces marketers to examine their ethics. *PR Daily.* https://www.prdaily.com/facebooks-scandal-forces-marketers-to-examine-their-ethics/

Yuhas, A. (2018, November 1). Gritty's first month: The heroic ascendance of a "ghastly empty-eyed Muppet." *New York Times.* https://www.nytimes.com/2018/11/01/sports/hockey/gritty-philadelphia-flyers.html

Zimmer, M. (2010). "But the data is already public": On the ethics of research in Facebook. *Ethics & Information Technology, 12(4),* 313–325. https://doi.org/10.1007/s10676-010-9227-5

Index

Milton Keynes UK
Ingram Content Group UK Ltd.
UKHW050156171023
430732UK00005B/51